DICTIONARY of STRATEGY

To my parents, Maureen and Joe Kelly, with love and thanks.
To Rosemarie with love.

DICTIONARY of STRATEGY
Strategic Management A-Z

Louise Kelly
Alliant International University

Chris Booth
Alliant International University

SAGE Publications
International Educational and Professional Publisher
Thousand Oaks ▪ London ▪ New Delhi

For information:

Sage Publications, Inc.
2455 Teller Road
Thousand Oaks, California 91320
E-mail: order@sagepub.com

Sage Publications Ltd.
1 Oliver's Yard
55 City Road
London EC1Y 1SP
United Kingdom

Sage Publications India Pvt. Ltd.
B-42, Panchsheel Enclave
Post Box 4109
New Delhi 110 017 India

Printed in the United States of America

Library of Congress Cataloging-in-Publication Data

Dictionary of strategy: Strategic management A-Z / Louise Kelly, Chris Booth.
    p. cm.
Includes bibliographical references and index.
ISBN 0-7619-3072-8 (cloth) — ISBN 0-7619-3073-6 (pbk.)
  1. Strategic planning—Dictionaries. I. Booth, Chris II. Title.

HD30.28.K454 2004
658′.003—dc22

                      2003028043

This book is printed on acid-free paper.

04   05   06   07   10 9 8 7 6 5 4 3 2 1

Acquisitions Editor:	Al Bruckner
Editorial Assistant:	MaryAnn Vail
Production Editor:	Diane S. Foster
Copy Editor:	Kevin Gleason
Typesetter:	C & M Digitals (P) Ltd.
Proofreader:	Cheryl Rivard
Cover Designer:	Janet Foulger

R
658. 401203
K 29 7d
2004

Contents

Preface

E xcellent leaders are excellent strategists. This dictionary is an invitation: an invitation to think strategically, an invitation to learn the words that allow for strategic debate. Some key words from this book that may form your view of strategy are strategy as algorithm, acronym, and aphorism. This is not a comprehensive dictionary; instead it is eclectic, it is cutting edge.

I hope the dictionary is full of information and provides a nice balance of theory and example. I have tried to handle many of the technical issues such as the Delphi Technique or Game Theory in a definitive way.

Why did I write the dictionary? When I looked at strategy as a consultant, student, and professor, I realized that this field has a tricky, complex language that is at times difficult to understand. I also wondered if it was a purely masculine world. I discovered that only the persona of strategy is masculine; there is a deep underlying complexity that could be understood as being feminine.

I believe that the dictionary format of conveying the basics of strategy solved some of the dilemmas of presenting strategic management as a linear, hierarchical process that one encounters in the classic textbooks. In writing in the dictionary format, I discovered you could start anywhere to go somewhere, and get there. I believe this is true of the creative process as well as the strategy process—which is, in its essence, a creative process. Unlike a mechanical decision, such as where you situate a factory (near railroads, major highways), strategy is difficult: It involves an imaginative approach. The basic philosophy of strategic management presented in this book is the idea that one can embark from any point in strategy. It is an existential view: Once one takes a decision, defines a problem, starts the process of strategic action—once a start-up sets up a UPS account, for example—then one bumps up against the constraints of the system or environment. Choices become crystallized, as William Burroughs said, in that frozen moment he called "Naked Lunch" when everyone realizes what is at the end of her fork. It is at this point that the various trade-offs among competing priorities must be resolved on a continual, and imperfect, basis: the suboptimizing and satisficing concepts that helped Herbert Simon to win the Nobel Prize in 1978. In reading this dictionary, you will be exposed to these historical tidbits as well as being introduced to the chief protagonists who helped to define the field.

The complexity of strategy as a disciplined way of thought arises because of the nonlinear interaction of different disciplines such as the military, computers, sports, politics, history, psychology, and plain old management thought. When we have covered economic, game theory, and militaristic views of OODA loops, we are left with something metaphysical, intuitive, nonlinear.

Many strategic management books emphasize the technical aspect of the subject. This dictionary tries to strike a balance between the hard side and soft side, answering the question that Henry Mintzberg famously asked at the Academy of Management in Denver 2002, Whatever happened to the management in strategic management? Strategic management always involves getting things done through people, just on a grander scale than basic management. Strategic management can become so enamored of the complex econometric industry analysis and the linear programming-based implementation schedules that the tricky matter of getting results through people can be ignored. This dictionary happily embraces those tricky soft-side issues.

Viewpoints that had the most influence on me in writing this dictionary are Henry Mintzberg's emergent view of strategy, Igor Ansoff's linear programming systems thinking, and military inspiration from Sun Tzu's wisdom to Donald Rumsfeld and his existential Zen koan approach to military strategy.

The kind of question this dictionary invites you to ask yourself is, What is the greatest strategic decision you know of?

What about GM's decision in 1929 to bring out a new model every year? Ford owned the market with the Model T—the design of which was static, with no changes in model from year to year.

GM's strategic decision: Build a car for every pocketbook, change the model every year. That decision brought GM ahead of Ford. That later led to the analysis of the decision in the now famous book by Alfred Chandler, *Strategy and Structure,* that in 1962 officially inaugurated the separate field of strategy.

Chandler asked the chicken and egg question, Which came first, the strategy or the structure to implement that strategy? The answer, through his analysis of GM and three other American firms, led to his conclusion: A change to a multiproduct strategy, such as GM's, necessitated the administrative innovation of a multidivision or M-form structure that allowed the pushing down of strategic and operational decisions to lower levels in the hierarchy. And so, the Pontiac, Buick, Chevrolet, and Oldsmobile divisions are born. Heady stuff for the students of strategic management. Of course, this dictionary clearly recognizes that one can convincingly argue the opposite: that a change in structure could drive a change in strategy.

That is what is important. In strategy, one has to get the magnitude right. Strategy requires breadth of mind, perspicacity to in fact deal with it. This dictionary will provide an opening to some of this sweeping view that is necessary for strategic thinking.

We, my fellow author Chris Booth and myself, will leave you with an acronym for strategy that should capture the eclectic and sometimes whimsical view of strategy that this dictionary presents.

"Strategy" by Acronym

Are you into strategy?

Scenario setting: Mapping the future.

Tasking: Assigning tasks and defining roles.

Reconnaissance: Reconnaissance time is time well spent.

Attack: Attack only when you know you can win.

Target setting: Target goals to solve the main problem.

Existentialism: Defining oneself through choices that reflect values.

Generalship: You have to be a general.

Y: The why of the actual strategy, the mission.

This dictionary is an invitation to make up your own acronyms. Go ahead, use some of the words defined here.

The goal of this dictionary is to move the field forward by codifying in a dictionary format some of the best thinking so far in the field while providing tools to the practicing manager to enter the strategic debate, *strategos*—the game of the generals—with confidence and a certain élan.

—Louise Kelly

Acknowledgments

Thanks to all the doctoral and MBA students at Alliant International University who inspired and tested these definitions.

Thanks to Sage editors Al Bruckner and MaryAnn Vail for encouraging support and Kevin Gleason for meticulous editing and patience.

A special thanks to Aung Z. Lwin for his care and safeguarding of the manuscript as it was written.

A

A–Z of Strategic Management   The approach is based on strategic debate, addressing the big issues. There is an existential view of strategy: The strategist can pick any starting point, and this will bring her up against the constraints of the situation. These constraints are unknowable until some action is taken (as Donald Rumsfeld says, "there are the unknowns that are known and then there are the unknowns that are unknown"), so the situation cannot be strategically assessed in any complete sense without the element of action—of making a strategic choice.

Absence of Strategy   Reactive approach to the market or environment. Passive, at times indicating confusion, disarray.

Accretion   The growth of a company through additions and purchases of plant or value-adding services.

Acquisitions and Mergers   (*See also* Mergers and Acquisitions.) Falls under corporate strategy, meaning those strategies that answer the question, "What business or set of businesses do we want to be in?" M&A refers to the purchase of a company that is already in operation. An acquisition is a strategy by which one firm buys controlling or 100% interest in another firm, with the intent of using a core competence more effectively by making the acquired firm a subsidiary business within its corporate portfolio. Acquisitions have become a strategy for many giant firms in the software and pharmaceutical industries that are no longer able to achieve entrepreneurial Schumpeterian innovation through internal investment and R&D, and therefore "buy rather than build" new technologies.

Acquisitions can also be a human resource strategy for large firms. In a knowledge-based economy, social capital becomes the most critical factor of production and can be a bottleneck for implementing innovation-based strategies especially in high-tech industries. Examples are Microsoft's acquisition of smaller firms and IBM's acquisition of Lotus. Acquisition strategies are common in industries that are consolidating, such as the DaimlerChrysler acquisition in the automobile manufacturing industry. Acquisitions are notoriously difficult to manage. The costs of incorporating the acquired company into the parent company are significant, and paper synergies (those that appear in the planning stage—*see* Formal Strategic Planning) often disappear in battles of dueling cultures and systems and the "them versus us" quagmire. After an acquisition is announced, the stock of the acquiring company typically falls while that of the smaller acquiree rises. Thus, acquisitions are notoriously unstable, risky, and difficult to manage. Many firms look for more flexible arrangements such as alliances, networks, and joint ventures in lieu of acquisitions. Acquisition capability is a distinctive competence that can be developed through a series of acquisitions.

Acronyms An acronym is a linguistic invention in which the first letters of the words in a phrase form a newly coined or previously existing word to distill the essence of at-times complex concepts and programs into a memorable, inspiring word. A key idea in strategy is for leadership to capture and convey a concept in a brief, memorable manner. An acronym to be effective must sound like a word. This highlights the artistic side of strategy, where thinking in imagery, soundbites, and off-beat, seemingly off-the-cuff insights often can be very effective. Many examples of memorable acronyms come from the U.S. military:

MOPP: Mission Oriented Protective Posture, the acronym used to describe a military unit's alert level against gas attacks and the like. Marines call their protective gear "MOPP suits."

USA PATRIOT ACT: Uniting and Strengthening America by Providing Appropriate Tools Required to Intercept and Obstruct Terrorism.

OK: "0 (zero)" killed.

Are you into strategy?

Scenario setting: Mapping the future.
Tasking: Assigning tasks and defining roles.
Reconnaissance: Reconnaissance time is time well spent.
Attack: Attack only when you know you can win.
Target setting: Target goals to solve the main problem.
Existentialism: Defining oneself through choices that reflect values.
Generalship: You have to be a general.
Y: The why of the actual strategy, the mission.

As a WW II veteran notes, "SNAFU" brought back memories, good, bad, and funny. During his time in the military, the word was so completely appropriate so very many times that they often speculated on how incredibly screwed up the enemy must be, since the Allies seemed to be winning. This is a common theme in the military; for example, recently in Iraq, American military are frequently quoted as saying that they were saved only because "the Iraqi could not shoot straight."

Recent news should provide a plethora of acronyms that reflect the various stages of disarray that emerge when strategy implementation goes awry. *See* Murphy's Law.

Some acronyms help to communicate the organizational hierarchy such as POTUS, FLOTUS, SCOTUS, VPOTUS. These are President, First Lady, Supreme Court, or Vice President of the United States, respectively. Many strategic initiatives in companies are given acronyms such as GE's FMP (financial management program) or general leadership theory in the army's "Be, Know, Do" (BKD) model of leader development (LD). An acronym often gives followers energy and makes them feel part of something special. Another example is the U.S. military's HUA (heard, understood, acknowledged), now written as it's pronounced: Hoo-ah.

Action   Action is something that happens while you are strategizing, or as a result of strategizing.

Action-Centered Leadership   A leadership model that focuses on what leaders actually have to do in order to be effective. There are three main activities: achieving the task, building and maintaining the team, and developing the individual.

Action Learning   The concept of action learning is based on a simple equation: L = P + Q. Learning (L) occurs through a combination of programmed knowledge (P) and the ability to ask insightful questions (Q). Learning must be free-flowing and "opened up" through asking questions.

Action Plan   Pertains to the behavioral side of learning—what we do differently as a result of new discoveries. Action is akin to the strategy implementation process.

Reminiscent of Winston Churchill's famous dictum in memoranda to bomber command—action this day! This often motivated and energized subordinates to complete a specific task. Nowadays the action plan process still requires motivating and energizing players in the organization; however, the impetus for change can no longer be top-down directives from the command center.

Action Research   The researcher takes an active role as a participant in planning and implementing change in an organization. Experiments are conducted by making changes while simultaneously observing the results. Employees are encouraged to participate in developing practical solutions to real organizational challenges.

Active Supporter   (*See* Sponsor.)

Acts of Symbolism   Odd or unusual behavior that seems to run contrary to common sense but turns out to be deeply significant for employees and other stakeholders. For example, William Watson, the CEO of IBM, by allowing himself to be challenged by the security guard, shows that IBM is democratic and nobody is above the rules. The effect was instantaneous, though many outsiders may have thought that IBM was oversensitive to security.

Adaptability   Not indicated by measures; however, measures can help people to see the areas of adaptability or lack of adaptability to adapt.

Adaptive Strategy   Emphasizes fitness with the environment.

Adding Value   Adding value to a product consists of any activity that increases the product's worth to the customer, such as design, manufacturing, packaging, service, and so forth. The mouse added value to the keyboard on the personal computer. The mouse was invented, and subsequently lost, by researchers at Xerox PARC in Palo Alto, California, who could not grasp its added value. Steven Jobs instantly recognized the practicality of the mouse and hence the added value to the Macintosh computer.

Ad Hoc Management   Ad hoc management necessarily involves the ability of a manager to respond without consulting a formal plan. Ad hoc management gives more flexibility to managers.

Administration   The management of the affairs of a business, especially the planning and control of its operations.

Administrative Behavior   "Organization is not an organizational chart, but a complex pattern of communications and other relationships in a group of human beings."—Herbert Simon. Simon, in his landmark book *Administrative Behavior* (for which he won the Nobel Prize in 1978), says that "administrative man" usually does enough to "get by" (satisficing) when making decisions.

Advice Networks   Informal networks that connect people who turn to one another to seek counsel, get technical answers, and solve specific problems. Some say it is a phony concept, false nomenclature for friendly relationships. This can be extremely valuable to women and minorities in top management. Often a useful communication circle prior to successful self-establishment or getting your foot in the door. The neophyte's crutch.

Agency Theory   The basic conflict between owners and managers. How can the owners ensure that the managers are acting in the owners' interests and not toward maximizing their own wealth and power? For example, a CEO can go on a wild spending and acquisition spree and end up with a much bigger compensation package as she is now managing and leading a much larger and more complex organization. However, eventually these acquisitions may need to be divested if they were not made with the strategic intent of the firm. Was Carly Fiorina's acquisition of Compaq for HP empire building or strategic positioning? Only time will tell.

One area of research known as agency theory suggests that managers frequently place their own interests above those of their shareholders. This appears to be true when strategic decisions involve diversification. While stockholder value may be maximized by selling a company, managers in the acquired field may lose their jobs—a potential conflict of interest.

Aggressive Accounting   Pushing the envelope of generally accepted accounting principles (GAAP), as Enron did. Sometimes unethical, sometimes illegal, always innovative.

Aggressive Action   Relating to investment strategy marked by a willingness to accept high risk while trying to realize higher-than-average gains. Typically, such a strategy involves investing in rapidly growing companies.

Aggressive Expansion   Devoting considerable resources to a market penetration strategy. Used in describing BMW's strategy in trying to capture the automotive

Algorithm **5**

market in China. Despite a weak economic situation in Europe and North America, BMW is taking an aggressive approach in reaching out to the Chinese market.[1]

Aggressive Posturing   Reminiscent of the jungle warfare among alpha males but carried over into internecine struggles among corporate giants. Many firms under the threat of hostile takeover develop poison pill policies. Firms that are losing ground or in financial trouble often react aggressively by acquiring smaller rivals, introducing new products, discounting prices, and so on. Such actions can heighten cross-company rivalry and can trigger a hotly contested battle for market share.

Agility   "The starting point for next year's strategy is almost always this year's strategy. . . . the company sticks to what it knows, even though the real opportunities may be elsewhere."—Gary Hamel. A company that builds a more agile platform is one that will exploit future opportunities and respond more quickly to change.

Algorithm   A solution to a problem that is certain to work; for example, the formula to solve quadratic equations that always gets the answer to any quadratic problem. If a company in NYC wants to make sure that it has a seat on a plane going to London every day, it uses the algorithm *book on, cancel off*. This is an example of an algorithm, or decision rule, that allows strategists to move forward through a complex set of situations and information and make effective choices. An algorithm is certain to work. Fear of flying can be alleviated by the same principle: Book on, cancel off. You need to find surefire solutions that can't fail.

Often in an undertaking, such as introducing a new product, the developers are confronted with a problem like distribution. FedEx turns this problem into an algorithm. American air war policy in Iraq is based on algorithms. American policy allows the American planes to hit their targets but not be hit. Without this aerial algorithm, the air war would not be possible as one American pilot downed could destroy their whole strategy. Both the military and business are intensely interested in algorithmic solutions and strategies.

FedEx works on an algorithm: A plane is not going to leave Tennessee empty. You have to achieve a certain size or scale to be profitable. The same is true of McDonald's or Starbucks.

The Gulf War in 1991 was turned into an algorithm, surefire win, done by bringing 500,000 American troops to Kuwait. Had to be guaranteed absolutely to win.

September 11, each plane had five men. Onboard, two competing algorithms. The pilots' first reaction: "This is just a hijacking." The hijackers were working on a different algorithm: "We are going to die." This is the algorithm of the suicide bomber. People are looking for surefire solutions.

Another algorithm: To increase learning in a company and facilitate the distribution of knowledge, take a gatekeeper in an innovation network and put him or her with a pulsetaker in an expert network.

The RAND Corporation transformed the question about the siting of nuclear bomber bases (to save them from a preemptive strike) into an algorithmic solution: Keep a proportion of the bombers airborne at all times.

Herbert Simon argues that experts in a given area can solve a problem more quickly and more effectively than novices because they have in mind a pattern or algorithm that they can overlay on a particular problem and use to quickly detect a solution.

Alignment   Getting one's "ducks in a row" behind the implementation of a new strategy. Process of building a corporate culture to achieve strategic goals.

Alliances and Alliance Networks   Two or more firms that band together on a loose, noncontractual basis, to achieve certain objectives such as new product development or penetration of new geographic markets. Many computer firms no longer manufacture the actual computers but "agree" to have a third firm do the manufacturing and simply stick on the badge and their peripherals. Other examples would be IKEA and Benetton, the Swedish and Italian firms that do not manufacture their furniture and brightly colored sweaters, but instead have a complex network of alliances with many small European manufacturers with whom their design engineers work very closely.

Allocation of Time   Allocation of top management time is allocation of attention, which is a strategic and costly firm resource. Allocation of time is a magical idea that gets people thinking that time is being lost and can never be recovered and therefore has to be allocated with extreme care, such as by keeping colleagues out of your hair. Hence the expression "putting the monkey (or parrot) on the other guy's shoulders"—casually and briefly telling your boss about a problem instead of responding to his salutation.

Time is of the essence, hence the revolution in management theorizing with the arrival of Sune Carlson's and Henry Mintzberg's executive behavior studies of the 1950s and 1960s. A short-sighted view, as it turns out, that had dramatic significance at the time and led to many books and courses on time management that became a fetish among practicing managers, even to this day (*see* Executive Behavior and Time Management).

A Mechanism and a Man   Unfortunately, the gender-neutral version of this phrase is not an alliteration, so we will leave well enough alone this time. To run an operation there needs to be an office (it is hoped with a good acronym, *see* Strategy by Acronym) and a person to run it.

Analytical Knowledge   Analytical knowledge is objective, scientific knowledge. It requires the formulation of operations, definitions, and concepts in reference to the properties of the phenomena and to the relations between the properties.

Anchoring   To institutionalize a new approach in the culture.

Andrews, Kenneth (1916–)   Proponent and popularizer of the Harvard Business School approach to strategic management, which emphasized leadership, the role of the general manager, and the mission statement. General management responsibilities include (1) securing the attainment of present results, (2) developing organizational capability, (3) distinctive personal contribution, and (4) planning and executing policies for future results. Authored one of the first books on strategy to recognize the green movement by addressing the ecological and environmental concerns of key stakeholders. Andrews sees the CEO as the architect of purpose.

Annual Reports   Annual reports are complex, symbolic constructions of what management wants to communicate to its audiences, a vivid narrative of corporate performance. There is also a financial information section that summarizes and again shows the firm's performance. The rhetoric must then persuasively argue that description to the organization's audience. More recent annual reports have less financial data and more management text. Annual report narrative content and themes are important information about corporate strategy.

Ansoff, Igor (1918–2002)   Author of one of the first books in strategic management, the 1965 *Concept of Corporate Strategy*, and so considered a father of the discipline. This was only the second business book to use the word "strategy," after Alfred Chandler's 1962 classic *Strategy and Structure*. Ansoff frequently cites Chandler in this book, and Ansoff's model builds on a similar focus on corporate strategy (as opposed to business-level or competitive strategy).

Ansoff was trained in the Carnegie Mellon systems approach of George Steiner and others. Systems thinking ambitiously tries to define, predict, and tie together all the elements of a given system, with the view that if the system's elements can be specified, understood, and manipulated, the system as a whole can be directed to produce a given outcome. Closed systems are rational; all the variables can be predicted; even outside forces and their effects can be predicted. Open systems are influenced by unpredictable changes in the environment.

Ansoff provided strategic management with a methodology, which is essentially an engineering approach and involves a series of checklists. Systems thinking has been largely discredited as a way to either study or do strategic management and is associated with an overemphasis on formal strategic planning. However, chaos theory and complexity theory try to rehabilitate the systems model and update it with a nonlinear approach.

Ansoff succeeds in being the first to define the strategy universe. However, his model can be misleading, suggesting that the strategy-making job can be captured within a defined system. It minimizes the aspect of strategy as a human construction that is responsive to human needs. It is important to remember the concept of bounded rationality, from the Nobel Prize-winning thinker Herbert Simon, which highlights the limited capabilities of humans to define and solve problems.

Simon also differentiates between programmed and unprogrammed tasks. Strategy making is by definition an unprogrammed task that happens at largely unprogrammable moments. The danger of Ansoff's model is that in his brilliant summing up of the strategy universe, he misleads us to believe that these mechanistic manipulations ensure winning strategies. We cannot simply break down the strategy task into its component parts as we run the risk of ignoring deus ex machina events. These deus ex machina events, such as the September 11, 2001, terrorist attacks, change the whole nature of the system, the whole basis of competition. Gary Hamel maintains that if it is not revolutionary, it is not strategic.

Some key concepts Ansoff introduced are (1) the importance of the diversification decision (the key component of corporate strategy), (2) the importance of synergy $(2 + 2 = 5)$ in diversification decisions, (3) the make-or-buy choice (he labels this organic growth versus acquisition), and (4) the Ansoff matrix as a good tool for making decisions about investing in new areas. Ansoff suggests that there must be a common thread that runs through all of a company's business. This insight was a forerunner of Rumelt's and Porter's studies that proved that related diversification outperforms unrelated diversification. These findings were a foundation and precursor of the core competence concept (Prahalad and Hamel), a unifying thread that runs through business units.

In his later writings, Ansoff noted, "For optimum profitability the levels of both the strategic aggressiveness and general management responsiveness of the firm must be aligned with the environmental turbulence level." This is his fundamental formula for the firm that explains the relation among strategic capabilities and environmental turbulence levels; if both gaps are less than one, the firm is strategically ready for the future (although some improvements may be needed). If the general management capability gap is greater than one, a discontinuous transformation of the general management capability must be made.

Ansoff spent his last 20 years at Alliant International University testing his theories and having them validated by a series of doctoral theses.

Antitakeover Tactics Tactics used to ward off being acquired. Often controversial, these antitakeover tactics appear to serve the needs of managers (who are likely to lose their jobs in the newly merged entity) more than the owners. These tactics include "scorched earth," "golden parachute," and "poison pill."

Apple Strategy "From the garage to the desktop." Getting it out of the garage and into the market. The guy who invented the semiconductor left the company where he was working and joined with seven other PhDs; within three months there were seven other garages working. This is an apocryphal but illustrative example of the Apple strategy.

Architecture of Strategy A framework or building blocks used in strategic management to create a successful firm. This framework includes organizational capacity, enterprise synergies, structural position, process execution, competitive advantage, and financial performance.

Argyris, Chris (1923–) Considered by many a humanizing force in business and academia, Argyris has done extensive research into how executives and organizations learn—or fail to learn. He saw strategy as a learning process. Argyris emphasized single- and double-loop learning; the two types of learning refer to the way that people respond to changes in their environment. Single-loop learning occurs when a manager responds to a problem with a simple application of the rules. Double-loop learning goes beyond this simple feedback response and questions the assumptions on which the response is based.

Key books include *Personality and Organization* (1957), *Theory and Practice* (1974), and *Organizational Learning* (1978).

Artificial Crisis Leaders often create artificial crises rather than waiting for something to happen. They drain scarce resources from the firm and thus leave less maneuvering room. "Don't just do something, sit there" can often be the most appropriate response.

Assessing the Environment The objective of assessing the environment is to determine the timing and significance of the effects of environmental changes and trends on the strategic management of the firm. Without the assessment, a firm is left with data that are interesting but of unknown competitive relevance.

Assets The factors of production a firm may draw on in providing its customers with valuable goods and services are called assets. There are both tangible (a firm's property) and intangible (brand name) assets.

Attention Management A method of ensuring that employees are focused on their work as well as organizational goals. An important factor in winning and sustaining attention is tapping into people's emotions as developed in Daniel Goleman's theory of emotional intelligence.

Authority The character of communication in a formal organization that determines how it is accepted by an actor in the organization and how it governs the action she contributes.

When Henry Ford II used to argue with Lee Iacocca, his final words were, "Why don't you go outside and see whose name is on the building?"

During the past decade, the term "authority" has taken on a new meaning as organizations move from authoritarian control to one of decentralized structures that stress employee development and empowerment.

Avoided Competition Avoiding head-to-head competition, versus seeking out and taking on the next biggest rival.

Awareness of Competition Refers to whether or not the attacking or responding firm is aware of the competitive market characteristics, such as market commonality and resource similarity of a potential attacker or respondent.

A Way Forward/a Bridge A way to transition from an antiquated or no longer viable policy and segue into a new way of doing things. For example, an Air Force Academy commander was quoted recently as saying that a cadet who said she was raped would not be punished for violating the honor code under the academy's new policy for handling assault allegations. "We tried to look at a way forward for this cadet in line with the agenda for change," said Col. Debra Gray. Gray went on to say that the case was a "bridge" between how the academy used to handle assault allegations and what it would do now.

Endnote

1. http://www.fortune.com/fortune/ceo/articles/0,15114,444769,00.html

B

"B" Players   Although "A" players are considered the company's stars, "B" players play a vital role in any organization's success. "B"s are the steady, dependable workers within the organization.

Ba   A Japanese term that means a shared space for emerging relationships. This space can be physical (office), virtual (e-mail, teleconferencing), mental (shared experience, ideas, ideals) or any combination. *Ba* provides a platform for advancing individual and collective knowledge. *Ba* is a shared place that serves as a foundation for knowledge creation. Knowledge resides in *ba,* it is intangible. Sharp, for example, employs teams as a platform for knowledge creation. Toshiba utilizes *ba* through establishing a platform for cross-functional knowledge creation in one of its divisions. Other firms use *ba* to establish an intimacy and immediacy in their relationship with customers.[1]

Back Channel   Previously a noun, now a verb to indicate private meetings or conference calls behind the scenes to quietly make your point. For example, a small biotech company that is struggling with a depressed economy, a competitor like Merck and Pfizer developing competing products, competition from the generic drugs, and a pending lawsuit about their development process may choose to back channel meetings with Wall Street analysts rather than try to address all these issues at their general annual meeting, where the events in such a public arena could backfire and turn into a PR debacle.

Backward Integration   Generates cost savings when the volume needed is big enough to capture the same scale of economies suppliers have. An example of backward integration would be acquiring a supplier whose technical skills would be easily mastered.

Balanced Scorecard   Actually a top-down approach to implementing strategic change that is currently used by numerous companies to assess their position in the marketplace.

Bargaining, or "Let's Make a Deal"   Offering up a position designed both to secure your own advantage and gain mutual agreement and benefit. The essence of business: In Spanish, the word for business is *"negocios,"* meaning negotiations. "Let's make a deal" were the words that Michael Eisner, head of Walt Disney, said to Steve Jobs of Pixar Animation Studios, on a popular weekly TV program, "Topic A." At the time, Disney and Pixar split production and marketing costs and shared profit. However, Disney took more than a 50% share because it receives a distribution fee for releasing movies in theaters and on video and DVD. A new deal, proposed after the record-breaking success of *Finding Nemo*—which is on its way to becoming the most successful animated movie of all time with projected U.S. ticket sales of more than $300 million—would be more favorable to Pixar. "Let's make a deal" arises when relative strategic positions shift and new options open up. In this case, Pixar is trying to leverage the fact that with five consecutive hits, it seems to be the only entertainment company at that level working with a perfect track record. However, Disney will try to leverage its "ownership" of every Pixar film from *Toy Story* to *Cars*. A key is to emphasize mutual benefit, synergy, and shared destiny, not to mention the win-win approach. As Eisner said of Disney and Pixar, "We are Martin and Lewis. We are Abbott and Costello. We are a good team. We are a better team together than separate. I know it. I hope he knows it."

Barnard, Chester (1886–1961)   Articulated in his classic 1938 book *The Functions of the Executive* was the view that corporate leaders have to manage employees and inspire in them the values of the firm. Barnard saw the firm as a community, and in a community, "all acts of employees and leaders are directly and/or indirectly interconnected and interdependent."

Barnard was a humanist who saw in the organization the external conflict of man in society; however, he saw the firm as a vehicle for providing a contribution to "man" as a whole. Barnard was a philosopher, a practitioner, a scholar, an economist, a statesman, a person who has significantly influenced American life. His book simply describes what executives do and how they do it.

Barriers to Entry   A barrier to entry exists whenever it is hard for a newcomer to break into the market or economic factors put a potential entrant at a disadvantage relative to its competitors. Barriers to entry can be erected by specific firm strategic choices such as branding or preemptive capital investments, or barriers can emerge from the structure of the industry (*see* Five Forces Industry Analysis).

"New entrants to a market bring new production capacity, the desire to establish a secure place in the market, and sometimes substantial resources with which to compete." —Michael Porter.

BCG Matrix "Cash Cows"   Cash cows are businesses with a high market share in relatively low-growth markets or industries. Because of their strong positions and their minimal reinvestment requirements, these businesses often generate cash in excess of their needs. Therefore, they are selectively "milked" as a source of corporate resources for deployment elsewhere (to stars and question marks) within the firm's portfolio. Cash cows can be thought of as yesterday's "stars" and as the current foundation of corporate portfolios.

BCG Matrix "Dogs"   Businesses with low market share and low market growth are the dogs of the firm's portfolio. Facing mature markets with intense competition and low profit margins, they are managed for short-term cash flow reasons (through ruthless cost cutting, for example) to supplement corporate-level resource needs. Oftentimes, dogs are divested or liquidated once this short-term harvesting has been maximized.

BCG Matrix Question Marks   Question marks are businesses whose high growth rate gives them considerable appeal but whose low market share makes their profit potential uncertain. Question marks can be cash guzzlers because their rapid growth results in high cash demands, while their small market share results in low cash generation. Where this long-term shift from question mark to star is somewhat unlikely, the BCG Matrix suggests divesting the question mark and repositioning its resources more effectively in the remainder of the corporate portfolio.

BCG Matrix Stars   The stars are businesses in rapidly growing markets with the largest market shares. These businesses represent the best opportunity for long-term growth and profitability in their firm's portfolio. They require substantial investment to maintain (and expand) their dominant position in a growing market. This investment requirement is often in excess of the funds that they can generate internally. Therefore, these businesses (or stars) are often short-term, primarily consumers of corporate resources.

BCG Portfolio Matrix   Tool for CEOs to manage strategic planning and capital budgeting and resource allocation process according to quadrants of industry market growth rate and relative market share. Products or business units can be classified, say, as dogs, question marks, cows, and stars. The idea is to get rid of the dogs and to promote the stars, financing them with cash generated from cash cows. The idea is that CEOs can balance the portfolio of firms' businesses among the quadrants to grow faster. Dogs, for example, would receive no investment if no rapid payback, while stars would receive a lot to be cash cows. The limitation of the BCG matrix is that it ignored relatedness among businesses in the matrix, the concept of synergy that later came to be known as core competence. This tool fell out of favor in the 1980s.

Behind the Curve   According to Donald Rumsfeld, what happens in life is that in any given year, you can get by without making an investment. For example, if the roof on your house leaks a little bit, you can decide, "We'll fix it next year." If you do that for several years, you are behind the curve.

Benchmarking   A tool that allows a company to determine whether the manner in which it performs a particular function or activity represents the best practices when both cost and effectiveness are taken into consideration. Not only compares a company with its rival on cost but also compares itself to others on its most relevant activity or competitively important measure. Benchmarking has never lived up to its promise. It's simply too time-consuming and expensive.

Sears and General Electric are major rivals in the home appliance industry. Sears' principal strength is its retail network. Conversely, GE possesses the financial resources needed to support modernization of mass production of its products, which has enabled it to maintain a competitive advantage (both cost and technological) over its rivals, particularly Sears.

Bennis, Warren (1925–)   USC professor famous for transformative leadership. A transformative leadership style is described as one that motivates through identification with the leader's vision: pulling rather than pushing others on.

Best Product Strategy   Competitive strategy that entails choosing a different set of activities to deliver a unique mix of value. For example, Coke's overriding strategy is a consistent quality product at an affordable price. This is illustrated in Coca-Cola's mission:

> More than a billion times every day, thirsty people around the world reach for Coca-Cola products for refreshment. They deserve the highest quality—every time. Our promise to deliver that quality is the most important promise we make. And it involves a world-wide, yet distinctly local, network of bottling partners, suppliers, distributors and retailers whose success is paramount to our own. Our investment in local communities in over 200 countries totals billions of dollars in jobs, facilities, marketing, the purchase of local goods and services, and local business partnerships. Always and everywhere, we pursue continuous innovation in the products we offer, the processes we use to make them, the packages we develop and the ways we bring them to market.

Big Picture   Taking the broad picture or perspective on issues that encompass the firm's surroundings, context, and long-term implications.

BlackBerrying   The postcard-size BlackBerry communicator holds a CEO's Rolodex as well as her e-mail system. Many CEOs use this communicator to squirt orders and suggestions to employees and other top managers, typically using only a few words. It is like a haiku. During a meeting, these hyped-up executives constantly spin the BlackBerry's dial and punch out text on its tiny keyboard. "Sometimes we're in a meeting talking to each other and BlackBerrying each other at the same time," said one of George W's political advisors. Sometimes the voltage of BlackBerrying can get too hot, and executives have been known to break into song in midsentence.

Black Box   The part of the system that is unknown and unknowable. Donald Rumsfeld muses, "As we know, there are known knowns. . . . But there are also unknown unknowns—the ones we don't know we don't know." Rumsfeld was referring to the concept of the black box in his cryptic, philosophical, and poetic musings on the preparation for war in Iraq and in the process highlighting the inherent limitations of systems theory to arrive at strategic solutions.

The black box concept can be used as a means to limit our need to control and understand. Strategy as a field is by its very nature dealing with the unknowable (the future) and the partially unexplainable (firm success).

Black Hawk Down Syndrome Situations in which the mission is unclear and success is a remote possibility. The U.S. Army Rangers' motto, "No one left behind," led to disastrous consequences when a combined Special Forces (Delta and Army Rangers) operation to capture Somali warlord Mohammed Farah Aidid in Mogadishu went terribly wrong. After one of the Black Hawk helicopters went down, the resulting rescue mission left 18 American dead, and one American serviceman's corpse was dragged through the streets of Mogadishu. It was a bitter and demoralizing experience. The fallout was the perception by many that Americans won't fight, won't get involved. Some argue that this perception contributed to the proliferation of al-Qaeda training camps and the ensuing al-Qaeda attack on the World Trade Center and the Pentagon on September 11, 2001.

Another example of this syndrome is Japan's continued commitment to lifetime employment, consensual decision making, and kereitsu even though the economy is suffering a 10-year recession.

Blocker A blocker is an upholder of the status quo who resolutely resists change. Sometimes blockers can join together to form a hindrance network, which can be even more troubling. Two examples of traditional blockers are the receptionist and the department head. Often "experts" are blockers to the innovators because they do not want to lose their power base. Knowledge management systems need to track these blockers.

Blue-Sky Free-wheeling brainstorming sessions that consider the future of the industry in a very open-ended, unfettered manner. American culture is particularly suited to this type of discussion and investigation as the culture is not afraid to tear down the tradition and past way of doing things, if doing them in a different and new way promises a payoff in profit or efficiency.

Boot Camp Boot camp is that period of intense training and indoctrination in the military. In business, this term denotes any intense immersion experience that separates "A" players from the "B" players.

Boots per Square Meter The false or misleading idea that throwing more money or resources at a problem will solve it. There needs to be higher-order thinking. Lieutenant General Abizaid assumed duties as the Deputy Commander (Forward) for Combined Forces Command, U.S. Central Command in January 2003. He noted, "It is not a matter of boots per square meter. Everybody wants to think that, but that's just not so. If I could do one thing as a commander right, I would focus my intelligence like a laser on where the problem is, which is mid-level Baathist leaders." Abizaid betrays his international perspective by using the metric system, rather than maintaining the quaint U.S. attachment to the imperial system.

Boundarylessness A management philosophy, perfected at General Electric under Jack Welch, which basically means, "Good ideas can come from anywhere." Some companies have forums where employees at all levels get together and discuss strategic issues and everyone is entitled to air his or her opinion. In this way, employees see their stake in the organization, so it's easier for them to accept change rather than oppose it, since they contributed to the goal setting (ownership). Boundarylessness makes all employees feel important and motivated to work toward achieving the firm's objectives.

Brand(s)   Diversified companies with well-known brand names have lower barriers to entry into new businesses than do firms without established brand names. Well-known brand names that have had success in diversifying include Sony and Nike.

Call it the Pepsi Blue Generation. So much for the one-soda-fits-all strategy. When 130 million viewers tuned in to Super Bowl XXXVII, Pepsi didn't disappoint those who count on it to deliver glitzy and entertaining ads. There was not, however, a single commercial devoted to Pepsi's flagship cola. Instead, three of the four slots, purchased for $2 million apiece, went to newer and narrower brands such as lemon-lime Sierra Mist and lemon-flavored Pepsi Twist. It's a sign of how the soft-drink giant has reformulated its missions from bolstering core brands like Pepsi-Cola and Mountain Dew to covering the market with niche products and brand extension. Its strategy is creating value through diversification. It is creating niche products, new brands that appeal to specific target markets and thereby spread all over the beverage market and get a high portion of it.

Bringing the Market Inside   The structural changes that can be made to encourage entrepreneurial behavior. The term suggests how large firms can manage their resource allocation and people management systems to be more entrepreneurial and responsive. Some examples include market techniques such as spin-offs and corporate venture capital operations. Originally this view came from the works of Joseph Schumpeter and has later been applied through the works of Hamel (1996)[2] and Kaplan (1996).[3]

British Officer Requirements   Show initiative. Bash on. Be nonchalant.

Budgeting   An important lever for implementing strategy is a firm's system for allocating capital resources. The availability of capital to pay for proposed actions strongly determines managers' efforts; it is a direct way of influencing what strategic action will be taken and what realized strategies will emerge.

Budgeting and Performance Assessment   Budgeting is a tool for performance assessment. Budgeting is used in planning expenditures, capital purchases, and growth. Knowing how to budget gives a firm more chances to succeed. A firm should have a budget and use it effectively while analyzing its performance by variance or exception analysis, matching the estimate budget and the actual budget. An expense item that has an underexpenditure to budget can be of equal concern to one that has an overexpenditure to budget.[4] Whenever underexpenditure or overexpenditure takes place, a firm is responsible to find out its underlying causes and then initiate actions needed to correct for the future.

Bunker Mentality Paranoid mind-set popularized by Andy Grove in *Only the Paranoid Survive:* seeing strategy as war and enemies within and outside the company. Often appropriate in fast-paced industries. Microsoft often exhibits a bunker mentality in its dealings with competitors like Sun Microsystems.

Bureaucratic Controls Formalized supervisory and behavioral rules and policies that are designed to ensure consistency of decisions and actions across different units of a firm. Across time, relatively rigid and standardized managerial behavior tends to be the product of strict adherence to formalized rules and/or policies. It often results in less innovation. Standard operating procedures (SOP) are an example of behavioral control.

Business According to Peter Drucker, the definition of a business is the creation of a customer through marketing and innovation. Managing a business must always be entrepreneurial in character; it cannot be bureaucratic, administrative, or even a policy-making job. "There is only one valid definition of business purpose: to create a customer, markets are not created by God, nature or economic forces, but by businessmen." The purpose of business lies outside of itself. The purpose is the enrichment of customers and society.

Business Ecosystem The system in which companies work cooperatively and competitively to support new products, satisfy customers, and create innovation in key market segments.

Business-Level Strategies A business-level strategy is an integrated and coordinated set of commitments and actions designed to provide value to customers and gain competitive advantage by exploiting core competencies in specific, individual product markets.

Business Model A management plan for making money in a particular business. It deals with the revenue-cost-profit economics of its strategy—the actual and projected revenue streams generated by the company's product offerings and competitive approaches, and the resulting earnings streams and return on investment.

Business Philosophy A company's values, policies, practices, and culture are all part of the business philosophy, which dominates the kinds of strategic moves it considers or rejects.

Business Policy The name of the capstone course at the Harvard Business School that stressed integration of previous course material. Business Policy, for many years, was the term for the area of management we now denote as strategic management. It was originally viewed as a course, not a field. However, this dictionary helps to mark the 42nd anniversary of strategic management as a separate field of inquiry and not just a course.

At the time the course was instituted, there were no professional societies, no specialized journals, or formal academic training of faculty. Basically, all the "ex"es taught business policy: ex-CEOs, ex-CFOs, ex-high-level government bureaucrats.

Business Position Matrix   A framework designed to assess the attractiveness of entering into an industry or business area. Items such as industry attractiveness via suppliers, threats of new entrants, and economic factors are looked at and assessed. Additionally, factors of the business position of firm via cost position, financial strength, and public approval are looked at and assessed.

Business Priorities   Strategy is an exercise in setting priorities. Priorities involve an opportunity cost: Pursuing one objective with certain resources precludes other uses of those resources. Coca-Cola's 2003 annual report outlines their strategic business priorities.

1. "Accelerate carbonated soft-drink growth, led by Coca-Cola."

2. "Selectively broaden our family of beverage brands to drive profitable growth."

3. "Grow system profitability and capability together with our bottling partners."

4. "Serve customers with creativity and consistency to generate growth across all channels."

5. "Direct investments to highest-potential areas across markets."

6. "Drive efficiency and cost effectiveness everywhere."

Coca-Cola has been able to continually outperform its arch rival Pepsi through the pursuit of these business priorities.

Business Strategy   The "game plan" for a single business. It is mirrored in the pattern of approaches and moves crafted by management to produce successful performance in one specific area of business.

Endnotes

1. Nanaka, I., & Konno, N. (1988). Creating organizational order out of chaos: Self-renewal in Japanese firms. *California Management Review*, 30:3, 57.

2. Hamel, G., & Prahalad, C. K. (1996). *Competing for the future*. Boston: Harvard Business School Press.

3. Kaplan, R. S., & Norton, D. P. (1996). *The balanced scorecard: Translating strategy into action*. Boston: Harvard Business School Press.

4. Lazof, R. C. (2002). *Planned Performance*. Retrieved May 1, 2003, from the World Wide Web: http://ww.refresher.com/!rclplanned.html

Calling Audibles   The football term for calling plays from the line of scrimmage. L. Paul Bremer, the occupation administrator and overseer in Iraq, adapts strategy as hurdles arise. "I think I said at my first press conference that I expected we would be calling a lot of audibles," he said, "but our strategy hasn't changed." Mr. Bremer has strong credentials as the tough counterterrorism chief in the Reagan administration and as a longtime protégé of Henry A. Kissinger, the former secretary of state and for 23 years a career diplomat.

Can-Do Attitude (American)   Mayor of Galveston on Hurricane Claudette: "I'll take this minimal hurricane, so they can go ahead and bring this one on and we'll make it through this."

Capabilities   The firm's capacity to deploy resources that have been purposely integrated to achieve a desired end state. Often thought of as the glue that holds the organization together; capabilities emerge over time through complex interactions among tangible and intangible resources.

Knowing the company's resources, knowledge, potential, and abilities helps to make decisions on strategic planning. It was not easy for Lou Gerstner to change IBM in the early 1990s. He carefully analyzed the company and found that IBM's structure was not adaptive enough to changes. He had to restructure the company so that new capabilities could be developed to meet environmental demand. One key capability that emerged after the restructuring was IBM's e-business service consulting.

Capability Responsiveness   A term used by Igor Ansoff in his later writings to denote the level of the organization's internal capability to meet challenges from its environment. Capability responsiveness is linked to concepts such as attitude toward change, success model, and focus of power.

Case Method and Strategic Management   The case method as problem-solving algorithm comes from the Harvard Business School (HBS) via books like Christensen's first business policy case book. The HBS in turn borrowed the case approach from the Harvard Law School. (Remember the disclaimer at the bottom of every HBS case study: This case is meant to illustrate administrative situation and is not meant to demonstrate the correct or incorrect handling of an administrative situation.) The most important aspect of the case method is that there is no right or wrong. There is, however, a systematic methodology to analyze the situation and come up with a solution. This approach grounds strategic management in the area of practice, anecdote, and precedent rather than the strictly analytical approach of the Carnegie Mellon mathematical systems thinking.

The strategic manager is capable of evolving a set of alternatives that will help her reach her goals. She is then able to evaluate each of these alternatives against a set of criteria and make an intelligent selection. Having selected an alternative, she can then spot blockages impeding her intention and develop tactics to circumvent or remove them. The achieving executive using the case method algorithm has a strong need for feedback to monitor her efforts and to give her satisfaction as she moves toward her goals and the organization's goals. Think of the case of George W. Bush's executive style; it is not accidental that the first MBA president of the United States relies heavily on this decision-making algorithm. Typically, when he was faced with questions like stem cell research or the war in Iraq, he responded, We are going to analyze the alternatives and come up with a course of action in due time. It is not necessary to agree with the final course of action, but to see the simple elegance of the HBS method of the case study.

Cash Cow   Contrary to the belief of brand-new MBA students, a cash cow is not a particularly heavily uddered bovine that produces prodigious amounts of milk on a regular basis. Instead, a cash cow business is a valuable part of a diversified company's business portfolio because it generates cash for financing new acquisitions, funding the capital requirements of cash hogs, and paying dividends.

Cash Hog   A business whose internal cash flows are inadequate to fully fund its needs for working capital and new capital investments.

Cassandra Complex   A self-fulfilling prophecy that predicts doom and misfortune. From Greek mythology, portrayed in Aeschylus' play *Agamemnon*. Cassandra was the daughter of Priam, the king of Troy, and her prophecies of doom and gloom were fated to never be believed. This often happens in mergers and acquisitions, where the us-versus-them division becomes a self-fulfilling prophecy.

Catastrophic Success   Tommy Franks, when he was leading Central Command in Iraq, warned of the perils of "catastrophic success." The swift drive to Baghdad, while in one sense wildly successful, left large areas of Iraq and millions of Iraqis under minimal or nominal coalition control and with a very small force to handle an unmanageable country. The answer may not have been to go slower, but the speed did leave major holes to be filled in. To what extent can those holes be planned for and filled in advance?

This applies in a business context to rolling out new products such as Apple's iPod digital music download service. A proposed idea for marketing Apple's new iPod and digital download service from a Mac discussion forum on the Internet: "a revival of the 1984 Apple Super Bowl commercial . . . same scene . . . just this time it's a shattering of the Orwellian control these guys want to impose on your Digital lifestyle, . . . instead of a sledgehammer, it's an iPod."[1] Apple's success with the innovative iPod could be catastrophic if Wintel-based competitors with incompatible music formats drive Apple's market share in the music download market downward into single digits like its PC share. Apple is known for its catastrophic success. The Mac versus Microsoft battle is now playing itself out again, only this time, it is a musical!

Catch-22   A situation in which a desired outcome is not possible because the rules prohibit it. The term was coined by Joseph Heller in his novel of that name. The catch-22 in the book applied to pilots who had already flown beyond their maximum number of missions with no relief in sight and were actually going crazy with fatigue and fear; so they wanted to get out of the military by pleading that they were crazy. Their wanting to get out of potentially fatal combat was presented to them as proof they were not crazy. This is the catch-22: Claiming to be crazy proved they were not. In strategy, every strategic decision usually involves some catch-22, inherent logical inconsistencies or unintended consequences of following a rule or mandate.

A catch-22 would be the unintended consequence for American companies of globalization. For example, in the global marketplace, as the CEO of Intel, Craig Barrett, points out, political events—the fall of the Soviet Union, China's moving toward capitalism—brought half the world's population, or about 3 billion people, into free markets. Once these markets are stimulated, these people increasingly can buy U.S. products, compete against U.S. companies, and ultimately compete for jobs and markets once firmly held by U.S. citizens and firms.

Causal Ambiguity   Refers to a situation where there is difficulty relating the consequences or effects to initial states or causes. The complexity of causal structures is best illustrated by investigations of aircraft crashes that are often presumed in the first instance to be due to terrorist acts. Indeed, this may be so, but there are often complex causes at work.

For example, in 1998, a TWA plane disintegrated and fell into the sea; the immediate conclusion was that the cause was an act of terrorism. It was subsequently ascertained to be an electrical fault in the plane's fuel line. The explosion originated in the electrical line in the central fuel tank, which was not properly insulated: a technological defect in the design of the aircraft.

In business, there is this type of uncertainty as to the actual cause of an event. Corporate problems with multiple causation often lead to dramatic changes in strategy. It is as well to keep in mind what David Hume, the great Scottish philosopher, said, "Events that are seen as contiguous in time and space are perceived as causally linked." So, for example, in many firms, the boards of directors, increasingly impatient with CEOs who don't deliver, dismiss them, perhaps on the basis of causal ambiguity. Booz Allen Hamilton's annual study of CEO succession trends showed that forced turnover of underperforming CEOs at major corporations reached a new high in 2002, rising 70% from 2001 and accounting for 39% of all chief executive transitions. Roy Disney's attack on Michael Eisner, attributing the Disney Corporation's underperformance to Eisner's mismanagement, may be a case of causal ambiguity. A classic case of possible causal ambiguity is the question whether one can attribute U.S. economic performance to the president who is in office.

Centralization The degree to which decision-making authority is retained at higher managerial levels. Today, the trend is toward decentralization—the movement of decision-making authority down to people in the firm who have the most direct and frequent contact with customers.

CFCD *See* Concept Formulation, Contract Definition.

Champion A maverick iconoclast who gets a fire in the belly to pursue a project or innovation.

Chandler, Alfred Dupont (1918–) Author of arguably the first book on strategic management, at least the first with strategy in the title: *Strategy and Structure*. Chandler, a scion of the DuPont family, is essentially a business historian from the Harvard Business School. His groundbreaking book is actually a detailed history of the transition of four of the giants in American business (Sears, Standard Oil, General Motors, and DuPont) from a single product line to a multiproduct structure.

Chandler's brilliance was (1) to meticulously document this transition and anchor it in a historical context; (2) to recognize and label it as an "administrative innovation": American business is famous for not only innovating in product and production process but also in administrative process; and (3) to impute a linear directionality to the relationship of strategy and structure, arguing that a change in strategy causes a change in structure. This is like many chicken and egg arguments: At times it is hard to defend, as one can argue convincingly that a change in structure can lead to a change in strategy.

The administrative form that Chandler documents is the birth in the late 1950s and early 1960s of the multidivisional structure. In 1949, only 24% of the big American companies were divisionalized, and by 1969, 80% were. This administrative innovation allowed for the emergence of the corporate headquarters as a center of strategic control and direction. Paradoxically, the more decentralized structure allows for more corporate control to occur because the divisional form makes financial monitoring possible through the profit center or cost center. This financial control allows for greater strategic freedom and initiative for the division or subsidiary manager and the general manager in the division, pushing strategy making to lower levels in the organization.

This administrative innovation seemed like a winning formula for large, complex, multiproduct and multidivision firms. The divisional structure can also be easily translated to a multicountry strategy with the country manager in the multinational corporation (MNC, now called MNEs because smaller firms are getting on the global strategy bandwagon).

However, in the mid-1980s, this approach to structuring firms came under fire in the works of Gary Hamel and C. K. Prahalad. They argued that the multidivisional form led to managing the firm as a portfolio of financial assets and doing so got away from the concept of synergy (Ansoff), or, to use the modern term, core competence. Chandler continues to write on topics like the invisible hand and multinational corporations.

Change   A definition of grace is the ability to accept change. One principal task of the top management team is to anticipate and welcome change in the environment and model this readiness to every level of change. Change is best understood by trying to understand the path between the beginning state and the end state. What systems theory is all about is showing that there are many paths from beginning state (BS) to end state (ES).

A good example of the complexity of these transitions is acceptance of the fact that it is better to enter a new field after the first inventor has bankrupted itself. A perfect example comes from World War II, when the failure and destruction of the German rocket industry gave the Americans a tremendous postwar jump forward into rocketry via Wernher Von Braun.

One well-recognized way of characterizing the change process focuses on unfreezing, change, and refreezing, from Kurt Lewin's research. During the unfreezing stage, old beliefs are discarded to make way for new understandings. Also called unlearning, this process is seen as a key preliminary stage in the change process. As old beliefs are discarded, new understandings about the environment can be achieved. Finally, the new worldview is solidified. These new patterns of attention are frozen in the anticipation of future events.

Even beneficial change is quite difficult. It is human nature to resist it, and there is only one way to overcome it and that is leadership.

Kurt Lewin's research during World War II and the Hawthorne studies demonstrated that allowing greater participation in the change process increases the likelihood of acceptance of the change and positive impact.[3]

Weick (1999) distinguished between episodic change and continuous change.[4] Episodic changes are infrequent, discontinuous, and intentional, while continuous changes are constant, evolving, and cumulative.[5]

Change Management   Coordination of a structured period of transition from one situation to another in order to achieve lasting change within an organization. This can involve continuous change, which usually involves small changes, or radical change, which involves looking at change from the macro level.

Change Process   John Kotter wrote the best-selling book ever published by the Harvard Business School Press. In it he lists eight steps in the change process at the strategic level:[6]

1. Establishing a sense of urgency

2. Creating the guiding coalition

3. Developing a vision and strategy

4. Communicating the change vision

5. Empowering broad-based action

6. Generating short-term wins

7. Consolidating gains and producing more change

8. Anchoring new approaches in the culture

Channel Conflict   Conflicts that arise from external forces that include suppliers, customers, investors, and regulators and result in internal obstacles. An example is resistance from existing sales organizations to new ways of marketing and selling products to customers.

Chaos   In describing conditions in Iraq following the war, a senior Washington official said, "I wish I could tell you differently but I can't. Things are fairly chaotic there. When my people want secure communications, they go find an M1A1 tank or a Bradley and beg the army sergeant in charge for a few minutes on the vehicle's secure computer."

Chicken Little Syndrome   A defeatist attitude such as "The sky is falling." Opposite of can-do attitude. The Chicken Little syndrome is common after mergers.

Chief Executive Officer (CEO)   CEOs originated when there was a transition from owner-founders running companies to what Chandler refers to as the "salaried manager": a professional who is not owner of the company and is hired to act in the interest of a group of shareholders. An early example of this original CEO is Alfred P. Sloan, who became president of GM when the founder was no longer able to administrate a company that had slipped into chaos and inefficiency. The success of Sloan's management approach with commissions, meetings, and open discussions led to the trend for CEOs managing corporation in the 1940s and 1950s.

At the beginning of the 1980s a new management era was inaugurated when Jack Welch became the CEO of GE. Bad performance, unproductive units, and old management were the first things that Welch fixed. Welch introduced employees' performance measures, fired unproductive managers, and sold off unproductive units. His commitment toward the shareholders' interests brought him to focus on GE's stock price. The result was incredible: In the 20 years of the Welch era the stock price rose more than 5,000% and the notion of the charismatic CEO superstar was born.

It is interesting to note that an executive holding the titles of both CEO and chairman of the board is more likely to deliver greater returns to shareholders and higher net income growth. The higher up you go on the corporate ladder, the more you need to make other people winners, and not make it about winning yourself.[2]

Chinese Wall   A Chinese wall is a surreal wall that exists to separate two functions. That is the wall that people walk through all the time and that is what causes problems, as happened between Anderson Consulting and Enron. At Anderson, one division was involved in auditing and another division in consulting.

Resulting conflicts evolved, such as giving the heads of the companies advance notice to buy into stocks before they went public. If you are in the vice squad, you will sleep with the girls; if you go undercover, you eventually become a gangster. In other words, Chinese walls do not work. For example, in an investment bank, part of the firm could be concerned with mergers and acquisitions. On the other side of the Chinese wall are the honest brokers who advise investors. With the Chinese wall, the M&A people are supposedly separate from those that give advice on investing. But it's not really possible to maintain that division.

Chronic Mediocrity   Continuous average or mediocre performance by a company; according to the management guru Jim Collins, the reason behind this mediocrity is as follows: "A real turnaround can take seven years, and failing to embrace that fact is one of the primary causes of chronic mediocrity." This can be applied to many companies for many reasons. Performing poorly can depend on many reasons, and unless the companies can identify these reasons, the mediocre behavior of the organization might very well become chronic.[7]

Clinician   A clinician is a practitioner who excels in practice and implementation over theory. Clinicians base their knowledge on specific practical situations.

Closing Window Situation   Typically occurs when there is less than a year to accomplish a goal, as in a rapidly deteriorating situation due to increased competition or technology change.

Clusters   Clusters are geographic concentrations of interconnected companies and institutions in a particular field. Often an industry spins off a number of supporting organizations in the same area. One example is the Silicon Valley, where dominant semiconductor manufacturers are located near Stanford University and there are also producers of electronics, computing equipment, and software. There are great synergistic benefits and strategic externalities that derive from these clusters; for example, there are terrific tidbits of industry information to be gleaned in the chitchat at the grocery store checkout. Or consider the synergies of writers, producers, and stars that emerge in the Hollywood entertainment cluster.

Clusters are related and supporting industries that spring up from an initial industry. Take the example of the online auction marketplace such as eBay. This industry has successfully spun off side industries, such as the service industry of trading assistants who make digital photos of items for clients who would like to sell online. In addition, these trading assistants upload the picture, write a description, do enough research to make a realistic assessment of price, and follow through on the sale. The goal of a trading assistant is to help people who are too strapped for time or timid about the Internet to sell their belongings online. Some of these trading assistants studied e-commerce at universities like Columbia. So, the education industry expands to fill the training needs of this new spin-off, the trading assistant cluster from the online auction industry. This expanding cluster cycle is one of the reasons that the U.S. economy is the most full and complete economy in the world. Try and dream up the most obscure or absurd occupation that you could imagine and it is likely to exist in the United States. This is why Marlon Brando, playing Don Corleone in *The Godfather*, says in the opening line of the trilogy of films, "I love America." These clusters extend out from themselves and help to create an economic system that sustains the land of opportunity.

Coalitions   Coalitions are power structures that influence strategic choice. The use of power to further individual or group interest is common in organizational life. Coalitions are power sources that influence strategic choice, such as in large firms, where subunits and individuals (particularly top managers) have reason to support some alternative and oppose another. Coalitions, particularly the more powerful ones (dominant coalitions), exert considerable influence on the strategic choice process. Many academic studies have confirmed the frequent use of power and coalitions in the strategic decision-making process.

Coase, Ronald (1910–)   Won the Nobel Prize in 1991 for a 1937 article that questioned the very existence of the firm. His question was, Why do firms exist? Why are there not a series of market transactions that are entered into anew for each strategic goal? This was almost 70 years before the concept of the virtual firm became accepted. The answer to Coase's question comes in the form of transaction cost (transaction cost theory and, later, agency theory), which are the costs of setting up a new transaction. That is, it is too costly to set up a series of transactions in the marketplace. For example, joint ventures are very difficult to manage successfully because the transaction costs and the risks (technology transfer/pirating) often outweigh the financial performance.

Coercive Power   A form of commanding power, coercive power explicitly uses institutionally granted power to achieve a position or end result. This heavy-handed approach has been largely discredited because of its ineffectiveness with employees.

Conformity is exacted through the control of rewards or sanctions. Coercive power goes beyond authority and is by definition illegitimate and thus attracts illegitimate people. Enron executives were using coercive power when they disallowed the selling of company stock by employees while they were free to sell their own stock before the bankruptcy.

Co-Evolution and the Business Ecosystem   Buzzwords created for a new approach to strategic management. It denotes creating networks of relationships with customers, suppliers, and rivals to gain greater competitive advantage and create new businesses, markets, and industries. Here's how it sounds in practice: "In a global market, companies should learn how to work in a world of business ecosystems where they can get other players to co-evolve with their visions of the future," says James F. Moore, founder and chairman of GeoPartners Research Inc. in Cambridge, MA.

Co-Market   Marketing your product with another company's product or service. For example, Apple could address its brand from a business perspective and co-market with IBM. It can be a great platform to base a business on. Starbucks has been very successful with this strategy, co-marketing with many partners like grocery stores, airlines, and bookstores. *See also* Cross-Branding.

Commitment, Managerial   Commitments exert both an immediacy and a lasting impact on the company. A commitment is anything from hiring decisions to capital investments. Like organizational culture, a commitment can shape a business's identity and direction.

Common Language   Sharing a common language is key to strategic success. A U.S. general in Iraq commented on the difficulties of creating a civilian authority: "When you create a civilian authority, you have to be very selective. Unlike the military, they have no common language, no hardware. It takes a lot more planning and a lot more thought."

Communication   Strategic vision should be communicated to managers and workers and ought to convey a larger sense of purpose—so that employees see themselves as "building a cathedral rather than laying stones."
   A well-articulated strategic vision creates enthusiasm for the course that management has charted and engages members of an organization.

Competencies   A competency is nearly always a product of experience, representing an accumulation of learning and real proficiency that are consciously built and developed over a period of time.

Competency Sharing   Stopping in the middle of something, taking time to reflect in a busy day and share tips/tricks. They say that you can keep only what you give away and the best way to learn something is to teach it. Often executives are required to teach what they have learned at a conference or a seminar within 48 hours of returning to work.

Competition   Refers to the context facing an organization within its specific arena of operation. In considering competition, one must naturally considers a firm's immediate rivals. A company's strategy should be tailored to fit industry and competitive conditions.

Competitive Action   Competitive action is a significant competitive move made by a firm that is designed to gain competitive advantage in a market. Examples of competitive actions: bring new products to market more quickly; diversify (Barnes and Noble into music); shift product emphasis (U-Haul to accessories); consolidate (merger of Exxon and Mobil); combine online and physical stores (CompUSA).

Competitive Advantage   A phrase coined by Michael Porter in his book of the same name. A company has competitive advantage whenever it has an edge over rivals in attracting customers and defending against competitive forces.
   Competitive advantage entails something that is unique, that is difficult for competitors to duplicate, and that is valuable to customers. Jack Welch said that if you don't have some advantage on which to compete, don't bother.

Competitive advantage is a condition that enables a company to operate in a more efficient or otherwise higher-quality manner than the companies it competes with, and that results in benefits accruing to that company. Southwest is able to turn their airplanes around the fastest in the industry, which leads to customer satisfaction through more on-time arrivals than its competitors. This more efficient use of the planes also leads to lower costs.

Hyundai got started by skipping the design stage. Instead, they bought an out-of-date model from Toyota. This gave Hyundai a competitive advantage.

Competitive advantage means being the first choice for a customer or consumer because the company or organization has positioned itself in the marketplace to secure a positive impression with a discrete set of buyers. When a firm sustains profits that exceed the average for its industry, the firm is said to possess a competitive advantage over its rivals. The goal of much of business strategy is to achieve a sustainable competitive advantage.

Michael Porter identified two basic types of competitive advantage:

- Cost advantage
- Differentiation advantage

Cost and differentiation advantages are known as positional advantages, since they describe the firm's position in the industry as a leader in either cost or differentiation. To gain competitive advantage, an organization must have the best market intelligence, the right resources in the right place at the right time, and products and services that meet the needs and expectations of customers at the right price.

Fry's Electronics provides a good example of competitive advantage through offering a unique shopping experience, a one-stop-shopping environment for the high-tech professionals, in its large super electronics stores. With 21 stores in California, Texas, Arizona, Nevada, and Oregon, Fry's Electronics is a rapidly expanding consumer electronics retail chain. It was founded in 1985 in Sunnyvale, California, by three brothers, John, Randy, and Dave Fry, along with Kathryn Kolder. The company initially set out to serve the growing community of high-tech professionals in the Silicon Valley. Fry's is a closely held private company, and all of the founders are actively involved in the daily operation of the business.

The stores, which range from 50,000 to 180,000 square feet, stock around 50,000 electronics items, including computer hardware and software products, technical books, I.C.s, electronic components, and accessories; audio, car audio, video, telecommunications, appliances, and personal electronics; and music CDs and DVDs, as well as convenience and general merchandise items. And the shopping experience is designed to be fun and efficient. Each store has its own theme; for example, in Sunnyvale, the store has marble floors, a grand piano, and a display of Silicon Valley museum pieces. The Anaheim store places customers on the NASA flight deck for the Endeavor Space Shuttle, complete with launches on big-screen TVs. Other themes range from an homage to the astronomers of Mayan Indian culture to a salute to the Industrial Revolution at the store in the City of Industry, outside Los Angeles.

The company has a sort of technophile culture that derived from its initial success, which made the management very conservative in its operation and not willing to share its success with the public.

By delivering benefits that exceed those of competitors (differentiation advantage), the company offers many products warehouse style. Thus, a competitive advantage enables the firm to create superior value for its customers and superior profits for itself.

Competitive Capabilities   The skills a firm needs in order to take full advantage of its assets. Competitive capabilities are considered part of a company's core competence when they differentiate it from its competitors and when they also enhance its own competitiveness.

Competitive Dynamics   Competitive actions and responses in an industry. For example, the HP-Compaq merger also made a player out of HP in the growing technology services sector, moving from being an afterthought in the services industry to No. 2 or No. 3. It has actually threatened IBM's position with its innovations. In certain cases, HP has been able to take on IBM, through lower prices and more choices. In the process, HP was able to win major deals such as a far-reaching $3 billion contract with Procter & Gamble, and others with organizations ranging from the Bank of Ireland to the U.S. Department of Agriculture.

IBM is now fighting back. It has recently launched a major marketing campaign for its services business and pushing into new areas thanks to its own merger with Pricewaterhouse Coopers. Partly as a result, IBM's services revenues rose by nearly 17% last quarter, while HP's fell 9%. This proves that in competitive dynamics, what is true one minute may not be the next.

Competitive Environment   Refers to that segment of the industry that includes a firm's immediate rivals. Michael Porter developed the concept of *strategic groups* as a tool to identify and analyze this part of the firm's environment.

Competitive Forces (Porter's Five Forces)   Even though competitive pressures in various industries are never precisely the same, the competitive process works similarly enough to use a common analytical framework engaging the nature and intensity of competitive forces. As Michael Porter has demonstrated, the state of competition in an industry is a composite of five competitive forces:

1. The rivalry among competing sellers in the industry

2. The potential entry of new competitors

3. The attempts of companies in other industries to win customers by marketing their own substitute products

4. The competitive pressures stemming from supplier-seller collaboration and bargaining

5. The competitive pressures stemming from seller-buyer collaboration and bargaining

Competitive Intelligence   Information relevant to strategy formulation regarding the environmental context within which a firm competes. Beneficial because it can provide a description of the competitive environment, challenge common assumptions held about the environment, forecast future developments, determine when a strategy is no longer viable, and indicate when and how to adjust strategy to compensate for changing environment.

Competitive Position   One measure of corporate success is relative dominance in the marketplace. Larger firms commonly establish an objective in terms of competitive position, often using total sales or market share as measures of their competitive advantage or position. For example, Gulf Oil set a five-year objective of moving from third to second place as a producer of high-density polypropylene. Total sales were the measure.

Competitive Reaction   In weighing strategic choices, top managers frequently incorporate perceptions of likely competitor reactions to those choices. In the early 1970s, Anheuser-Busch (A-B) dominated the industry, and Miller Brewing Company, recently acquired by Philip Morris, was a weak, declining competitor. Miller's management decided on an expensive advertising-oriented strategy to directly challenge the "big three"(A-B, Pabst, and Schlitz) head-on because it assumed that their reactions would be delayed due to Miller's current declining status in the industry. This assumption, of course, proved correct, and Miller was able to reverse its trend in market share before A-B countered with an equally intense campaign of its own.

Competitive Response   A competitive response is a move taken to counter the effects of an action by a competitor. When Dell offers music online with their Dell DJ and Dell Music Store, this is a competitive response to Apple's launching of their iTunes music online three months earlier.

Competitive Rivalry   Competitive rivalry is how firms interact in pursuit of competitive advantage. If two or more companies heavily concentrate on very similar business segments, it could cause a competitive rivalry. An interesting example of rivalry could be Cisco versus Huawei (China's largest telecom and datacom equipment supplier). Nowadays, while American companies are trying to capture the Chinese market, Huawei is preparing to fight with Cisco in the United States.

Competitive Strategy   Focuses on management's plan to compete successfully. Moves to attract customers, overcome competitive pressures, and strengthen the firm's market position. The five generic strategies are overall low-cost leadership, broad differentiation, focused low cost, focused differentiation, and best-cost provider.

A good example is Sony's Playstation 2, where it competes on the basis of complementary products such as third-party software support. With this competitive strategy, Sony was able to dominate the game console market with Playstation2 capturing 70% of global sales.

In Porter's (1985) words, competitive strategy is "the search for a favorable competitive position in an industry" and an aim "to establish a profitable and sustainable position against the forces that determine industry competition." He argues that anyone formulating competitive strategy must answer two central questions: How attractive is the industry with respect to long-term profitability, and what are the determinants of relative competitive position within the industry? He calls the answers to these questions dynamic, which means that they will change over time, since industry attractiveness and competitive positions rarely remain constant over time in any industry. Porter's perhaps most famous model is that of the five competitive forces, which is used to determine industry attractiveness and profitability.

The objectives of competitive strategy are to gain competitive advantage, create a bunch of loyal customers, and knock down (out) the rivals—ethically and honorably, of course.

Competitor   A rival that operates in the same area as another. Example: Wal-Mart versus KMart.

Complexity   "Management is about coping with complexity, leadership by contrast is about coping with change." —John Kotter

Complexity Theory   Complexity theory has its roots in evolutionary biology, computer science, mathematics, and chemistry. It is now being applied by writers, consultants, and researchers to the behavioral sciences, and to organizations in particular. In complexity theory, new conditions emerge spontaneously from the repeated interaction of numerous events. The events may be based on human interaction or technological events that disrupt the system. In complexity theory, equilibrium is not a desirable state (in contrast to neoclassical economics, where the intersection of market demand and supply sets a desirable equilibrium state); equilibrium is seen as leading to deterioration. For example, being number one in an industry can be an undesirable equilibrium state in which the will and discipline to improve can erode.

Concentrated Growth   Concentrated growth is the strategy of the firm that directs its resources to the profitable growth of a single product, in a single market, with a single dominant technology. The main rationale for this approach, sometimes called market penetration or concentration strategy, is that the firm thoroughly develops and exploits its expertise in a delimited competitive arena. Many firms that have fallen victim to mergers were once mistakenly convinced that the best way to achieve their objective was to pursue unrelated diversification in search of other financial opportunities.

One firm that has enjoyed special success through a strategic emphasis on increasing market share through concentration is Chemlawn. Chemlawn's approach to increasing market share hinges on addressing quality, price, and value issues.

Concentric Diversification   Grand strategies involving diversification represent distinctive departures from a firm's existing base of operations, typically the acquisition or internal generation (spin-off) of separate businesses with strengths and weaknesses counterbalancing one another. For example, Head Ski initially sought to diversify into summer sporting goods and clothing in order to offset the seasonality of its snow business. Another example is AT&T, which made the Crosspad with partner IBM in a strategy designed to expand its sales potential.

Concept Formulation, Contract Definition.   How the U.S. Air Force has its planes built. The air force subcontracted the whole thing: Come up with the concept and we will award the contract on that basis. In contrast, the navy designs its own ships.

Conglomerate Diversification   Occasionally a firm, particularly a very large one, plans to acquire another business because it represents the most promising investment opportunity available. The principal, and often only, concern of the acquiring firm is the profit pattern of the venture. Unlike concentric diversification, conglomerate diversification gives little concern to creating synergy with existing businesses. Many companies seek to balance their portfolios between current businesses with cyclical sales and acquired businesses with countercyclical sales. An example of conglomerate diversification was the acquisition of Universal studios by Seagram, a Canadian firm whose main business was distilled spirits. This was an example of unsuccessful diversification, and, like most conglomerate diversifications, was ultimately divested.

An international example of a successful conglomerate strategy is agribusiness giant Charoen Pokphand (CP), the third-biggest company in Thailand, winning polls in Thailand for "visionary leadership" and the "company most likely to emulate." CP is Thailand's most diverse conglomerate, with interests ranging from shopping malls in China to chicken production in Turkey. This year, CP moved into the car parts production business.

Consensus Management   Let us begin by saying what it is not. It is not decision making by unanimity, nor is it rule by the majority. It is subtler. Consensus is often achieved through the exertion of the powerful clique or minority agreeing on a solution that the majority agrees not to oppose or make unworkable.

Consolidation Strategy   The "consolidation" includes fusion, union, or mergers, which are effective growth strategies being used by companies around the world today.[8] The automobile industry worldwide seems to be operating on a relentless consolidation strategy.

Constant Monitoring   Constantly scanning the environment beyond one's horizon. Strategy is a continuous opportunity search. Dell, for instance, constantly monitors the environment for possible opportunities. Dell, therefore, foresaw the opportunity of the Internet and gained an advantage through its Internet-based sales. However, the newly gained competitive advantage from Internet sales required Dell to adjust its structure to fulfill this new demand.

Constraints   One approach to strategic management argues that you can start anywhere to achieve an endpoint. Once you start, you will bump up against the constraints of the situation. This awareness gives you the strategic insights and inputs to move forward. For example, in the United States, an entrepreneur with a résumé of a couple of failed businesses is seen as strategically savvy because she is aware of and familiar with the constraints of the situation.

Constructive Confrontation   The term Andy Grove used, when he was CEO at Intel, to describe the atmosphere of tough openness that prevailed at Intel.

Contingency Theory of Organizing   Based on the idea that there is no one way of organizing that is best in all circumstances: Think of the Hershey-Blanchard model of leadership, in which there is an ever-shifting mix of attention to people and tasks based on follower readiness. "It all depends," is the motto of the contingency theory. Now you know that that statement is not just a lame response but a strategic management theory.

Continuum   A conceptual term that indicates that the aspect of a phenomenon is not black or white or "0" or "1," but is spread out over a range of scores, so there is a lot of gray area in a continuum. Traditionally, in strategy we divide businesses into industries or business segments (*see* NAICS); however, because of convergence, these classifications are emerging as more of a continuum or moving target. (*See* Convergence.)

Control Systems   Control systems look at how supporting resources are allocated and used across primary processes. Financial budgeting is an example of a dominating control system. The danger of strict adherence to control systems is managing by numbers instead of value creation. Financial control measures are needed to help people see. They can promote decentralization of decision making by allowing participants to agree to the goal and then do their own self-reflection.

Convergence   With the increasing complexity of technology, industries are converging. A good example is Intel's strategy, which is based on a complex set of alliances with the PC, entertainment, and consumer electronics industries. As a result, it is difficult to define Intel's core industry. Convergence requires rethinking of some strategic management tools such as Porter's five forces industry analysis. For example, how does one define the industry one is meant to analyze when it may entail the intersection of a number of industries such as banking, insurance, and financial services?

Co-Opetition   Coined from the words "cooperation" and "competition." With markets constantly emerging, more firms are being set up to meet market needs, but are all competing for the same resources, which unfortunately are not growing in proportion to the growth of firms. Thus, firms and their competitors collaborate because of increasing competition and decreasing margins and costs and a short product life span. Firms combine strengths and form co-opetitive alliances that are forward thinking and flexible enough to change with the marketplace and with customer demands.

It is not safe to assume that cutting-edge technologies will remain cutting edge. New technologies will evolve. For this reason, firms must cooperate and engage in healthy competition that will see that customers get the best products or services available. The opposite of co-opetition is "mutually destructive competition": Your opponent has to fail for you to succeed. IBM and Intel are "frenemies," as are Apple and Microsoft.[9]

Core Competence   Prahalad and Hamel introduced the notion of core competence: "A capability or skill that provided the thread running through a firm's businesses, weaving them together into a coherent whole."[10] A core competence is an internal activity that a company performs better than do other competitors. A core competence is also something that a company does well relative to other internal activities: resources and capabilities that serve as a source of competitive advantage for a firm over its rivals. When developed, nurtured, and applied throughout the firm, core competences can result in strategic competitiveness. An example might be the capability to develop innovative new products and to reengineer existing products to satisfy changing consumer tastes. Sources of these competences are usually production marketing and human resources (now called social capital).

The keyword in Hamel and Prahalad's book *Competing for the Future* (1994) is core competence. Despite the fact that this important term is repeated over and over throughout the book, no short or convenient definition is really provided by the authors. It can be described as the major thing that a company does the very best; a core competence is ". . . a fundamental knowledge, ability, or expertise in a specific subject area or skill set."[11]

Hamel and Prahalad argue that the base of a firm's competitive advantage can be found in its core competences. They illustrate this theory by describing the corporation as a tree that grows from its roots: The roots of the tree are considered the core competences of the corporation, and they nourish the trunk of the tree, which consists of the company's core product. They further describe the smaller branches as business units, while the leaves, flowers, and fruits are the end products of the firm.

Corporate (Organizational) Culture   Refers to the complex set of ideologies, symbols, and core values shared throughout the firm and that influence the way it conducts business. It can also be construed as the social energy that drives (or fails to drive) the organization.

Corporate Conspiracy Novel   Not the work of John Grisham, instead this was the Senate Finance Committee's description of a report by the staff of the Joint Committee on Taxation on Enron's illegal corporate financial reporting. Wall Street banks, encouraged and directed by lawyers and accounting firms, helped Enron devise tax shelters that let the company operate tax-free for years while inflating its reported profits by billions. Enron's tax department had been transformed into a business unit, a profit center with annual revenue targets. The tax savings and manufactured profit were mostly smoke and mirrors, not reflecting any real business activity. The title of one tax shelter deal was "Show Me the Money," a quote from the film *Jerry Maguire*, with Tom Cruise.

It seems that Enron relied on technical interpretations of the differences between tax and accounting rules that allowed it to deduct dollars from its tax liabilities more than once. It also treated some capital as expenses so as to generate tax losses while at the same time maintaining the appearance of profit. The *New York Times* described one triad of Cayman Island entities explicitly set up to hide money from the IRS as being so complex and so much pushing the envelope that the IRS lacked the capacity to deal with them. This circumstance does raise the question whether in a knowledge economy Enron's pushing the envelope on accounting rules—which are, after all, only generally accepted accounting principles (GAAP)—was not financial innovation. In five years, will some of these accounting innovations be generally accepted principles? This is the argument that Enron's rampant greed and dissimulation was an example of Nietzsche's concept of the overman (Ubermensch), who is essentially above the law, because his action changes the course of history and consequently the laws. Or was it merely, as one senator noted, "unbridled greed and blatant disregard for the law of fairness"? As Senator John Breaux put it, the Texas company, instead of drilling for oil and gas, was drilling the tax code for ways to find more tax shelters. Thinking of firm strategy as a creative act of writing a novel is a good literary view of strategy that can provide additional insights.

Corporate Ethics (an appropriate term to follow the previous one) What guides companies that make ethical behaviors a fundamental component of their corporate culture. Values statements and codes of ethical conduct are used as benchmarks for judging both company policies and conduct, as well as how the public views a company.

Corporate Governance Corporate governance is the art of governing—in a princi-pled fashion—so as to maximize the welfare of the company and of its relevant stake-holders. Corporate governance encompasses issues ranging from how companies should behave on the Internet and how management can best motivate employees and board members, to how institutional investors should discharge their responsibilities to the beneficiaries whom they represent. Firms with stronger advisers and share-holder rights have higher firm value, higher profits, higher sales growth, lower capital expenditures, and fewer corporate acquisitions.

Corporate governance is often identified with shareholder activism and with efforts to make top executives more accountable and responsive to those who own stock in the companies they manage.

Poor, inadequate, or unethical corporate governance can lead to corporate melt-downs such as Enron's. Investors and employees with their defunct 401(k)s suffer through a bankruptcy while consultants and lawyers often make lots of money in the process.

Corporate governance concerns the relationship between managers (as agents of the owners) and the board of directors. The key is the system of checks and balances to ensure company performance, direct strategic action, reduce the risk of fraud, and help the firm to maintain social responsibility.

The term "corporate governance" is often mentioned in connection with the very high payments of executives in the United States. For example, Disney's net income fell from $1.9 billion to $920 million from 1997 to 2000, but Eisner's salary was raised while he was additionally rewarded with stock options that had a value of almost

$40 million. This is just one example of an often-seen problem that can be addressed through corporate governance systems. Many consider that the United States is in the midst of a crisis in corporate governance.

Corporate Health or Effectiveness   The ability to mobilize the power centers of an organization to maintain flexibility, growth, and adaptation to the turbulence of the environment.

Corporate Identity Crisis   When a corporation goes through an existential crisis or confusion regarding what it is in the business world. Gateway is an example of a company about which one can ask, How many identity crises can one company have over the years? How many times can you change a logo or a name? First it was Gateway 2000 with a stylized "G," then it was changed to just Gateway with a cowbox logo, now it is Gateway with a "power switch." This is all in, what, 5 years? It seems that changing a logo was not working, so then they copied Apple marketing. What is next? An "Apple" with a cowhide pattern? Gateway next launched an ad campaign promoting their digital music packages—which also promoted MP3 services, Listen.com, and Emusic.com. This campaign coincided with Apple's launching of its digital music technology iPod. Gateway's campaign used the motto "Rip, Burn, Respect" (www.ripburnrespect.com/music)—a not-so-oblique reference to Apple's "Rip, Mix, Burn" campaign of 2002—in their television ads that saturated the United States in the summer of 2003, which were aimed mostly at showing how Gateway's digital music packages simplify online music. It can be argued that Gateway's corporate identity crisis is being played out through copying Apple's marketing and product lines. Perhaps as one Internet pundit put it, Apple should respond quickly with an "Operation Liberate Gateway users" advertising campaign.

Apple seemingly couldn't care less about this corporate imitation. Gateway may have made a mistake by getting into the retail store business because they have too much competition. As long as Dell is around, Gateway will have a hard time competing, and the corporate identity crisis does not help the matter.

Another example of corporate identity crisis is Burger King. At one time, it was at the top of the heap—"Have It Your Way," "The Burger King Character," etc. For the past several years, the company hasn't known what it is or who it caters to, and it shows in its schizophrenic ad campaigns over the past few years.

That moment when one's previous way of business seems to be hitting a wall, perhaps the company is a victim of its own success and must try to reinvent itself. Think of the example of Boeing. Boeing is the American company that in the past fifteen years had been most dominant in its global industry. Since 1958 when Boeing introduced the first U.S. commercial jet, the 707, it has experienced unqualified success. Recently, Boeing was falling behind its rivals McDonnell Douglas and Europe's Airbus—many say because of overconfidence and skimping on research and development to deliver better profitability. In 2001, Boeing underwent a corporate identity crisis when it moved its headquarters from Seattle, where the jets are assembled, to Chicago, apparently to demonstrate that it is more than a plane company. Its latest reinvention depends on the success of the 7E7: a wide-body plane being developed that would seat 200 and have lower operating costs than current jets.

Corporate Power   The antiglobalizers (or anti the negative effects of globalizationers, as a friend puts it) have cottoned onto a key issue in our modern times: Multinational corporations are taking on the role of national governments. They are to some extent driving foreign policy, social policy, environmental policy, and general geopolitics, including influencing wars. What the antiglobalizers seem to overlook is the possibility of this corporate power to be facilitators of positive change. *See* Pluralism and Stakeholders.

Corporate power is at times stronger than government power, because it is independent of and survives the change of governments. Corporate power often derives from alliances that are not necessarily political.

Corporate Social Responsibility   In the modern pluralistic world, where fringe groups have a strong voice in the carnival that is life, corporations, which are, after all, a legal entity or person, need to conduct themselves in such a way as to placate or, even better, proactively engage with what used to be considered the lunatic fringe or voice in the wilderness (greens, feminists, antiglobalizers, eco-preneurs).

BP, for example, has changed its name from British Petroleum to Beyond Petroleum. The company is looking at the big picture, looking for alternative sources of energy. Another example is Unilever, which is trying to act as a good corporate citizen. In India, Unilever has established itself in poor villages that others have written off, educating villagers about the importance of washing with soap and how this will help end dysentery. Then it will sell soap in affordable packets for one rupee each.

Social responsibility is supposedly very important for Nike. In its Web page, the company mentions some of its social and environmental focuses like education and recycling. It explains that its mission is "simple in concept, complex and long-range in execution: Through the adoption of sustainable business practices Nike is committed to securing quality of life, restoring the environment and increasing value for our customers, shareholders and business partners." However, this could be construed as backpedaling and greenwashing after its major PR debacle over its use of sweatshops in Asia. Nike's main strategy has been to engage in a series of alliances with NGOs.

Corporate Strategy   It is the overall organizational strategy that addresses the questions, What business or businesses are we in or should we be in? What is the current strategy? What is happening in the larger social, political, technical, and financial environments? What are our growth, size, and profitability goals? In which markets will we compete? Which businesses? Which geographic areas?

For example, in recent years, Ford Motor Company has decided to focus more on its core business of manufacturing cars. Consequently, Ford decided to sell three companies that it owned: Budget Rent-a-Car (the fifth-largest rental car company), its heavy truck operations, and a financial unit called USL Capital.

Corporate Venturing The idea that new business ventures need to be managed separately from the mainstream business, otherwise they will not survive long enough to deliver benefit to the sponsoring company. Special organizational arrangements need to be put in place so that the new ventures' processes can be aligned with the company's existing activities. Corporate venturing is a key way for companies to handle disruptive technologies.

Corporate Voodoo This term is actually a book title by Rene Carayol, who asks:

> Why do many companies find it so hard to escape the pull of the past? Why do many individuals keep resorting to learned behavior, the habits and ideas that may have brought them success in the past, but which will leave them adrift in the fast-moving currents of the new economy? What is the spell that keeps them so immobilized? It's the Voodoo. . . . And what is the magic that can release us all—organizations and individuals, leaders and the led, employees and free agents, parents and children and candlestick makers—into a world of power, creativity, connection and achievement? It's also the Voodoo. . . .

IBM gives an instructive example of the dangers of corporate voodoo. IBM was caught up so often in antitrust suits that when it was looking for an operating system for its original PC, it approached an innovative couple who were software writers. As soon as the couple saw the IBM lawyers coming at them, the couple balked at the deal. In the end, IBM got the DOS operating system but did not negotiate exclusive rights.

The voodoo in IBM's case is that they were constantly involved in antitrust suits. IBM's history is replete with these examples of corporate voodoo. Thomas Watson Sr. was in a state of collapse over being sued for IBM's punch card technology. However, the younger Watson said let them have it, and IBM moved on to new technology, as Watson Jr. recounts in his memoirs *Father, Son and Co.: My life at IBM and Beyond* (1990).

Corporation The perfect entity that evolved as a means for men and women to stop making war and start to cooperate. A legal entity, a "person" in the eyes of the law.

Correlation Seeker/Tester Correlation seekers/testers use surveys and questionnaires to discover how variables do or do not correlate with each other. Just about every professor who teaches strategy has engaged in this kind of research.

Cost Leadership A generic strategy coined by Michael Porter whereby a firm leads the industry by maintaining the lowest costs and offering its products or services to a broad market at the lowest prices.

After the terrorist attacks on September 11, 2001, the low-cost leader Southwest watched its competitors struggle, some in and out of bankruptcy court. Southwest is the only major carrier to remain profitable in every quarter since September 11. While its six biggest rivals have grounded 240 aircraft and laid off more than 70,000 workers, Southwest—which has never laid off a soul in its 31 years—has kept all of its 375 planes and 35,000 people flying.

Southwest's strategy is a good example of cost leadership. This is its competitive advantage and the main thing that saved it from financial crisis while the airline markets crashed. Southwest keeps its costs so low chiefly by being the short-haul airline that flies directly from city to city, with just one type of plane, the Boeing 737. While other airlines are struggling with bankruptcies, Southwest is planning to increase its market share by 8%.

Counterintuitive Strategy   Logic and rational thinking would lead you in a particular direction. Counterintuitive thinking involves striking up a paradox. The Hegelian dialectic is thesis, antithesis, and synthesis. Instead of stopping with the thesis, you go to the antithesis hoping that it will develop into synthesis.

While working as a spokesman for General Electric, Ronald Reagan began thinking about how to defeat the Soviet Union. Instead of arms control, he suggested an intensified arms race. "In an all-out race, our system is stronger," he told audiences. If Moscow tried to keep up, the communist system would become "unhinged." When Ronald and Nancy Reagan met with Pope John Paul II, he told the pope that God had spared his life after his assassination attempt (an experience the pope had also shared) so he could defeat communism. Reagan and Gorbachev met for the first time in Geneva in 1985 and Reagan told Gorbachev that when it came to an arms race, "I assure you, we won't lose." This was a winning counterintuitive strategy.

Countervailing Power   A term made popular by John Kenneth Galbraith, a professor of economics at Harvard, economic advisor to numerous presidents, and onetime ambassador to India. He developed the theory that there will always be powers to create balance in this world. His idea was based on economics: Wherever we find power dominating, some equal and opposite power will eventually balance it. It is evident in the case of Microsoft. While enormously powerful, it can't just have its way with the world. For right or wrong, either its competitors will step in, the government will legislate against it, or as consumers, we'll buy something else. According to Michael Porter's five forces industry analysis, there are powers that help make an industry attractive. And for each of these powers, from Galbraith's point of view, lurking somewhere in the shadows, if not overtly, will be a countervailing power to bring balance: Unions are countervailing powers to big business, antiglobalizers are countervailing forces to global corporate dominance.

Covert Leadership   Mintzberg uses the model of a symphony orchestra conductor to show how leadership really works. Through covert leadership, conductors—and senior corporate officers—lead without seeming to. They don't seek absolute control over others; rather, through many unobtrusive actions, they inspire others to perform and use their talent.

Creativity   The new focus on innovation and creativity redefined the role of manager to be receptive to suggestions made by team members. Idea innovation networks were observed and used to expand organizational innovation and organizational learning.

Credibility   What the "word on the street" is about one's competency and commitment.

Crisis Management   Dealing with crises that have arisen through failure to deal with strategic issues beforehand. *See also* Dentist Syndrome.

Critical Systems (CS)   CS has highly complex interfaces with the rest of the end product and is relatively expensive, but tends to influence consumer behavior and perceptions. Black and Decker outsourced the entire design and production of its glue gun, effectively defining the product as a critical system.

Cross-Branding   Enhancing your original brand name through an association with a powerful brand name. Amazon.com has pursued a cross-branding strategy; the most recent example is their Ruby Project, carrying clothing lines like GAP. Another example of wildly successful cross-branding is Cole Haan's upscale shoes, which now include Nike Air sole technology. *See* Co-Market.

Cultural Convergence   Can be described by looking at managers in industrial countries and the fact that they exhibit common values regarding economic and work-related behavior.

As nations industrialize, the values automatically change toward behavior embracing free-market capitalism. For example, as many Eastern European nations are becoming more and more industrialized, and joining the European Union, their values will become more and more like the values of Western Europe, so the cultural convergence in Europe will become more prevalent. A recent brilliant article in *Strategic Management Journal* discussed ethical cultural convergence amongst Eastern European managers as they adopted Western management techniques.[12]

Cultural Synergy   The harmonization of the direction and operation of separate organizations into a whole. The lack of cultural and strategic fit is the main cause of failures in mergers. Cultural integration needs to be carefully analyzed, planned, and implemented.

Culture, Marine Corps   *See* Marine Corps.

Culture, Organizational   Embedded understandings of the current power structure and operating philosophy of a company that can limit (or help) how individuals and groups can generate new ideas and ways to implement those ideas.

One need look no further than Southwest's online reservations approach and one immediately sees the innovative culture Southwest fosters.

The late Bill Hewlett and David Packard pioneered the "HP Way," which valued people as well as profits. HP was long famous for promoting a culture that prizes innovation.

Current Strategy   Current business strategies are often based on past strategies. If strategists have invested substantial time, resources, and interest in strategies, they typically are more comfortable with a choice that closely parallels or involves only incremental alterations to the past strategy to develop a current strategy.

Research by Henry Mintzberg suggests that past strategy strongly influences current strategic choice. The older and more successful a strategy has been, the harder it is to replace. Similarly, once a strategy has been implemented, it is hard to replace because organizational momentum keeps it going. Even as a strategy begins to fail due to changing conditions, strategists often increase their commitment to it. Consequently, one could conclude that many firms replace top executives when performance has been inadequate for an extended period of time because replacing these executives lessens the influence of unsuccessful past strategy on future strategic choice.

Customerization The process of customizing to an individual customer's needs, wants, and desires. Customerization is based on the idea of individualism, treating a customer as an individual rather than classifying him/her in a market.

Customer Orientation Herb Kelleher would take exception to the conventional wisdom that the customer always comes first. Kelleher popularized the "employee comes first" philosophy. If you take care of the employee first, then the customer will inevitably be satisfied.

Customer Value A function of factors that usually fall into one of three categories: those that differentiate the product, those that lower its costs, or those that allow the organization to respond to customer needs more quickly.

Cutting Edge/Bleeding Edge In terms of strategy, it is always being a step ahead, often to the point where launching a new system or new technology is emerging. It calls for and delivers greater flexibility; having room to maneuver. For example, the invention of the Boeing 707 jet airliner was cutting edge for Pan Am in the late 1950s, when transatlantic air travel took 14 hours. The head of Pan Am, Juan Trippe, was offered Boeing's KC-127. Trippe accepted on the condition that Boeing install fighter jet engines so the planes could get tremendous acceleration and range. Pan Am had a cutting-edge advantage over all the other airlines, until the competitors too switched from propeller planes to jets.

Cybernetics The science of control and communication in animals and machines. In the cybernetic approach, it is assumed that the system is to some extent self-regulating, based on a feedback loop of information.

Endnotes

1. http://forums.macrumors.com/archive/topic/23149-1.html
2. Mintzberg, H. (1973). *Nature of managerial work*. Englewood Cliffs, NJ: Prentice Hall.
3. Lewin, K. (1951). *Field theory in social science: Selected theoretical papers*. New York: Harper.
4. Weick, K. E. (1999). Organizational change and development. *Annual Review of Psychology*.

5. Axelrod, R. H. (2001). Why change management needs changing. *Reflections: The SOL Journal*, 2:3.

6. Kotter, J. P. (1996). *Leading change*. Boston: Harvard Business School Press.

7. Lenzer, R. (2003, April 28). Room at the top. *Forbes*.

8. Brady, D. (2003, April 21). Plugging in to the network war. *BusinessWeek*.

9. Brandenburger, A., & Nalebuff, B. (1996). *Co-opetition*. New York: Doubleday Dell.

10. http://whatis.techtarget.com/definition/0%2C%2Csid9_gci214621%2C00.htm (Gutierrez, R., July 24, 2001).

11. Messmer, M. (2001). Encouraging employee creativity. *Strategic Finance*, 83:6, p. 16.

12. Robertson, C., & Crittenden, W. (2003). Mapping moral philosophies—Strategic implications for multinational firms. *Strategic Management Journal*, 24:4.

D

Dataholic   Someone who is obsessed with obtaining information, especially from the Internet.

"Day in the Sun"   Time period during which a product is successful in the marketplace.

D Day   A useful planning technique from WWII. Though you cannot define the day, and you don't know which day it will be, you can start to count backward or forward from D day: D day minus one, D day minus two, D day plus one, D day plus two.

Deal, or "Cutting a Deal"   General management term used to indicate agreement on terms for a business arrangement with another entity.

"Death Valley Curve"   A point in development of new business when losses begin to erode the company's equity base, so that it becomes difficult to raise new equity.

Decentralization   Has become the theory of choice of almost every industrial and financial enterprise. The idea is simple: to move decision making closer to the customer and to serve that customer better. Give decentralized managers control over everything they do so they can make decisions more quickly.

Decentralized Corporate Structure   Decentralized corporate structure can be understood using the Catholic Church as the example. We can look at the church as a corporation and how the hierarchy is separating its many entities legally in order to insulate them from liability when priests get involved in moral and legal transgressions. By decentralizing, they are able to effectively shield their assets from legal claims and hence foil any attacks aimed at the church as a corporation.

Decision Loop   In Gulf War II, coalition commanders were always two or three days ahead of the Iraqis. For example, U.S. troops racing toward Baghdad crossed bridges rigged with explosives before the Iraqis could blow them up. Soldiers and marines passed through the Iraqis' so-called red zone around Baghdad before Saddam Hussein's forces could unleash any chemical or biological weapons. And U.S. forces drove into the heart of the Iraqi capital before Hussein could drag them into a bloody, protracted urban street fight.

"We are inside their decision loop" is how the military describes the process of collecting and analyzing information, then acting on it. "That's what's turning this thing. We are doing things before he [Hussein] can expect them."

Decision Making   The process of choosing between alternative courses of action. This process can be lengthy; it includes establishing objectives, gathering relevant information, identifying alternatives, setting criteria for the decision, and selecting the best available option. An example of making a decision would be the wise decision to purchase this book.

Decision Support System   A computer system designed to collect, store, process, and provide access to information to support managerial decision making. Developed in the 1970s to facilitate unstructured decision making, DSSs use modeling techniques to examine the results of possible alternative courses of action.

Decision Theory   A body of knowledge that attempts to describe, analyze, and model the process of decision making and the factors influencing it. Decision theory encompasses both formal mathematical and statistical approaches to solving decision problems by using quantitative techniques such as game theory and probability as well as more informal behavioral approaches. It is used to inform and assist decision making in organizations.

Decision theory looks at what is at the heart of the modern executive life: the continual process of decision making. Decisions are needed as to whether to buy or sell, whether to fire a troublesome subordinate or remonstrate with him, whether to send a memo increasing controls or to call a conference call to talk the problem out, whether to order a new computer system or have the current one updated. Decision theory presumes that executives cannot master all the information available. It assumes that individuals operate under bounded rationality, accommodating the trade-offs of cost and benefit, value and utility, within an intuitively derived framework of probability. In decision theory, there are two kinds of decisions: programmable and nonprogrammable. The latter is the domain of strategic management, which is why so far we have not seen a software that successfully captures and codifies the strategic management decision-making process.

Graham Allison, in *Essence of Decision,* quotes JFK on the mysteries of decision making: "the essence of ultimate decision remains impenetrable to the observer—often indeed to the decider himself. . . . There will always be the dark and tangled stretches in the decision-making process—mysterious even to those who may be most intimately involved." In this unusual classic of strategic management, Allison gives a vivid account of the crucial decisions surrounding the Cuban missile crisis, which in the end provides a stunning insight into organizational politics and decision making. Allison proposes three basic models of decision making that range from the rational actor to the organizational process to the mechanics of game theory.

Deconstruction   The breaking up of traditional business structures to meet requirements of the modern economy.

De-Diversify   To sell off parts of a company that are not considered directly relevant to a corporation's main area of interest.

De-Escalation Strategy   A de-escalation strategy is an attempt to reduce overly heated competition that has become self-defeating and is destroying the profit potential of the industry. Oracle's attempt to purchase PeopleSoft can be seen as a de-escalation strategy, to reduce the level of competition in that segment of the software industry.

Defense Tactics   Tactics are maneuvers a business uses in combat with its rivals to address threats and help ensure that a firm's broader strategy is carried out successfully. Defensive tactics protect the status quo or react to events as they unfold.

Defrost   To make a hardened status quo more flexible.

Delayering   The removal of supposedly unproductive layers of middle management to make a company more efficient and customer responsive. When delayering is taken to the extreme, it can lead to an anorexic organization.

Delphi Technique   The Delphi technique was developed by the RAND Corporation in the late 1950s as a forecasting methodology to obtain an intuitive consensus of group expert opinions. The Delphi technique was originally conceived as a way to obtain the opinion of experts without necessarily bringing them together face-to-face.

The Delphi procedure is designed for the systematic solicitation of expert opinion. Three characteristics distinguish it from interpersonal group interaction: anonymity, iteration with controlled feedback, and statistical group response.[1]

A questionnaire designed by a monitor team is sent to a select group of experts. After the responses are summarized, the results are sent back to the respondents, who have the opportunity to reevaluate their original answers, based upon the responses of the group. Incorporating a second and sometimes third round of questionnaires gives the respondents the opportunity to defend their original answers or change their position to agree with the majority of respondents.

The Delphi technique and consensus building are both founded on the same principle—the Hegelian dialectic of thesis, antithesis, and synthesis, with synthesis becoming the new thesis. The goal is a continual evolution to "oneness of mind," a solidarity of belief—in effect, the collective mind. In thesis and antithesis, opinions or views are presented on a subject to establish views and opposing views. In synthesis, opposites are brought together to form the new thesis. All participants in the process are then to accept ownership of the new thesis and support it, changing their views to align with the new thesis. Through a continual process of evolution, consensus will emerge. Alan Cline discusses the 10 steps of the Delphi technique.

1. Pick a facilitation leader, preferably not a stakeholder.

2. Select a panel of experts, which can and should include stakeholders.

3. Identify a brainstorming criteria list from the panel.

4. Rank the criteria.

5. Calculate the mean and deviation and eliminate outliers.

6. Rerank the criteria.

7. Identify project constraints and preferences.

8. Rank projects by constraint and preference.

9. Analyze the results and feedback to panel.

10. Rerank the projects until the ranking stabilizes.

The setting or type of group is immaterial for the success of this technique. When people are in groups that tend to share a particular knowledge base, they display certain identifiable characteristics, known as group dynamics, which allow a facilitator to apply the basic strategy of the Delphi technique.

Dematerialize   To become independent of material items.

Democratic or Participative Management   Approach to management that encourages input from those who are affected by a decision. An extreme example of commitment to participative management occurred when a CEO of a Brazilian manufacturing firm invited all his employees to vote on a potential acquisition. The employees voted against the acquisition, although all strategic indicators seemed to support it. Participative management works fairly well in American culture. However, in Mexico, for example, attempts at participative management can be seen as a sign of weakness by Mexican employees. *See* Hershey-Blanchard Situational Leadership Model, where the readiness of the followers is key.

Dentist Syndrome   Not going to the dentist till the pain we expect to experience is less than the pain we are presently experiencing.

Deregulation   The dismantling, loosening, or entirely doing away with laws and government control of given industries. The deregulation and softening of antitrust laws are factors in the proliferation of mergers and acquisitions. It has been observed that most mergers and acquisitions take place in those countries pursuing intensive deregulation policies.

Dictionary   An organized group of coherent words that have meaning. In our case, this dictionary applies to a certain genre: strategic management.

Differentiation Strategy   In pursuing competitive advantage based on differentiation, firms attempt to create unique bundles of products and/or services that will be highly valued by customers. An example of a differentiation strategy is GarageBand that Apple has added to the Macintosh-only family of applications that make up Apple's iLife 2004 software suite. It is composed of iPhoto (organizing pictures), iTunes (digital jukebox), iMovie (homemade videos), and iDVD (creating custom DVDs).

This is an entertaining, light-hearted differentiation strategy designed to appeal to the frustrated rock star in all of us.

Digital Convergence   Many industries are converging, merging new technologies with more traditional ones. For example, traditional consumer electronics firms such as Philips and Sony have begun to harmonize the domains of telecommunications, computing, and software. Products like cellular phones, palm tops, and WebTV are examples of the integration that is digital convergence. E-commerce is facilitating the convergence of banking, retailing, database management, and communications. The food processing industry is engaged in integrating genetic engineering and biotechnology.

Convergence means that industry structures are being radically altered. Often this is achieved through megamergers, such as Citigroup's, or through the emergence of nontraditional competitors, such as Virgin's entry into the airline industry.

Disaggregation   The breaking apart of an alliance of companies to review their strengths and contributions as a basis for rebuilding an effective business web.

This is when strategy falters, as it is bound to sometimes, and the complex cycle created fails and the venture becomes less profitable. This is when disaggregation comes into play and the firm is broken into smaller units, the books are straightened out and are opened to investors, and hence shareholder value increases.

Disaster Management (Disaster Recovery Plan)   The actions taken by an organization in response to unexpected events that are adversely affecting people or resources and threatening the continued operation of the organization. For example, three years after the disastrous merger of Time Warner and America Online, the world's largest media company instigated a disaster recovery plan and expects earnings growth in 2004.

Disclosure of Information   The release of information that may be considered confidential to a third party. For example, whistle-blowing legislation allows employees to divulge information relating to unethical or illegal conduct in the workplace.

Discontinuity   An event that a company, industry, or technology has never experienced before and may change the whole strategy. For example, NASA's experience with the Challenger disaster.

Disintermediation   Traditional channel structures are being challenged. Manufacturers are more likely to be in direct contact with end users by eliminating intermediaries—wholesalers, dealers, and distributors. The Internet provides a new approach to customer access and distribution. Managers are gaining increasingly sophisticated knowledge of consumers and are therefore able to serve them better. A good example is Dell's direct marketing, whereby they access the consumer directly through the Internet.

Disruptive Technology   A new technology that shifts the existing technology paradigm. The introduction of a disruptive technology often makes an existing technology obsolete and represents a major disruption in an industry. Firms that compete within tumultuous high-technology environments are wise to constantly scan their environment for advances that represent potential disruptive technologies so as to not be surprised and lose ground.

An example of a disruptive technology is the fact that for the first time, smart cell phones this year are expected to outsell PDAs. But smart phones are an improvement over PDAs because they are smarter, they are replaced often by consumers, and their price is subsidized by the cell phone carriers as a means to lure new customers. Even Palm is investing to produce smartphones and cannibalize its own PDA market. If you can't beat a disruptive technology, you may as well join it.

Divergent and Convergent Thinking   Liam Hudson in *The Cult of the Fact* distinguished between the convergers ("unemotional and objective engineers who like working with things and who work towards the answers at the back of the book") and divergers ("dreamy wide-ranging social scientists" who keep moving "up the funnel," creating more issues and questions and fewer answers). Perhaps it is more helpful to think of these as cognitive styles that may be employed alternately by the same or different people at different points in the problem-solving cycle.

Diversification   To diversify means to invest in other product/market segments and broaden the strategic scope of the firm. Although diversification is usually justifiable only if it builds shareholder value, it can also be a form of personal narcissism or empire building on the part of CEOs or can be a desperate attempt to shore up a shaky financial situation. Firms need to decide whether to diversify into related or unrelated businesses. Most research on firm diversification suggests that unrelated or conglomerate diversification is the least successful. Also, diversification from a position of financial and strategic strength seems to give better results. Igor Ansoff in his 1965 book *Concept of Corporate Strategy* was the first to deal with these issues in his diversification and portfolio models.

Product / Mission	Present	New
Present	Market Penetration	Product Development
New	Market Development	Diversification

Figure D.1   Ansoff Product Mission Matrix

An alternative to diversification is sticking to a single-business strategy, which has been very successful for firms such as Wal-Mart and Southwest.

General Cinema is the leader in the nationwide movie exhibition industry. Although the firm started out in drive-ins, it diversified into the multicinema market, then diversified further, becoming the largest bottler of soft drinks (Pepsi) in North America. Its stock value correspondingly rose 2,000% in just under a decade.

Diversified Firms   Firms that are invested in more than one line of business. A big risk in remaining concentrated on a single business is putting all the proverbial eggs in one proverbial basket. Seagram's investment in Universal studios (subsequently divested) and recent acquisition of Warner Music Group were both attempts to make a hard liquor manufacturer more diversified.

Diversity in Management Development   Since most older managers are male, women often have more difficulty finding mentors and entering the network. "Men only" clubs were declared illegal, allowing women access to areas where contacts are made. African American managers also are learning the benefits of networking. A few principles apply to developing female and minority managers: Grooming women and minorities for management positions is the key to long-term profitability. The best women and minorities will become harder to attract and retain. More women and minorities means that businesses can serve female and minority customers better.

Divestiture   Includes divesting extraneous businesses because resources are being stretched too thin. Focusing corporate resources on a few core businesses is usually a superior strategy to diversifying too broadly and potentially stretching resources and management too thin.

Downshifting   The concept of giving up all or part of your work commitment and income in exchange for a greater quality of life. This concept can be contrasted with the "organizational man," who essentially lives to work for the organization. Downshifting is integral to the idea of portfolio working, whereby individuals opt out of formal employee relationships and sell their services at a pace and price to suit themselves.

Downsizing   Otherwise known as corporate liposuction, it can possibly lead to corporate anorexia. One key danger is that cutting the corporate fat can needlessly sacrifice morale and tacit knowledge.

Downstream Progress   Movement by a company toward achieving its objective(s) fairly easily by riding a wave or trend and benefiting from favorable conditions. An example of downstream progress, in this case jumping on a bandwagon, is Pepsi-Cola's 2004 launch of the first high-profile ad campaign for online music. Pepsi is promoting a contest to offer 100 million free downloads at Apple's iTunes Music Store. Pepsi shipped specially marked 20-ounce bottles wherein consumers who find a numerical code in the bottle cap can type it into the iTunes program for a free download.

Driving Forces Industry conditions change because important forces are driving industry participants (competitors, customers, or suppliers) to alter their actions. The driving forces in an industry are the major underlying causes of changing industry and competitive conditions. In the 1970s, most cars were designed as a body sitting on a frame. Today, Crown Victoria and Grand Marquis are among the last cars that use body-on-frame design. Most automakers have switched to building a car as one total unit—or unibody—to reduce weight. This has been a driving force in the auto industry due to competition, even though for consumers it means a less quiet ride.

Drucker, Peter (1909–) Peter Drucker is considered by many to be the sharpest and consequently most important business thinker/philosopher of our time. His credo is, "There is only one valid definition of business . . . to create a customer." Drucker focused his analysis chiefly on management. Although he significantly influenced the theory and practice of management, many of his ideas are untestable empirically. His contribution can be characterized as eminently useful generalizations. For example, in 1994, Drucker predicted that the United States was going to lose ground economically to India and China and soon. His method was essentially journalistic: observation, searching for patterns, finding truths such as his sweeping statement on India and China.

Chief economist in the Austrian civil service, Drucker later moved to England, where he worked as a clerk, then became a journalist and still later an economist. He moved to the United States in 1937. He has had a career as noted consultant, writer, and academic. Drucker was the first to advocate decentralization of large corporations. He invented the concept of the knowledge worker decades before it came to be widely used. He was first to advocate privatization of publicly owned utilities, airlines, and the like; first to advocate that government should steer the economy rather than engage in economic activity; and one of the first to acknowledge that the large corporation had its day. He formulated management by objectives: clear objectives with both strategic and operational focus achieved through participative agreement between manager and subordinates. Features were worker participation and quality circles. A maxim was, "Do the right thing," not just do things right (effectiveness versus efficiency, which is at the heart of strategy: prioritizing and making the hard trade-off decisions).

Dynamic Efficiency Dynamic efficiency is derived from new resources or extending and leveraging existing resources in a new way. Dynamic efficiency is necessary for strategic change. Offshoring of, for example, programming jobs to India can be seen as a form of inevitable dynamic efficiency.

Dynamic Programming A mathematical technique used in management science to solve complex problems in the fields of production planning and inventory control. Term comes from Richard Bellman in the 1950s and 1960s.

Dynamic View of Strategy Taking advantage of your current market position while concurrently creating new opportunities for exploiting the innovation of others. For example, Samsung for the past 10 years has been one of the leading TV manufacturers in the world. Samsung's main competitors are Sony, Philips, and Sanyo. Samsung has always focused on competing and creating better products than its competitors. Samsung's main philosophy is being No. 1. Traditionally Samsung focused on producing low-end TV sets, very cheap but poor quality. However, applying a dynamic view of strategy, Samsung had to change and focus on producing the best products in the market. In the past several years, it has been very successful.

About five years ago, Samsung was producing TV sets that had good sales but very low profits because the competition was very tough. The R&D team came up with a great idea. They developed the Samsung "Extreme Sound" TV set. This TV had the best speaker system and was designed to be used with every video game station. Its futuristic design looked very different from all other TV sets. The price was reasonable, about $50 more than a regular TV set. In fact, Samsung took its competitors by surprise. Samsung was the only one in the market with a TV set like this one. Within a few months, sales increased by more than 100%.

Endnote

1. Martino, J. P. (1993). *Technological forecasting for decision making*. New York: McGraw-Hill.

E

E-Business/E-Commerce   A business area whose primary interaction with the customer is through the Internet.

Economics   Transaction cost, agency theory, game theory, and evolutionary economics are key economic theories from which strategic management derives its theories. Economics is a much more elegant and "scientific" discipline than strategy, which tends to be more nebulous and commonsense, "nailing Jell-O to the wall." When strategy borrows from economics, the models are usually very elegant and appealingly scientific, like Porter's five forces model.

Economic Value Added (EVA)   A new way of measuring firm performance that integrates the cost of capital by including both the cost of debt (the traditional approach) and the cost of equity (the EVA innovation). The firm's free cash flows are discounted at the business-specific weighted average cost of capital as a means to evaluate performance of the management or economic value added. At the business unit level, many projects can be evaluated and eliminated if they have negative EVA. At the corporate level, EVA offers insight needed to address many underperforming business units so as to improve the firm's stock performance.

Economies of Scale   Many of the industries of today are characterized by increasing returns, which means that the cost of production falls when a company increases its scale of operations, and mass production results in lower average cost.

Chris Malburg[1] claims, in his article "Competing on Costs," that the strategies of the twenty-first century will shift away from economies of scale and cost cuts through mass production and toward rethinking the whole core of the manufacturing process. According to Malburg, companies will outsource all activities except those in which they have a distinct cost advantage.

Economies of Scope   Economies of scope occur when the average costs of joint production of two products are less than the combined costs of producing these products separately. Economies of scope can exist in production, product development, marketing, and distribution. In production, economies of scope arise from synergies in the production of similar goods. In product development, a firm achieves economies of scope by using common science, equipment, and know-how to develop two or more products. Finally, firms can lower their distribution costs by carrying more and different products in their inventory. When Quaker Oats paid $1.3 billion to acquire Snapple, the company was hoping for economies of scope in the marketing and distribution of the two drinks, Snapple and Quaker's Gatorade. It was dismayed to find these synergies illusory and later sold the company for $300 million.

Eco-Preneur   An entrepreneur who is concerned with environmental issues.

Efficiency   Less is more. Don't let the best become the enemy of the good. The achievement of goals in an economic way. Involves seeking a good balance between the economical use of resources such as time, money, space, and materials and the achievement of an organization's aims and objectives. "Efficiency is doing the right things, effectiveness is doing the right things right," as Drucker points out.

Eighty-Twenty Rule   The principle that describes the natural balance between the causes and effects of business activities and that holds that all business activity displays an 80%-20% split. Originally called the Pareto principle after the economist who first postulated this relationship, the principle can be used to concentrate management control and identify problem areas. Examples might include 20% of the workforce accounting for 80% of the salary bill and, conversely, 80% of the company's profits coming from 20% of its products.

E-Lance   A freelance worker who makes use of the Internet, thereby being able to work freely around the world.

Emergent Approach   An ongoing process of constant learning, experimentation, and risk taking characterizes this approach. Criticisms of the emergent approach are that the approach is not clear-cut and orderly. In fact, the emergent approach involves a number of complex interdependencies. With an emergent approach, the manager can be more of a facilitator than a doer.

Emergent Strategies   The emergent strategy process breaks down problems into subproblems that are solved sequentially. It is described as an adaptive, incremental, complex learning process in which the ends and means are either specified simultaneously or are intertwined. The ends are rarely announced or recorded in a formal planning document, and when they are announced, they remain broad, general, and nonquantifiable. The means develop and evolve over time as organizations learn from environmental interactions.

It has been proposed that some stages of strategic decision making require a formal process while others may call for an emergent one. Mintzberg also observed a mixing of processes, which he indicated depended on the nature of the decision and the functional orientation of the department involved. Other studies suggest that a variety of contextual factors (firm size, environment, etc.) may explain why either a formal or emergent approach may be used. Most significantly, it is suggested that organizations not only employ both formal and emergent approaches, but that strategic processes may be formal on some characteristics and simultaneously emergent on others, all the while assuming conditions that are neither formal nor emergent on others.

Emotional Capital   The intangible organizational asset created by employees' cumulative emotional experiences, which give them the ability to successfully communicate and navigate interpersonal relationships. Low emotional capital is seen as resulting in conflict with staff, poor teamwork, and poor customer relations. By contrast, high emotional capital is evidence of emotional intelligence and an ability to think and feel in a positive way that results in good interpersonal communication and self-motivation. For example, Marion Sandler, Co-CEO, Golden West Financial, comments on the emotional capital of the women competing on Donald Trump's *The Apprentice,* the TV business show where young executives compete for a job in Trump's organization: "The women go through a ritual dance of beating each other up on every show. Perhaps it gets their adrenaline flowing. More likely it reflects their reaction to pressure. They mistake haggling for negotiating and continue using their cute shtick. The latter tactic is a turnoff in the real business world. To build a winning team the prima donnas must go, and the rest need to drop their sophomoric, self-centered attitude."

Emotions of Strategy   The emotions of strategy include fear, greed, courage, dedication, and the selflessness to go beyond themselves to help the team. The emotions of strategy really run the gamut, as Robert Dickman says: "It is a slice of humanity." Business and strategy and innovation are all built on trust: Ultimately one has to trust one's partners, inside and outside the organization, to take that risk to collaborate, "co-opete," innovate, or just get something done.

Empowerment   Empowerment involves the redistribution of power and decision-making responsibilities, usually to employees, where previously such responsibility and authority was a management prerogative. Based on the assumptions that employee abilities and skills are frequently underused, empowerment is an attempt to give employees and lower-level managers more control over their situation.

Enacted Environment   An idea introduced by Karl Weick, the eminent social scientist and theorist, to emphasize that the environment of the firm is not passively received by the firm and the firm has the chance to influence the environment through its choices, strategic moves, and innovations. Example of the enacted environment is Gary Hamel's exhortation to be a rule maker not a rule taker.

End-Around   An approach to a problem that does not attack it directly but rather tries to avoid it. For instance, concerning the media empire of Conrad Black, which includes Hollinger International's newspaper holdings like the *Chicago Sun-Times,* London's *Daily Telegraph,* and the *Jerusalem Post,* which is currently up for sale. Hollinger International's board in Chicago is trying to thwart Black's proposed $466 million sale of his 78% stake in Toronto-based Hollinger Inc. Meanwhile, Black is seeking help from Canadian courts to make sure the deal goes through. By suing to halt the sale, the board is attempting an end run strategy that could block a divestiture of Hollinger International's newspaper holdings.

Endorsement   The public approval of a product or service by a person or organization. Can be used to promote the product. Athletes are often paid to endorse products and are successful until they get involved in scandals, such as the Kobe Bryant trial that resulted in dropped endorsement contracts.

End-to-End Services   An interesting way of referring to the "all inclusive" packages that are becoming more and more common in industry today. Indian software companies offer "end-to-end services" that they hope will help them compete with the global consulting giants. This strategy involves a one-stop-shopping approach for clients such that if an Indian firm like Wipro offers a call center, it will also write the software that will train the call center workers and manage the client-information database.

Enemy, The   In business terms, this is often a belittling term for the competition to allow the firm to move forward and meet objectives. Soldiers of the Third Infantry Division that in the Second Gulf War led the assault into Baghdad and secured Fallujah reported that their convoys were routinely fired on, especially in the night, with bullets striking the first and last vehicles and rocket-propelled grenades going over gunners' heads and between jeeps. "We are just lucky they are bad shots" was a familiar refrain of soldiers involved in the operation. Denigrating the enemy in such a way often seems necessary to sustain the energy and enthusiasm for sustained competition or combat.

Enterprise Culture   An organization or social environment that encourages and makes possible initiative and innovation. Considered to be more rewarding and stimulating to work in on a daily basis. 3M is a good example of an enterprise culture.

Enterprise Resilience   Gary Hamel speaks of the ability and capacity of a firm to withstand economic and systematic discontinuities and adapt to new risk environments. A resilient organization can effectively align its strategy, operations, management systems, governance structure, supply chain, and decision-support capabilities so that it can detect and adjust to continually changing environments with risks of disruptions to its primary earnings drivers. This ability to adapt creates advantages over less-adaptive competitors. Cisco Systems' survival of the dot-com bust is an example of enterprise resilience. The demand for Cisco's routers, which can cost as much as $1 million and act as gateways and make up much of the plumbing of the Internet and corporate networks, fell off a cliff with the turndown in the tech and telecom industry. Many attribute this survival and enterprise resilience to CEO John Chambers's leadership.

Entitlement   The expectation that an organization or individual will make large profits regardless of its or her contribution to the economy. Many have accused Microsoft of an attitude of entitlement and a failure to meaningfully innovate.

Entrepreneur Somebody who sets up a business or enterprise. The individual displays attributes like creativity, initiative, risk taking, and problem solving. Setting up a business typically puts capital at risk as well.

Entrepreneurial Orientation The specific dimensions of entrepreneurial orientation describe an entrepreneurial firm as one that engages in product market innovation, undertakes somewhat risky ventures, and is first to come up with proactive innovations, "beating competitors to the punch." Some dimensions of innovativeness, risk taking, and proactiveness characterize entrepreneurial orientation.

Entrepreneurial Spirit of American Business The Microsoft "Agile Business" television ads are really effective in capturing that spirit. These ads tap into the entrepreneurial spirit of American business; they express the hopeful ring and business zeal that are characteristic of American business and marketing in general. *See* Can-Do Attitude.

Entrepreneurial Transformation Large firms need to adapt to an ever-changing environment through entrepreneurial transformation, which involves manipulating the firm's culture and organization systems so that individuals act in a more entrepreneurial way. This approach has been advocated by Peters and Waterman (1982), Ghoshal and Bartlett (1997), and Kanter (1989).

Entrepreneurship Entrepreneurship involves the process of creating something new with value by devoting the time, money, and sweat equity and assuming the accompanying financial, psychic, and social risks to receive the rewards of monetary and personal satisfaction and independence.[2]

Entry Barriers A perceived or real obstacle preventing a competitor from entering a market. Established brand names like Starbucks make other possible start-ups think twice before entering the coffee market.

Environment The pattern of all external conditions and influences that affect the life and development of the firm, according to Kenneth Andrews (1971).

Environmental Scanning The monitoring of changes in the external environment in which an organization operates in order to identify threats and opportunities for the future and to maintain competitive advantage.

Environmental Turbulence Environmental turbulence is attributed to the increasing rate of change and to the drastic nature of many changes, especially those related to technology, that increase the difficulty of identifying causes or predicting results of competitive initiatives with reasonable certainty.[3]

Equilibrium The concept that things always go back to their natural balance after certain modifications have been made, such as cost reductions. Equilibrium theory serves as a useful basis, but has many problems: Reality is not always of one piece; complex systems theory rejects the notion of equilibrium as good, instead viewing it as degradation of the system. Another way of looking at it is that if you are not growing, you are declining—or as Bob Dylan said, "those not busy being born are busy dying."

Essential Messages   Charles Kepner in his book *The New Rational Manager* (1981) states that truly strategic managers need to identify, capture, and transmit essential messages. These messages are actually being delivered impersonally by the external environment and market forces. Managers are the filters; they translate this external information and use it as a basis for establishing priorities. Although limited in their ability to control (or "enact"—the word used by Karl Weick, the eminent social scientist and theorist) the external environment, managers use this information to alter the more controllable internal environment and to position the firm for future success. An example of failure to grasp an essential message is the case of Wang. Once the leader in word-processing terminals, Wang missed a major technological shift to personal computers. The company crumbled: the pitfalls of stubbornly sticking to a technology and missing an essential message of the environment.

Estimate   An approximate calculation of an uncertain value. An estimate may be a reasonable guess based on knowledge and experience or it may be calculated using more sophisticated techniques designed to forecast projected costs, profits, and losses. A related term, guestimate, highlights the unknowable aspect of estimates.

Ethics   An example of ethics gone bad is a *New Yorker* cartoon of an accountant in his office on the phone replying, "Oh, THAT 3 billion dollars!"

Excellence and Inspiration   What every organization is striving to achieve, to be able to succeed in whatever it does despite the dispiriting setbacks—doing things better, less expensively. An example is Parkland Hospital, which delivers the most babies in the United States. It attributes its success to "a strategy for performance, innovation and customer care."

Execution, Strategy   If the first thing that springs to mind when you hear strategy execution is Sun Tzu's beheading of the concubines for not following his orders, then you score some points for strategy knowledge because it means that you have read, digested, and remembered the anecdotes from *The Art of War,* by Sun Tzu. However, this is not what we are referring to here.

Strategy execution has to do with implementing agreed-upon strategies. There has been a traditional distinction between strategy formulation and implementation—as when the general formulates and articulates the strategy and foot soldiers implement it. Just as the command and control model has fallen by the wayside in most cultures (including, interestingly enough, the military), the idea of the top level formulating and the lower levels implementing has fallen out of favor.

The key to strategy execution is getting the executors to think. Good strategy execution has a lot to do with inducing strategic thinking. *Hey, wait a minute, I thought the strategy executors were the doers, not the thinkers. I thought the top managers were doing the thinking.* Wrong. Sure, upper management needs to do strategic thinking, but perhaps a more important upper-level task is strategic decision making. So good strategy execution has to do with encouraging the lower levels to think before, during, and after their "doing."

According to Bertrand Russell, "most men would rather die than think. Many do." Most of us like to avoid thinking at all costs, and one of our favorite modes is automatic pilot, blindly implementing. However, the "foot soldiers" need to self-reflect and self-analyze as they execute and continually reflect on whether what they are doing is contributing to the overall strategy for the firm, or perhaps more importantly, creating value for the customer.

One way to achieve this reflection is to prevent employees from doing things they know how to do (blind execution) and encourage them to get out of their comfort zone. They need to be brought to an area outside the zone and essentially boxed into that area, where they will create value for the customer. Good strategy execution is about getting employees focused in that area of value creation.

Strategy execution involves getting people out of their normal mode, out of one box and into another—the value-creation box. One of the favorite dictums of strategy execution is Stephen Covey's "Begin with the end in mind."

Execution has a lot to do with reprioritizing, overcoming obstacles (or at the very least, identifying and articulating obstacles), and aligning priorities. Strategy execution often has to do with getting employees to ask the right questions that identify the obstacles. Obstacles need to clearly be things that employees don't know how to do, not simply a to-do list. Prioritizing and reprioritizing means getting rid of those activities that do not map onto the core strategies.

The idea of project management and task management has the unintended effect of reinforcing the problem. Instead of project managers, perhaps we need to start referring to problem managers.

Strategy execution has to do, above all, with guiding people's thinking. Suggesting solutions to employees can result in short-circuiting all the wisdom of the world. Managing strategy execution means guiding managers where they need to be engaged. However, all too often execution kills thinking. People need to evolve in their skills and capabilities, leveraging their talents in new ways to extend the core competences of the firm. This requires self-assessment and adjustment, the double-loop learning that Argyris talks about. Without this self-assessment and self-adjustment, employees and the organization are less likely to adapt.

Strategy execution: Get people to agree on the goal and let them do their own self-reflecting. This was the essence of Drucker's management by objectives (MBO) and the concept of getting "buy in."

Executive   An employee in a position of senior responsibility in an organization. The executive is involved in planning, strategy, policy making, and/or line management.

Executive Angst and Anxiety   Anxiety is characterized by diffusion of emotion, in that the cause of the fear and unease may be difficult to specify. Rollo May defines anxiety as "the apprehension cued off by a threat to some value which the individual holds essential to her existence as a personality." Downsizing, mergers, job uncertainty, and complex ethical issues in the workplace can lead to a diffuse sense of anxiety that a well-defined, articulated, and inspiring mission can help to dissipate or lessen. *See* Existential Strategy.

Executive Behavior   Executive behavior is the scientific study of what managers actually do. Studies show that managers spend no time developing strategies, whereas in the real world, as Adam Smith reminds us, merchants (the "managers" of Smith's day) rarely got together either at funerals or weddings without trying to figure out how to get the better of the customer. As Mintzberg showed in *The Nature of Managerial Work,* managers had very little or no time alone and seemed to spend all their days in a web of brief encounters in which horizontal communication was the order of the day. All in all, it was a picture of managers trapped in their cages, rattling the bars. Mintzberg's subsequent career showed a different bent when he turned his attention to strategy but seemed to ignore outcomes and focused exclusively on the process (*see* Mintzberg, Henry).

Both Carlson's and Mintzberg's revolutionary research highlighted the fact that managers seemed to work incredibly long hours, were constantly "in conference," and seemed to have little or no time for contemplation and reflection. However, we know from newspaper reports, biographies, and television that in reality, top managers lead a pretty full life that often lands them in court for insider trading, illicit love affairs, and other fraudulent activities. Naturally, they neither exhibit nor reveal any of these activities while they are under observation for these brief periods of study.

Top executives and executives at other levels are indeed complex human beings who strategize not only corporate affairs but their own personal affairs, and often casual interactions lead to dramatic changes in strategy. The Pacific War is dramatically transformed when a naval officer looks out the window of a plane landing in the Baltimore airport in early 1942. He sees neophyte carrier pilots learning to take off on a chalked-off "carrier deck" on the runway and realizes that the pilots of medium bombers such as the Mitchell B-25 could practice this maneuver for take-off only, but cannot re-land on the carrier. Hence the Dolittle raid on Tokyo in early 1942 that surprised and provoked the Japanese into the Battle of Midway, which was the decisive naval engagement of the Pacific.

Executive Bifocals   Executive bifocals explain how top managers look up and look down the hierarchy. Executives typically use human-relations lenses to look up hopefully and expectantly at their bosses and use task-oriented lenses to look down on their subordinates. This is not always true, but can be a tempting trap.

Existentialism   Existentialism is a philosophy based on the idea that a person is defined by free choice and action from moment to moment, rather than being a set essence that is predefined. The famed Myers-Briggs test is antiexistential, as it seems to limit the possibility of creative freedom and existential choice by putting people in boxlike and confining categories.

Decision making is central to existentialism. To act unfreely denies one's humanness. In terms of behavior, existential individuals struggle to be authentic, to give their lives meaning, to achieve some kind of identity.

Existential approach to strategy emphasizes choice. However, freedom to choose sometimes means every choice seems somehow inauthentic, seems like role playing. For example, a Generation X- or Y-er, at 25, may cry all night unable to turn down a well-paying job at a bank for no good reason except "I am not the kind of girl who works at the bank, you know," as Strawberry Saroyan wrote in her memoir *Girl Walks into a Bar.*[5]

Existential Strategy   An approach based on the major concepts and principles of strategic management in Joe Kelly and Louise Kelly's *An Existential-Systems Approach to Managing Organizations.*[4] The structure-process-values model is used to understand strategy in a multidimensional organizational view focusing on the individual, the group, and the organization. An existential approach emphasizes *decision* (refusal to choose to act unfree), *authenticity* (real, not phony, relations must be the basis for the solution), and *good faith* (maximum information made available to all parties involved). People are accepted as they are and are not subject to prejudice or the use of stereotypes. Answers are not as important as the process used to reach them. Problems are not regarded as incapable of solution; a dialectical approach is invoked that assumes that evolving solutions will generate new problems. There is an emphasis on courage in the existential approach to strategy. Participants will emerge with new insights and metaphors to understand their own struggle with themselves, others, and the organization. Existential strategy offers tools for solving the problem of living (in organizations).

Exit Strategy   A firm-level strategy for getting out of a typically declining market. Exit strategies include dropping prices to recoup investment costs, and selling off divisions. Texas Instruments wrote off $600 million in PC inventory as an exit strategy from that industry.

Experience Curve Effects   The acquisition of knowledge or experience over time. A steep curve reflects a substantial amount of learning in a short period of time, a shallow curve reflects a slower learning process.

Expertise   Expertise is what top managers pay token respect to because they really believe that all that technical jazz is the nitty-gritty reserved for their subordinates. The kind of expertise they love is the sort shown by Lee Iacocca when in the early 1960s he worked a transformation on the Ford Falcon, a utility car designed by Robert S. McNamara to fight the European imports. The result was the Mustang, the sporty car that appealed to young families. The success of the Mustang had a revolutionary effect on the U.S. auto industry. As a marketing genius, Iacocca knew that men love red sports cars, which bring them into the auto showroom—though they leave with a family car.

Other examples of expertise are Steve Jobs finding a role for the mouse and Edwin Land inventing the Polaroid camera. The manifestation of expertise for most managers is in the exploitation of somebody else's invention that the inventor couldn't get to market. One of the best examples is Pan Am's husbanding development of the Boeing KC-135, a jet refueling plane for the B-52, into the Boeing 707, which revolutionized transatlantic flying and allowed airlines to fly directly from New York to Frankfurt. Goodbye transatlantic ocean liners. This transformation arose because the head of Pan Am insisted that Boeing install the latest jet fighter engines on the military midair refueling plane. This is the kind of synergy of ideas that CEOs love, whether it is putting extra seats in a sports car or bigger engines on a plane.

Expertise Power   Power based on expertise. Becoming increasingly important in a knowledge-based economy. Basis of credibility and idiosyncratic power—like those of the nerds and geeks.

External Dependence   If a firm is highly dependent on one environmental element, its strategic alternatives and its ultimate strategic choice must accommodate that dependence.

Bama Pies makes apple turnovers. For many years, Bama Pies sold to only one customer—McDonald's. Because McDonald's was the major external dependence for Bama, its demands strongly influenced Bama's strategic alternatives.

External (Open) Systems Thinking   A learning and problem-solving approach that involves describing the behavior of a system, then exploring the possibilities for improving it. External (open) systems thinking encourages creativity and is used widely by learning organizations.

Eyes on the Prize   Keeping the focus on the main mission and goals. When Louis Gerstner first met with John Akers to be handed the reins of IBM, Akers briefed him on important decisions, such as an imminent decision to form a joint venture with Motorola to secure a partial exit for IBM from the "technology business." Gerstner reports that what struck him upon reading his notes was that there was little or no mention of culture, teamwork, customers, or leadership—the elements that are critical to strategy execution.

A key to strategy execution is strategic thinking. Having your employees blindly implementing is a risk; instead they need to be self-assessing, self-reflecting to see if the execution is actually creating value for the company.

Endnotes

1. Malburg, C. (2000). Competing on costs. *Industry Week,* 249:17.

2   Hisrich, R., & Peters, M. (2002). *Entrepreneurship.* 5th ed. New York: McGraw-Hill.

3. Bower, J. L., & Christensen, C. M. (2000). *Disruptive technologies: Catching the wave.* Cambridge, MA: Harvard Business School Press; D'Aveni, R. A. (1994). *Hypercompetition.* New York: Free Press.

4. Kelly, J., & Kelly, L. (1998). *An existential-systems approach to managing organizations.* New York: Quorum Books.

5. Saroyan, S. (2003). *Girl walks into a bar.* New York: Random House.

F

Factoids   New information for which it is easy to measure mastery. Learning can be measured in linear terms and taught in lockstep fashion.

Fallacy of the Single Objective   Self-explanatory. One of the fundamentals of strategy. There is always a trade-off among multiple objectives; objectives can be pursued sequentially or simultaneously.

Fast-Cycle Markets   Those markets in which the product life cycle can be anywhere from 12 weeks (an Internet year) to 1 year.

Fast Track   A rapid route to success or advancement. The fast track involves competition and a race to get ahead of the competition. Associated with great ambition or high activity. Fast track can involve an upcoming promotion or even a product launch. Donald Trump's TV show *The Apprentice* is a good example of fast track.

Feasibility Study   An investigation into a proposed plan or project to determine whether it can be successfully and profitably implemented. This normally includes analysis of the technical, financial, and market issues, including an estimate of the resources that would be required in terms of materials, time, personnel, and finance, as well as the return on investment.

Feedback   The communication of responses and reactions to proposals and changes or of the findings of performance appraisals with the aim of enabling improvements to be made. The closer in time the feedback is to the events, the more effective.

Financial Information   Financial information is one of the essential criteria for assessing the performance of a firm. At the heart of strategy is performance improvement, and this improvement often needs to be quantified and compared to specific articulated goals.

First Mover Advantage   The benefit produced by being first to enter a market with a new product or service. Synonymous with market leader in a new service or product area. For example, Avon is investing heavily to build its presence in China with a $40 million factory in southern China. Although the door-to-door style Avon uses around the world is banned in China, Avon is investing now in the hope that direct selling may be allowed again as early as 2005, and then it will have a first mover advantage.

First to Market   Gateway seems to be first to market with a digital music download service (well, before Apple). Gateway's strategy is to align itself with other services, whereas Apple's strategy with their music service involves building the infrastructure themselves. First to market doesn't always guarantee success. For example, with the Internet, though Amazon and eBay are two shining examples of first to market working, there's a long list of firsts to market that are long gone.

Five Forces Industry Analysis   One of the most well-known and most widely used strategic management tools that is derived from economics, specifically industrial organization. Developed by Michael Porter in the early 1980s in his two books, *Competitive Strategy* and *Competitive Advantage,* the five forces analysis answers the question, What is the future profitability of this industry? This analytical tool looks at the underlying forces at work in the industry and gives insight as to how the firm needs to position itself to protect itself from excessive competition. Thus Porter's quote: "Hypercompetition is self-inflicted."

This tool takes the outside-in approach to strategy that is Porter' perspective in general: Begin with the industry analysis and work your way back to the firm's capabilities. So, the choice becomes how to position the firm within the industry. According to the inside-out approach (review resources, identify core competences), in contrast, the beginning should be identifying the firm's unique capabilities and then deciding how and where they can be leveraged.

Michael Porter has demonstrated that the state of competition in an industry is a composite of five competitive forces:

1. The rivalry among competing sellers in the industry

2. The potential entry of new competitors

3. The market attempts of companies in other industries to win customers to their own substitute products

4. The competitive pressures stemming from supplier-seller collaboration and bargaining

5. The competitive pressures stemming from seller-buyer collaboration and bargaining

The five forces in the model determine the industry profitability by influencing costs (through suppliers' bargaining power and rivalry among competitors), price (through buyers' bargaining power, the threat of choosing substitute products, and rivalry among competitors), and required investments of firms in an industry (because of the threat of new entrants). Strategy courses at the HBS are largely built around the five forces model.

Flat Organizations   Opposite of tall organizations. Flat organizations, with minimal hierarchy and bureaucracy, are the current trend. One of the tools to facilitate a flat organization is the creation of teams.

Flexibility   Having room to maneuver, building slack into the system.

Flip   A start-up company that aims to build market share quickly and generate short-term personal wealth for its founders through selling off.

Force Field Analysis   A technique for promoting change by identifying positive and negative factors and by working to lessen the negative forces while developing the positive ones.

Forecasting   The prediction of outcomes, trends, or expected future behavior of a business, industry, or the economy as a whole through the use of statistics. Types of forecasting include, but are not limited to, trend analysis, regression analysis, and exponential smoothing.

In a global marketplace characterized by accelerating change, the crucial responsibility for managers will be ensuring their firm's capacity for survival. This will be done by attempting to anticipate and adapt to environmental changes in ways that provide new opportunities for growth and profitability. The impact of changes in the remote industry and task environments must be understood and predicted.

Even large firms in established industries will be actively involved in scanning the external environment. The more than $5.5 billion loss in the early 1980s to the auto industry is an oft-cited example of what can happen when firms fail to place a priority on environmental scanning and forecasting.

Formal Strategic Planning (FSP)   Formal strategy uses a systematic method to solve an entire problem. Planning is a deliberate, rational, and linear process of specifying first the ends and then the means. Plans emerge from the strategy-formation process fully specified, ripe for implementation through detailed attention to objectives, programs, and operational plans of ever-increasing specificity. FSP is based on principles of rational decision making and assumes that purpose and integration are essential for a firm's long-term success.

Henry Mintzberg's *The Rise and Fall of Strategic Planning*, considered by some the bible for enlightened strategists (and by others as a diatribe against Igor Ansoff's theories), describes in great detail the drawbacks of planning. Larry Downes, in his 1998 book *Unleashing the Killer App*, describes the limitations of traditional strategic planning.

- Planning is relatively slow clock speed.
- Like algebra, do it because you have to and then put it aside.
- FSP never implemented, doesn't drive change.

"The real purpose of effective planning is not to make plans but to change the mental models that decision makers carry in their heads." —Henry Mintzberg

Sun Tzu wrote of FSP: "The general who wins a battle makes many calculations in his temple before the battle is fought. The general who loses a battle makes but few calculations beforehand. Thus do many calculations lead to victory, and few calculations to defeat; how much more no calculation at all! It is by attention to this point that I can foresee who is likely to win or lose."[1] Although in recent years there has been an emphasis on emergent or learn-as-you-go strategies, calculation and formal planning will always play a key part in strategic success.

Formulating Strategy   Rational process of determining opportunities and threats, performing risk assessment, and identifying strengths and weaknesses.

Formulation of Purposes and Objectives   One of the key functions of the executive.

Forward Integration   A form of vertical integration that involves investing in the downstream activities of the industry. An example of forward integration is Gateway's opening of the Country Stores to sell computers. Unfortunately, this forward integration has been largely unsuccessful, so much so that between 2000 and 2003, Gateway shut down at least 76 stores; 1,900 Gateway employees were laid off.

On a more encouraging note, Apple has opened 50+ successful Apple Stores and is rumored to be planning international stores as well.

Four Ps   Kotler and Armstrong[2] state that it is crucial for a company to:

- Have a strong *product,* or line of products (consisting of goods or services), to offer its target market in order to gain success.
- Keep a realistic and competitive *price* for this product or product line that the target customers are willing and likely to pay.
- Be located at a carefully selected *place* that makes sense for offering the target customers the product or products.
- Invest wisely in *promotion* in order to create an awareness of, communicate the strengths of, and build up a demand for the products offered.

Franchising   A strategy whereby the parent company (franchiser) grants the franchisee the right to use the parent's name, reputation, and business skills at a particular location or area; a specialized form of licensing in which the franchiser sells intangible property (i.e., a trademark) to the franchisee, but also insists that the franchisee agree to abide by rules as to how it does business. For example, McDonald's gives franchises for new branches to an individual person or a company.

Starbucks has entered into licensing agreements rather than franchise its stores, as this affords them more control. Growth of 5,506 stores and 25,000 people has been achieved largely without franchising, at least in the United States. "There is no doubt in my mind that Starbucks can realize its financial goals. A more fragile issue is whether our values and guiding principle will remain intact as we continue to expand." —Howard Schultz

Frenemies   "Friendly enemies" denotes competition with whom you may need to cooperate to achieve a strategic goal. If Microsoft were to partner with Google, this would be a case of frenemies. The term was originally coined at IBM.

Friction-Free Market   A market in which there is little difference between competing products and services, so that the customer has exceptional choice when choosing a product or service.

"Friendlies in Kandahar" This was the message the U.S. Air Force pilots heard 10 seconds after they dropped 500-lb guided missiles, killing four Canadian soldiers doing training exercises in Afghanistan. In mergers and acquisitions, when companies are looking to take over other firms, it is crucial to identify what is of value to you that you do not want to destroy or take out when you do the postmerger housecleaning. It also implies identifying those people that you can trust and not deliberately destroying that trust. The incident in Afghanistan weighed heavily in the Canadian decision not to support the United States in the Second Gulf War.

Frontal Assault Tactic Launching an offensive that involves taking on a competitor head-to-head in a given market.

Future Orientation The amount of time and top management attention that is devoted to positioning for future industry changes and discontinuities. Some argue, like Prahalad and Hamel in *Competing for the Future,* that this is the essence of strategy.

Endnotes

1. Sun Tzu. p. 11.
2. Armstrong, G., & Kotler, P. (1997). *Marketing: An introduction.* Englewood Cliffs, NJ: Prentice Hall.

G

Game Theory The Hollywood movie *A Beautiful Mind* introduced many to game theory as developed by John Nash. Game theory tries to predict outcomes based on interactive models in which the decisions of each party affect the decisions of others. Game theory allows for the systematic and quantitative analysis of these series of interactions; it is particularly applicable to business negotiations or anticipating market conditions that have not yet appeared. It can also be used to assess the viability of new ventures, products, technologies, and markets. Brandenburg and Nalebuff's *Co-Opetition* is one of the best strategic references on the subject, emphasizing in a non-mathematical way how cooperative strategies work.

According to Eatwell and Newman, game theory is an "interactive decision theory" that looks at the behavior of decision makers (players), whose decisions affect each other.[1] During the earlier years of game theory (1910–1930), the theory concentrated on competitive games such as two-person zero-sum games. In these games, there was no point for cooperation or joint action because if one player preferred one outcome over another, then the other player had the opposite preference. This is the case for most two-person "parlor games," such as chess, where each player's preferred outcome is the opposite of the other's.

Modern game theory began in the reflections of the Hungarian-born American John von Neumann, one of the greatest mathematicians of the twentieth century. In 1928, he wrote his first treatise on games. He believed that traditional games worked as models of human interaction. He found that through the study of games such as chess, one could develop algorithms (*see* Algorithms), and from the games he studied, he created the theory of free interactions that distinguished these games from games of pure chance. Now game theory has a different focus from that of its earlier years. There is more focus on the decision makers' use of cooperation and joint action.

- *Elements of Game Theory.* The elements include (1) the game: an interaction between or among mutually aware players; (2) each player's strategy: the action or plan of actions chosen from the player's set of strategies. "Pure" strategies specify nonrandom courses of action for players when there is no uncertainty, and "mixed" strategies specify that an action will be chosen randomly from a set of pure strategies with specific probabilities. A pure strategy would be for a goalkeeper to defend only one side of the net; a mixed strategy would be to try to cover the whole net; (3) the game's unique outcome: the consequence for each player of a specific combination of all players' strategies; and (4) a payoff, negative or positive, for each player: the number (ordinal or cardinal) attached to an outcome that reflects all that a player considers important about the game—profits, market share, envy of rivals' positions, and the like. In the hotel business, for example, one can say that the strategy of the management team (players) is to maximize the value of the company through profit and to maximize the value to the customer through excellent customer service and world-class hotel and restaurant facilities. Other players in this game are the other, competing hotels.

- *Maximin Decision Rule and Maximin Criterion.* The maximin criterion is utilized frequently by strategic decision makers in environments of high uncertainty. This criterion directs the decision maker to choose the alternative that provides the best of the worst possible outcomes. The decision maker finds the worst possible (minimum) outcome for each alternative and then chooses the alternative whose worst outcome provides the highest (maximum) payoff.[2] Therefore, this criterion focuses on the maximization of value, where decision makers should maximize on the minimum possible outcome. The disadvantage of this criterion is that it focuses on the most pessimistic outcome for each alternative. Despite its shortcomings, the maximin criterion is useful for decisions that involve the possibility of catastrophic outcomes. For example, the terrorist attacks in New York and Washington, DC, on September 11, 2001, had a catastrophic outcome in the hospitality industry in the United States, so this criterion can be helpful in these extreme cases.

- *Minimax Theorem.* In 1928, John von Neumann claimed that every zero-sum game with many pure strategies for each player is entirely determinable: There is always a rational solution to a precisely defined conflict between two people with completely opposite interests, because both parties assess the conflict in such a way that they do not expect to do any better. For many years, minimax was considered the main focus of game theory.

- *Bargaining Theory (Noncooperative and Cooperative).* In the 1950s, John Nash contributed significantly to game theory by laying the groundwork for the general noncooperative theory and for the cooperative bargaining theory. Bargaining refers to the negotiations between two or more parties about the terms of possible cooperation, which may involve trade or employment (collective bargaining) or the like. The outcome of bargaining is either an "agreement" about the terms of mutual cooperation or a "conflict" if no agreement can be reached.[3] Firms can benefit from utilizing the cooperative bargaining theory in dealing with labor unions. For example, in the 2003–2004 labor strike in Southern California, the four grocery chains involved entered into a (apparently illegal) revenue-sharing agreement to weather the strike.

- *Strategic Equilibrium.* Nash introduced the concept of strategic equilibrium (1951) as an outgrowth of the minimax theorem. Equilibrium arises when all players use strategies that are best responses to others' strategies. A strategic equilibrium occurs when, given that all players conform to the prescribed strategies, no player can gain from unilaterally switching to another strategy. Strategic equilibrium is the most frequently applied game theory concept used in economics. Economic applications include the following: oligopoly, entry and exit, market equilibrium, bargaining, product quality, principal agents, and discrimination.[4] Hotels utilize strategic equilibrium when increasing their hotel room rates every year. For example, if a competitor lowers its price, a rival can also lower its prices until equilibrium is reached. The goal is to balance competition through equilibrium.

• *Prisoner's Dilemma.* A game that dissects strategic equilibrium, as in the following situation. Two suspects in a crime (the players) are put into separate isolation cells. Each cares more about her own welfare than the other's, and each is presented with the following choices and their consequences. If they both confess, each will be sentenced to three years. If only one confesses, she will be freed and her testimony will be used against the other, who will be sentenced to 10 years. If neither confesses, they will both be convicted of a minor offense and spend just a year in prison. Each prisoner has a dominant strategy to confess. But if both confess, the outcome is worse for each than if neither had confessed. This dilemma provides the most famous argument that strategic equilibrium can lead to inefficient or worst possible outcomes. The prisoner's dilemma game illustrates the structure of interaction in an oil cartel, or any oligopolistic industry of quantity competition, where each firm has an incentive to "spoil" the market by unilaterally increasing its own output.

Game theory is a useful tool in strategic decision making in that it provides a framework for looking at human interactions in the real world. For example, the standard view of the neoclassical economics of free enterprise assumes that the players rarely influence one another's decisions. However, in a knowledge-based, global economy, clearly they do, and players can benefit from cooperating with each other. We are presently moving from a model of competition to one of imperfect cooperation, highlighted by recent strategic terms like co-opetition (*see* Co-Opetition) and IBM's frenemies (*see* Frenemies). A shortcoming of game theory is the fact that freedom of choice in free human interactions defies prediction. Therefore, game theory should be combined with other strategies in order for a company to make better predictions.

Gatekeepers   First identified by MIT professor Thomas J. Allen.[5] Information bottlenecks. Gatekeepers control the flow of contact to a particular part of the organization. Gatekeepers make themselves indispensable. In manufacturing, managers of key assembly plants are gatekeepers, protecting the plant's integrity; typically they keep a tight rein on information flowing in both directions.

Gate Posts and Stage Gates   Milestones of performance that are interspersed throughout a project to ensure control and on-time and on-target delivery of results. Researchers or product developers must pass through these sometimes narrowly defined gates to proceed further with funding and continued access to corporate resources. Gate posts act as a "nag factor" and control measure in project management, and stage gates force one to think of how the project is "chunked."

Gearhead   A technology enthusiast; for example, a person with a deep interest in the inner working of computers, automobiles, and the like. "[Mark] Pauline and his compatriots were true hard-core gearheads: they loved the oily complexities of machines, and understood the internal mechanics that are, to the rest of us, an inscrutable mesh of wires and servos."[6]

General Propositions Maker (GPM)   The general propositions maker searches for general propositions, using as a basis empirical findings and practical experience. General propositions are reached by intuition and invention and therefore require creativity and imagination: This can be considered the peak of knowledge creation. An example of a general proposition, though framed in the interrogatory, is R. Coase's brilliant question: Why does the firm exist, why not just enter into a series of market transactions?

Generic Strategy   A strategy introduced by Michael Porter for marketing products or services. Porter suggested that there are in fact three generic strategies:

- Cost leadership, achieved by supplying products in a more cost-effective way than other competitors
- Differentiation, achieved by adding value to a product or service
- Focus, achieved by establishing a monopoly for a particular strategic target in a specific market segment

According to Porter, a firm that positions itself well and performs above the average level of its industry through cost leadership, differentiation, or focus has, in the long run, a sustainable competitive advantage. He calls these three strategies generic competitive strategies, since they tend to be effective regardless of a firm's industry, but while cost leadership and differentiation seek competitive advantage in a broad range of industry segments, the focus strategies (on either cost or differentiation) aim at advantage in a narrow segment.[7]

The first strategy, cost leadership, requires a company to have a sustained capital investment and access to capital, to focus on developing process engineering skills and closely control labor costs, and to identify cost drivers in order to continuously get costs down year after year. The key to success is to get overall costs down, not just production and manufacturing costs.

The differentiation strategy is built on strong product engineering and marketing skills and on providing a product or service that offers unique attributes demanded by customers so as to limit the risk of their switching to a substitute product. The cost incurred in creating a perceived uniqueness of the product or service is covered by charging a premium price.

Lastly, the focus strategy is built up on the same basics as either cost leadership or differentiation, depending on what particular strategic target is the focus. The premise of this strategy is to serve customers better by focusing directly on them and thereby gain their loyalty.

According to Porter, it is important for companies to focus on only one of these strategies, or else they will find themselves getting stuck in the middle[8]—the worst-case scenario, in Porter's estimation.

While many people argue that Porter's theories on competitive strategy still are of great importance for competition today, there are almost as many that imply that they have outlived their broad usefulness and must be rewritten or at least reconsidered. Pitt et al.[9] argue in *Business Horizon* that while the distinct separation between the generic strategies might have been good for the 1970s and 1980s, recent developments in today's markets make a combination of cost leadership and differentiation not only desirable but crucial to survival and success.

Geoclustering   Used in multiattribute segmentation, it yields richer descriptions of consumers than traditional demographics. Its importance as a marketing tool and segmentation tool is growing as it can capture the increasing diversity of a population. It was developed by Claritas Inc., which calls it PRIZM (potential rating index by zip market); Claritas was able to classify more than half a million U.S. residential neighborhoods into 62 lifestyle groupings called PRIZM clusters.

Getting on the Same Page   Consensus and focus on mission, agreement on the *how* of strategy.

Gig   An individual project or assignment, typical of a working pattern made up of a series of one-off projects rather than a career with a single employer.

Global Citizenship   Jeffrey Garten, in *The Politics of Fortune: A New Agenda for Business Leaders,* coined the term "global citizenship." He argues that prices and competition should not govern everything; instead, businesses must adopt a sense of global citizenship and CEOs must lead the way or accept increased friction, insecurity, and even decline. This premise also fits with the economic diplomacy doctrine adopted by the United States that has fueled U.S. economic expansion since the 1990s. Economic diplomacy works, for example, when the United States first opens up markets and then hopes that democratic reforms will soon follow. This strategy worked in the case of Mexico: In 1994, the NAFTA free trade agreement opened up the markets, which in turn led to the first fully democratic election, in 2000, when Vicente Fox came to power. A similar strategy is being followed with China; the thinking is that admitting China to the WTO will lead to economic liberalization that in turn will lead to democratic reforms.

Global Corporate Evolution Strategy   As firms change in size and scope, the fundamental choice they make is whether to support this change internally or externally as their strategy for evolution. Should a firm expand into a new country by expanding current operations, or should it acquire an existing firm in the new country? When are mergers necessary? When are acquisitions needed? What drives these decisions, and what are the critical success factors? How well do alternatives work in practice? How do cultural and ethical issues affect these decisions? How do knowledge flows in firms vary according to the choice of evolution strategy?

Global Corporation   The evolution of a global corporation often can entail progressively more involved strategy levels to react to increasingly complex issues. Various levels can include import-export activities, technology transfer, and direct investment in overseas operations. If a firm is engaged in all three activities, it is most likely a true multinational corporation (MNC). At this level, a company begins to emerge as a global enterprise with global approaches to all aspects of strategy.

A global orientation is evident at IBM, which operates in more than 125 countries, conducts its everyday business in more than 30 languages, uses more than 100 currencies, and has 23 major manufacturing facilities in 14 countries.

Globalization   Integration of technology, markets, politics, culture, labor, and commerce on a global scale. Globalization can be seen as both the process and the result of this integration of numerous forces.

N. Napiet[10] has delineated three globalization dimensions, all of which play an important role in a company's strategy.

1. Globalization of production: encouraged by the cost advantages that can be won by establishing an international production network

2. Globalization of products: favored by the significant rise in costs generated through the constant need to present ever-newer products

3. Globalization of markets: access to more and more foreign markets since the fall of international trade barriers, creating new opportunities as well as stiffening competition

According to Koji Kodowaki, president of Honda Motors, "Establishing an operating system that incorporates the most effective use of global-scale manufacturing efficiently serviced by an optimal worldwide purchasing system is crucial," indicating the crucial role globalization plays in Honda's strategy. Today, Honda is not only challenging its European and American competitors, it is also investing in high-end and performance segments with luxury and sports car models. Honda's Acura line of cars is now a threat for European luxury car manufacturers BMW and Mercedes.

Global Matrix Structure   An organizational structure with product groups on the vertical axis and foreign divisions or strategic business units (SBUs) on the horizontal axis that allows companies to simultaneously reduce costs by increasing efficiency and differentiate their activities through superior innovation and customer responsiveness. General Electric applied a global matrix strategy in different SBUs for reducing costs by increasing efficiency.

Glocalization   The process of tailoring products or services to different local markets around the world. The word is a hybrid of globalization and localization.

Success in a globalized environment is more likely if products are not globalized or mass marketed (exceptions are McDonald's, IKEA), but glocalized and customized for individual local communities that have different needs from one another as well as different cultural approaches.

Gobbledygook   Overly wordy writing that is filled with passive voice constructions, weak noun forms instead of strong verbs, and deadwood that gets in the way of clear communication. A good example of this kind of talk:

> Although the Central Efficiency Rating Committee recognizes that there are many desirable changes that could be made in the present efficiency rating system in order to make it more realistic and more workable than it now is, this committee is of the opinion that no further change should be made in the present system during the current year. Because of conditions prevailing throughout the country and the resultant turnover in personnel, and difficulty in administering the Federal programs, further mechanical improvement in the present rating system would require staff retraining and other administrative expense which would seem best withheld until the official termination of hostilities, and until restoration of regular operation.

Keep it simple. The term "gobbledygook" was invented by Franklin Delano Roosevelt to describe a situation in which people are tying you up in knots.

Iraqi U.N. ambassador Mohammed Aldouri used gobbledygook when he was interviewed on PBS before the 2003 crisis and asked if Iraq was willing to meet the conditions UN inspectors set out for a meeting. An appropriate answer would have been yes or no. Instead, Aldouri, sounding like a parody of a diplomat, answered with 82 words of gobbledygook about how they asked the inspectors to attend the meeting "as much for the international community as Iraq."

Granulation   A strategy, according to Krogh and Cusumano,[11] of distinguishing the cell or smaller granules of the business and growing them aggressively. It works best when the company has already conquered all relevant markets and the product demand is flattening out, customers are changing their preferences, competition is increasing, the company is mature enough to monitor new business activities, and a new technology is flourishing that could become a substitute for the company's product. An example comes from 3M: When they had those original products, such as Scotch Tape, they encouraged every employee to be an inventor. One result was the Post-it. Kelly Johnson invented the skunk works when he was at Lockheed Martin to pursue this granulation strategy.

Grapevine   An informal communication network within an organization that conveys information through unofficial channels independent of management control. Information travels much more quickly on the grapevine than through formal channels of communication. It tends to strengthen social relationships within the organization. Instant messaging (IP) has heated up the grapevine.

Grass Ceiling   Set of social and cultural factors that discourage or prevent women from using golf to conduct business.

Greenwashing   Covering up ecological, environmental, or corporate social misdeeds through seemingly altruistic community, environmentally friendly acts in other areas. For example, Nike countered accusations of tolerating sweatshops by mounting an aggressive strategy of alliances with high-profile NGOs worldwide (*see* NGOs); this strategy could be construed as corporate greenwashing.

Groupthink   A phenomenon that occurs during decision making or problem solving when a team's desire to reach an agreement overrides its ability to appraise the problem properly. Not too dissimilar to the Abilene Paradox, which is based on people's desire to conform and please others. One of the most famous examples of the perils of groupthink was the Bay of Pigs invasion, where Kennedy's cabinet coalesced unanimously around the idea of an invasion of Cuba using Cuban exiles. The operation was an embarrassing failure; however, the cabinet learned that dissension is needed to avoid groupthink. When the Cuban missile crisis came along, cabinet members were able to solve that peacefully and creatively using a minimal amount of force (the naval blockade), diplomatic back channels, and a famous appeal to the United Nations.

Growth   "Growth without structural adjustment can lead to economic inefficiency, and strategic growth results from the awareness of the opportunities and needs."— Alfred Chandler.[12]

Guiding Coalition   The group that is influential in shaping the strategy. Can be from inside or outside the firm.

Gulag   The system of forced-labor camps in the former Soviet Union. Any prison or forced-labor camp, especially one for political prisoners. A place of great hardship, from the Russian Gulag, acronym from *G*lavnoe *u*pravlenie ispravitel'no-trudovykh *lag*erei.

Used in sports and business to denote paying one's dues in an outpost. "Kariya stands out, not only because he has been a prolific goal scorer throughout his career. For years, he has been fawned over by the Canadian media—particularly from his hometown of Vancouver—who saw playing for the Ducks as doing time in the NHL's gulag."[13]

Gurus   Fifty business gurus worldwide, according to a recent Internet survey, ranked according to influence:

1. Peter Drucker

2. Charles Handy

3. Michael Porter

4. Gary Hamel

5. Tom Peters

6. Jack Welch

7. Henry Mintzberg

8. C. K. Prahalad

9. Bill Gates

10. Philip Kotler

11. Peter Senge

12. Sumantra Ghoshal

13. Warren Bennis

14. Rosabeth Moss Kantor

15. Rober Kaplan and David Norton

16. Nicholas Negroponte

17. Kjell Nordstrom and Jonas Ridderstrale

18. Stephen Covey

19. Percy Barnevik

20. Jerry Porras and James Collins

21. Ed Schein

22. Kenichi Ohmae

23. James Champy and Michael Hammer

24. Andy Grove

25. Michael Dell

26. Chris Argyris

27. H. Igor Ansoff

28. Alan Greenspan

29. Richard Branson

30. Jeff Bezos

31. Scott Adams

32. Don Tapscott

33. Edward de Bono

34. Richard Pascale

35. John Chambers

36. Kevin Kelly

37. John Harvey-Jones

38. Lee Iacocca

39. Clay Christensen

40. John Kotter

41. Geoff Moore

42. Herbert Simon

43. Nelson Mandela

44. Fons Trompenaars and Charles Hamden-Turner

45. Chris Locke

46. Thomas Stewart

47. Watts Wacker

48. Geert Hofstede

49. Herb Kelleher

50. Meg Whitman

Endnotes

1. Eatwell, J., Milgate, M., & Newman, P. (1989). *Game theory*. New York: The Macmillan Press Limited.

2. Pappas, J., & Hirschey, M. (1989). *Fundamentals of managerial economics*. 3rd ed. Hindsdale, IL: Dryden Press.

3. Ibid., p. 18.

4. Ibid., p. 19.

5. Allen, T. J. (1984). *Managing the flow of technology: Technology transfer and the dissemination of technological information within the R&D organization*. Cambridge: MIT Press.

6. Brad Stone; Gearheads; Stone, B. (2003). *Gearheads: The turbulent rise of robotic sports*. New York: Simon & Schuster.

7. Porter, M. (1985). *Competitive advantage: Creating and sustaining superior performance*. New York: Free Press.

8. Garten, J. (2002). *The politics of fortune: A new agenda for business leaders*. Boston: Harvard Business School Press.

9. Pitt, L., Ewing, M., & Berthon, P. (2000). Turning competitive advantage into customer equity. *Business Horizons*, 43:5, p. 11.

10. Taylor, S., Beecheler, S., & Napiet, N. (1996). Toward an integrative model of strategic international human resource management. *Academy of Management Review*, 21:4, pp. 959–985.

11. Krogh, G., & Cusamano, M. (2001). Three strategies for managing fast growth. *MIT Sloan Management Review*, 42:2, p. 53; Cusumuo, M., & Murkides, C. (2001). *Strategic thinking for the next economy*. San Francisco: Jossey-Bass.

12. Chandler, A. (1962). *Strategy and structure.* Cambridge: MIT Press.

13. Foster, C. (2003, June 5). Vision of cup is no longer an illusion. *The Los Angeles Times*.

H

Hamel, Gary (1954–) Avid proponent of the resource-based school of strategy, favoring drastic strategy and putting reason and analysis as secondary. Most recognized book is *Competing for the Future,* coauthored with C. K. Prahalad.

Harvard Business School (HBS) Approach Harvard Business School (HBS) approach is a way of thinking about a firm holistically rather than as a collection of individual functions such as marketing, production, and finance. Kenneth Andrews and C. Roland Christensen were among its formulators. Corporate strategy is seen as defining the business, then focusing on resources to convert distinctive competence into competitive advantage. However, the strategy does not show how to translate distinctive competence into competitive advantage at the business unit level.

Harvard Business School's roots of strategic management, relying on the case method, can be contrasted with the Carnegie Mellon orientation, relying on theory and number crunching. Carnegie Mellon (formerly Carnegie Tech) brought the theory-driven, systems thinking, linear programming approach typical of the work of Herbert Simon, Igor Ansoff, and Cyert and March.[1] HBS practitioners write less-bureaucratic cases, being committed to getting insight from the personalities and emphasizing the pull of issues rather than the push of theory. The *Harvard Business Review* also typifies this personality- and issue-driven view of strategy. Practitioners often appreciate the HBS approach. However, Henry Mintzberg dismisses the HBS cases as brief, convenient packages of words and numbers.

Harvest Strategy Also called asset reduction, a strategy whereby a company limits or decreases its investment in a business and extracts or milks as much of the investment as it can; in a declining industry, a strategy by which a company optimizes cash flow. For example, Migros, the Turkish supermarket chain, used this strategy during a national economic crisis: It stopped opening branches in Turkey and instead focused on getting the most benefit from the current branches.

HDLD High demand, low density. Meaning: "Though we may need lots and we don't have many." It is a euphemism, according to Donald Rumsfeld, for error—for not buying what you need. You don't have what you need to do the job, but at least you have an acronym.

Heads Up Advance warning that something is coming down the pike.

Hershey-Blanchard Situational Leadership Model Based on the assumption that successful leaders adjust their style to the situation. The appropriate combination of relationship versus task behaviors depends on the follower's maturity or readiness level. *See* Contingency Theory. The more mature the follower or the higher the readiness level, the less attention and reward the follower needs from the leader either in task or relationship issues, so the follower doesn't need to be told how to do the task (task behavior) or be patted on the back (relationship) for doing the job well.

Hidden Agenda A motive, purpose, or goal behind, and differing from, the presented rationale or course of action. People who suspect hidden agendas tend to be suspicious of, indeed paranoid about, commonsense explanations of events. They tend to regard such explanations as facile, if not simpleminded. Such suspicions can have corrosive effects on morale, behavior, and employee effectiveness. An example of the force of the "hidden agenda" mind-set occurred when a California-based engineering company was bought out by a major defense contractor based in Massachusetts. A senior engineer in the California company commented on the distinct cultures of the two companies. Her company was fairly open, but when she met with her new colleagues in Massachusetts, she felt there was a paranoid sense of hidden agendas (consistent with my own experience of California versus Massachusetts culture).

She recounts a brainstorming session at which she was trying to generate possible solutions to the problem at hand. Her new colleagues kept interrupting, whispering concerns about why they were at the meeting, suspecting that their managers had some sort of hidden agenda for sending them there. She finally threw up her hands and gave up on the purpose of the meeting. Her attempts to get things back on track and into problem-solving mode were met by, "Oh, you can say that because you are from California." When she returned to California, her manager expressed his disappointment that she had not taken more control at the meeting. She rolled her eyes and muttered something about a loony bin. She was soon happy to leave the newly merged company.

Historical Analogy The use of analogy in forecasting involves a "systematic comparison of the technology to be forecast with some earlier technology that is believed to have been similar in all or most important respects."[2] However, many erroneous forecasts are based on comparisons with previous experiences. Though there is value to the historical analogy, there is always the issue of choosing the appropriate comparison or comparison technology.

The real challenge facing a forecaster, therefore, is the task of identifying a technological innovation that will truly serve as an accurate historical precedent upon which to base a forecast by analogy. For example, when the United States started operations in Afghanistan, in late 2001, there were many discussions of the historical analogy of the Soviet Union's defeat in Afghanistan.

An example of reasoning by historical analogy:

1. Define the failure of the concept of the First Gulf War: not going into Baghdad.

2. Pinpoint the failure of the Second Gulf War: going into Baghdad.

Enormous amounts of time spent formulating the mission and perhaps they got it wrong.

History of Strategy (Brief)   (Adapted from a *BusinessWeek* summary[3]) Early 1960s: Harvard professors Kenneth Andrews and C. Roland Christensen articulate the concept of strategy as a tool to link together the functions of a business and assess a company's strengths and weaknesses against competitors. Alfred Chandler says changes in strategy cause a change in the structure of the firm. Igor Ansoff emphasizes the importance of diversification and synergy in corporate strategy.

Early 1960s: General Electric emerges as the pioneer in strategic planning, creating a large, centralized staff of planners to ponder the future. Consultant McKinsey & Co. helps GE view its products in terms of strategic business units, identify competitors for each, and evaluate its position against them.

1963: Under founder Bruce D. Henderson, Boston Consulting Group becomes the first of many strategy boutiques. BCG pioneers a series of concepts that takes corporate America by storm, including the "experience curve" and the "growth and market-share matrix."

1980: Harvard professor Michael E. Porter's book *Competitive Strategy* provides a generation of MBA-trained executives with new models to plot strategy based on economic theories.

1983: New GE chairman Jack Welch slashes the corporate planning group and purges scores of planners from GE's operating units. Numerous companies follow his lead.

Early 1980s: Battered by global competition, companies turn away from strategic planning and begin to focus on operational improvement. Executives embrace the Total Quality Movement (TQM) and the teachings of guru Edward Deming.

Late 1980s: Corporate America begins massive downsizing and reengineering of operations to increase efficiency and productivity. Guru Michael Hammer leads the reengineering revolution.

1990s: After 10 years of downsizing, companies begin to focus on how to grow. Academics C. K. Prahalad and Gary Hamel become the most influential of a new group of strategists with the publication of *Competing for the Future*.

2000: A bevy of new books is out from a new group of strategy gurus who are capturing the attention of corporate executives and redefining the process of strategy creation to focus on strategic resilience and chaos theory.

Homogenization   The removal of characteristic differences between separate markets and cultures. Globalization is frequently blamed for homogenization. The United

States is seen as a chief exporter of this homogenization through McDonaldization or Hollywoodization of the world.

Horizontal Diversification or Expansion   Acquiring competitors to increase market share and attain a critical mass in the market. Many European utility companies have chosen to expand their operations horizontally into different areas, resulting in the creation of a multiutility.

Horizontal Integration   When a firm's long-term strategy is based on growth through the acquisition of one or more similar firms operating at the same stage of the production-marketing chain, its overall strategy is horizontal integration. One example is Warner-Lambert's acquisition of Parke Davis, which resulted in reduced competition in the drug field for Chilcott Laboratories, a firm that Lambert previously had acquired. Nike's acquisition in the dress shoe business (Cole Haan) and N. V. Homes' purchase of Ryan Homes have vividly exemplified the success that horizontal integration strategies can bring.

Horns and Halos   The good and bad of a person. Following Bush's sweeping reelection as Texas governor in 1998, *Fortunate Son* was commissioned by St. Martin's Press and published in 1999 to much controversy. The controversy focused on J. H. Hatfield's Afterword, which included an unattributed allegation that Bush had arranged to have a 1972 cocaine arrest expunged from his records through his father's political influence. Hatfield maintained that he was not attacking Bush, that a good biography will yield both the good and bad—"horns and halos." This denotes a realistically grounded view of a person or strategic situation.

Hostile Takeover   An acquisition that the acquired firm resists.

Hub   A person who becomes a gathering and sharing point for critical information. Shows up in social network diagram like the center of star clusters, sometimes with dozens of links radiating out from the person. The hub is the shortest route to information.

Hubris   Hubris is an exaggerated self-confidence, excessive pride. For example, the former CEO of Enron once declared, "We're on the side of the angels."

Humanistic Approach   That approach to strategic management that emphasizes the essential humanness of people, declining to treat them as well-oiled machines. The human relation school argues (not always convincingly) that the more people are treated as humans first, the more productive they will be. This was the main conclusion of the Hawthorne studies.

Hypercompetition   Describes a competitive situation in which technology changes with excessive speed or competitors execute moves and countermoves with excessive speed or severity. The term was coined by Richard D'Aveni in a book of the same title; in it he argues that the appropriate strategies for a firm in a hypercompetitive environment emphasize surprise and unpredictability. Similar advice was given by Sun Tzu: Be unpredictable and feign moves that you may not make.

Hypothesis Seeker/Tester   A hypothesis seeker/tester is concerned with the discovery and verification of causal hypotheses, predicting a relationship between A and B, then empirically testing, through careful observation or experiment, to confirm or disconfirm the hypothesized relationship.

Endnotes

1. Cyert, R., & March, J. (1963). *A behavioral theory of the firm.* Englewood Cliffs, NJ: Prentice Hall.
2. Martino, A. (1983). Fraudulent democracy. *Economic Affairs*, 4:1, p. 6.
3. *BusinessWeek*. (1996, September 16). Strategic planning: fundamental, fad—or dead? Readers Report.

I

Idea Practitioner The idea practitioner is often an unsung hero, the person who brings in new ideas about how to manage better. An idea practitioner would have been the first to utter the term "intellectual capital" in your company. Few business ideas take root purely on their own merits, but typically need a proselytizer. Idea practitioners tend to be boundary spanners in the organization. Steve Jobs is known as an idea practitioner.

Ideological Mission This kind of mission is an idealistic idea that drives company success. For Apple Computer, it was an idea—a lightbulb that went on—of empowering people through an easy-to-use computer on every desktop. This ideological mission eventually dimmed, not so much by itself but because other lights became brighter (Wintel, for example).

Idle Time Time spent waiting to continue working on a task while there is a delay in the process at some point along the line.

Implementation Implementation involves action, control, starting and completing an action sequence. Implementation is not easy: Humans resist change, either bashing the new or clinging to the inertia of bureaucracy.

Improvisational Strategy Improvisational strategy does not follow a script or recipe. It is interactive and face-to-face, and involves high-level conversations carried out on a regular basis.

There are not many tools on the improvisational end of strategizing. Improvisational strategy is continuous and ongoing, not periodic. It involves not necessarily planning but strategic thinking. Improvisational strategy seems to lack structure only because the underlying structure is not readily apparent. *See* Calling Audibles, Complexity Theory. Hewlett-Packard under the leadership of Carly Fiorina has experimented with improvisational strategy. HP uses an approach it calls "garage works," which HP managers describe as a "nowhere store in Palo Alto, California," and as "kindergarten for adults." Garage works is a space (mental and physical) for managers to work on improvisational strategy for HP, and sometimes the activities include donning costumes to stimulate creative thinking.

Incentives   Incentives are rewards that shape behavior for achieving strategic goals. An important consideration is that the various incentive systems be applied so that marginal revenue is equal to marginal cost. A prominent California university recently disregarded this aspect of incentives when, under a severe budgetary crisis, they decided to cut the tuition waiver benefit program for employees. This program had zero marginal cost, so cutting it contributed zero marginal revenue and acted as a disincentive and morale buster.

Incrementalism   A collective term for the many initiatives of the 1980s and 1990s that took relatively small steps to improving quality and productivity as well as reducing costs. This approach encompasses such initiatives as TQM, continuous improvement, and benchmarking. While considered a valid way to approach business challenges, it is generally recognized today that a more radical approach is often needed.

Incrementalism is often contrasted with more strategic solutions. Incrementalism can turn into "slowly bleeding to death." For example, John Akers was slowly bleeding IBM to death in the early 1990s, so when Lou Gerstner came on board, he decided to stop the incrementalism and made one dramatic cut of 50,000 employees. Gerstner said that keeping the company together was the first strategic decision and the most important strategic decision he made at IBM.[1]

Indeterminate Competitive Landscape   As Prahalad and Oosterveld have pointed out, convergence and deregulation are eliminating traditional industry boundaries among telecommunications, computing, and consumer electronics, and are doing the same thing among the investment, insurance, and banking industries. As a result, business models developed to compete in a traditional industry structure have become largely irrelevant in these new, evolving industries—territories for which there are no maps.

Indifference Curve   An indifference curve graphically depicts various combinations of goods that generate the same level of utility to an individual. In other words, an individual is "indifferent" among any of the bundles because they all provide the same satisfaction. In any kind of negotiations, whether it is to buy a car or a house or to negotiate a merger, it is useful to identify one's indifference curve; it is always there to be discovered and to be used to leverage one's position. A person can be described as being in an ideal dating situation when he or she has two potential dates for Saturday night and both are on an indifference curve.

Industrial Espionage   The practice of spying on a business competitor in order to obtain commercial secrets that can yield a competitive advantage. Espionage is strongly recommended in *The Art of War*.

Industrialization   Change from an agrarian-based economy to one based on manufacturing. Features of this include automation, scientific development, and the division of labor. The phase of development directly following industrialization is the postindustrial society or the knowledge-based economy.

Industry and Competitive Analysis   Analysis of an industry and the competitors within it, often using tools from Michael Porter such as the five forces analysis (*see* Five Forces Industry Analysis) and strategic groups (*see* Strategic Groups).

Industry Attractiveness   The future profit potential of an industry. For example, Quaker Oats paid $1.3 billion for Snapple because it saw the "New Age" beverage industry (made up of such products as flavored iced teas) as attractive.

Industry Consolidation   Consolidation of an industry or sector whereby the smaller and weaker competitors are acquired or driven out of business; also termed shakeout. The Money, Meaning & Life Institute, which coaches other start-ups and individuals suffering from "Sudden Wealth Syndrome" (a term this consulting firm invented during the dot-com bubble) on how to manage portfolios more efficiently and to gain inner peace, has been questioned about its own financial figures after the collapse of the dot-com frenzy. It claimed that it is doing much better than it did before the industry consolidation.

Industry consolidation can be thought of as a type of weeding, an inevitable transition from the "low-entry-barrier" stage into the "high-entry-barrier" stage, which can be best for industry profitability in the long run.

Industry Foresight   Prahalad and Hamel discuss how companies need to look at the future of their industries. In effect, how much time managers spend on exploring the possible impact of changes in their environment on their companies' future can be a key to strategic success. Industry foresight enables a company to "get to the future first"[2] and stake out a leadership position.

Inferring Strategy   Inferring strategy involves a systematic investigation of competitor documents to decipher corporate strategy. The annual report is a good data source, especially the letter to shareholders that provides extensive information.

Inflection Point   Term coined by Andy Grove, the former CEO of Intel, to describe a fork in the road, a point at which a firm has to make a decision that affects its strategic position. An example would be Grove's decision to bet the company by dropping memory chips, Intel's bread and butter, in favor of a complete focus on semiconductor chips. This was a very good response to a strategic inflection. The key is recognizing that a choice must be made in the first place.

Informal Networks   The informal networks shadow the formal networks or hierarchy of the organization. For example, although there is by definition no formal leader in a leaderless group scenario, usually a de facto leader emerges—the result being an informal network. *See* Informal Organization.

Informal Organization   The aggregate of personal contacts and interactions and associated groupings of people. Social networks analysis (SNA) studies the informal organization.

Information   Information reduces uncertainty. The value of information can be measured by the amount of surprise it induces in the receiver. The organization can then make strategic choices to bring the degree of surprise under control. A good example of this process is how Microsoft, which was slow to catch on to the opportunities of the Internet, was later able to incorporate that surprising information into an effective and profitable organization routine and product that is Internet Explorer. It is now trying to replicate that strategy in the search engine market to develop an effective project that would compete with Google.

Innovation   For a firm to grow or even survive, it has to innovate. Innovation involves the ability to think differently, to come up with a new idea, a fresh take, a unique offering. To innovate successfully, this playful approach needs to be coupled with tough-minded execution, discipline, and seriousness. So an innovative strategy requires out-thinking and out-executing the competition. The key is to take a smart risk and make it pay.

An example of a consistently innovative winning strategy is the millions of games produced and sold by Electronic Arts, the foremost video game company in the world. Another example is Anthropologie's sociologically sophisticated stores where they sell a sensibility and create a shopping experience that's unique.

Honda is one of the inventors of the gasoline-electric engine system, which is called hybrid; they adapted this system to the Civic model. This innovation comes from Honda's commitment to spending significant funds for research and development.

Wisdom from the Internet, passionately comparing Gateway and Apple innovation:

Whether it's an all-in-one, a retail store or this music service, Gateway's heart (deep deep down in their creative department . . .) seems to be in the right place. However, as the idea probably travels up the chains of command, it gets torn apart, jigsawed back together only to repeat that process. Sure, Gateway looks at the trends of industry and wants to capitalize on them. But it seems they always put out a product that is half-conceptualized and twice over shined on an older idea.

That's why I love Apple. They take ideas and develop them. They play, they wonder, they dream about the next big thing. Like the iPod. Or the new LCD iMac. Sure, I'm frustrated that there is no Apple PDA, but maybe Apple knows that I would never need something like that because they've done their research. It doesn't matter who copies who in the end. What matters most is that the product is something we all love. Apple delivers that about 98% of the time.[3]

For example, Intel, the leader in the semiconductor industry, pursues expansion through a strategic emphasis on innovation. Based in California, Intel is a designer and manufacturer of semiconductor components and related products, microcomputer systems, and software. Its Pentium processor chip gives desktop computing the capabilities of a small mainframe computer.

Another example of innovation is Polaroid, which heavily promotes each of its new cameras until competitors are able to match its technology, and consequently introduces a drastically new product. Polaroid introduced the Swinger, SX-70, One Step, and Sun Camera 660 in relatively quick succession.

Instrumental or Utilitarian Power   Instrumental or utilitarian power is related to the payment of inducements either to join the organization or do things for it.

Intellectual Capital   The combined intangible assets (tacit knowledge, experience, and social networks) of an organization. In a knowledge-based economy, the intellectual capital that exists within the organization is more valuable than the company's tangible assets and capital. Better management of knowledge assets like intellectual capital could lead to a competitive advantage.

The capacity to manage human intellect and convert it into useful products and services is fast becoming the critical executive skill of the present business climate.

Intellectual Foundation of Strategic Management   Kenneth Andrews, Igor Ansoff, Alfred Chandler, Henry Mintzberg, and consulting firms like McKinsey.

Intellectual Potholes   A term coined by Michael Porter to denote instances when companies have bought into a number of flawed or simplistic ideas about competition.

Internet Year   Three months.

Intrapreneurship   A corporate philosophy that focuses on encouraging the individual employee to act in an entrepreneurial way. Large firms by their very nature tend to put in place systems and structures that inhibit individual initiative. Instead of forcing mavericks to fight the system, a company that embraces intrapreneurship tries to facilitate entrepreneurial behavior. The word was coined by Pinchot.[4]

Intuitive Management   A management style that relies on "gut feeling" or a sixth sense, rather than analytical or objective reasoning. Closely linked to a style of decision making that encourages creativity and innovation.

Isolated CEO   A CEO who lacks centrality and density in her internal and external networks. Being connected with a wide number of people inside and outside of the organization has been demonstrated to increase creativity and innovation. CEO Tom Glocer of Reuters, the global information services giant, has rightsized his company into the black. But does he have the internal and external networks in place to make it grow?

Isolation, Strategic   Sun Tzu advises, "When in difficult country, do not encamp. In country where high roads intersect, join hands with your allies. Do not linger in dangerously isolated positions. In hemmed-in situations, you must resort to stratagem. In a desperate situation, you must fight. There are roads that must not be followed, towns that must not be besieged."[5]

This can be interpreted as advice to avoid isolation in difficult situations and instead make alliances with other companies to gain market share and to make it easier to compete. Pick your battles wisely.

Issues Management   The anticipation and assessment of key trends and themes of the next decade and the relation of these trends to the organization. Issues management is informed by future research in order to formulate strategic plans and actions.

Endnotes

1. Gertsner, L. (2002). *Who says elephants can't dance? Inside IBM's historic turnaround.* New York: HarperBusiness Press.

2. Hamel, G., & Prahalad, C. K. (1999). *Competing for the future.* Boston: Harvard Business School Press.

3. http://forums.macrumors.com/archive/topic/23149-1.html

4. Pinchot, G. (1985). *Intrapreneuring: Why you don't have to leave the company to become an entrepreneur.* New York: Harper & Row.

5. Sun Tzu. (1996). *The art of war.* (Ralph Sawyer, Trans.). Boulder, CO: Westview Press.

J

Japan Management System Japanese management is characterized by concern for the long-term, intensive competitive approach with an emphasis on market share fueled by internal growth. Ouchi described this as Type Z management style: greater collective orientation, less specialization, and more emphasis on informal controls. The Japanese management system is no longer as vigorously touted now that the country has been in a decade-long recession. *See* Kerietsu.

Java Language An open computer language promoted by Sun Microsystems in an attempt to break the lock-in effects of Microsoft and to deter Microsoft from entering the workstation market. Eventually Microsoft's Bill Gates announced his support of Java.

Joint Venture (JV) A partnering of two companies. Regarding multinational strategies, U.S. firms will look to target a foreign national company to JV with. AT&T used the JV strategy to produce its own personal computer; by entering into numerous JVs with European producers, it acquired the necessary technology and positioned itself for European expansion.

Jungian Approach Jungian psychology has emerged as a credible complement or alternative to Freudian psychology. Jung based his ideas on the concept of universal archetypes that cut across cultures. If the Freudian view shows affinities with the Judeo-Christian religious tradition, then the Jungian view is much closer to the Buddhist tradition and therefore more palatable for a certain mind-set. The Myers-Briggs Type Indicator is based on Jung's psychological types.

Junk Bonds Unsecured high-risk debt instruments that were often used to finance acquisitions. The thinking was that debt helped to discipline managers (*see* Agency Theory). Presently, junk bonds are used less frequently to finance acquisitions. Although debt can have a multiplying or leveraging effect on profits, too much debt can have a negative impact on firm competitiveness—for example, driving out funding for R&D necessary for long-term growth. Interesting to note that in 2003, California state bonds approached near junk bond status.

Just-in-Time (JIT) A manufacturing (and strategic) philosophy that aims to eliminate waste by supplying goods when the requesting organization needs them and not before. Critical components of JIT include TQM and employee involvement.

K

Kerietsu Kerietsu is a key aspect of Japan's corporate governance system that involves vertical integration, or quasi-integration, because it incorporates aspects of hierarchies and of the market system. Firms in certain industries in Japan have coordinated their activities so as to be able to flexibly respond to market exigencies and quickly respond to emergent technologies. Usually a kerietsu includes manufacturing firms, firms that supply the materials the manufacturers need, and a bank or financing institution.

Key Success Factors (KSF) Those factors without which one cannot compete effectively in an industry. KSF are dynamic, changing over time. Presently, having an online music store or music download device has become a critical factor of success in the PC industry.

KISS Keep it simple. The most effective plans are the simple ones. Ockham's razor: The hypothesis with the minimum number of assumptions wins.

Knowledge Information required for the interpretation of experience. Knowledge is built from interaction with the world and organized and stored in each individual's mind. It is also stored on an organizational level with the minds of employees and in paper and electronic records.

Knowledge Economy/Knowledge Worker "The capacity to manage human intellect and to convert it into useful products and services is fast becoming the critical executive skill of the age." Peter Drucker was the first to coin this term, prescient (as usual) of a major paradigm shift that then was dubbed the knowledge economy. In a knowledge economy, the critical asset of production is the intangible knowledge embodied in the knowledge worker. Many knowledge management systems try to capture, exploit, and nurture this intangible asset that is king in the knowledge economy.

Knowledge Management and Sustainable Competitive Advantage Knowledge management (KM) can be defined as the creative use of both written and unwritten information to develop new processes. KM is the formal process of determining what internally held information could be used to benefit a company and ensuring that this information is made easily available to those who need it. KM is the effective use of systems to collect, use, and reuse knowledge within the firm.

One of the biggest misconceptions is that knowledge management is about technology. While technology is a needed ingredient, there is no one silver bullet of technology that can assure successful implementation of knowledge management. The natural tendency is for CEOs and CIOs to focus on technology because it is a tangible investment that is easy to implement. The problem with this one-size-fits-all mentality is that this tendency to focus on technology rather than people and process has obscured some of the real benefits that KM can bring: Increasing workplace efficiency, saving time, reducing costs, and retaining, exchanging, and reusing knowledge are a few of the reasons companies introduce KM systems. There are four pillars of success in KM: content, process, culture, and technology.

L

Laissez-Faire Strategist   Laissez-faire: from the French, meaning let (people) do (as they choose). Adam Smith, an eighteenth-century professor of moral philosophy at Glasgow University, enunciated the concept of laissez-faire economics (though not by that term) by which the invisible hand of the market sets prices through demand and supply and encourages all participants in the market to pursue enlightened self-interest. One of the first tests of the laissez-faire philosophy was the Irish potato famine, in the 1840s, when the British government did not provide food aid to Ireland through a strict adherence to laissez-faire philosophies. The modern-day strategist faces a similar dilemma, as the negative effects of globalization can provoke a backlash against a corporation or government or both. *See also* Smith, Adam.

Large Group Interaction Methods (LGIM)   An increasingly popular set of methods for implementing large-scale changes. Characteristic methods include involving a large number of people, as many as 2,000 at one time. The communication method involves a large amount of interaction and participation. Usually many methods are used and a large number of stakeholders are involved through a series of workshops or conferences. Implementing strategic change through LGIM usually requires substantial follow-up as participants carry out action plans. GE conducts these LGIM at their Crotonville facility. Jack Welch was known to pontificate in front of large groups of managers very effectively.

Lateral Thinking   A creative and fresh approach to problem solving that attempts to ignore traditional approaches and tackles problems from unorthodox perspectives.

Two types of lateral thinking include vertical and horizontal (lateral). The former is based on logic (Spock's approach!) and the latter attempts to disregard rational trains of thought and branches out (thinking outside the box). Lateral thinking involves the examination of a problem and its possible solution from all possible angles.

Leadership   "The leader's job is not to provide energy but to release it from others."—Frances Hesselbein.

Leadership is seen when an individual is able to influence a group to achieve a common goal.[1] As Rudolph Giuliani explained in his memoirs, leadership is a privilege but also carries responsibility—from imposing a structure suitable to an organization's purpose, to forming a team of people who bring out the best in one another, to taking the right, unexpected risks. A leader must develop strong beliefs, articulate and act on those beliefs, and be held accountable for the results.

David Frum's recent book, *The Right Man*, offers a view of leadership that explains how George W. Bush was able to make an impact in his first year in office, through the combination of the events of September 11 and Bush's personality traits. Frum's portrait of Bush captures some of the contradiction of leadership:

> George W. Bush is a very unusual person: a good man who is not a weak man. He has many faults. He is impatient and quick to anger; sometimes glib, even dogmatic; often uncurious and as a result ill-informed; more conventional in his thinking than a leader probably should be. But outweighing the faults are his virtues: decency, honesty, rectitude, courage and tenacity.

Under Jack Welch, GE was able to successfully transform itself from an old-line industrial company to a diversified global manufacturing and services conglomerate. Welch endorsed one of the strategies of the Leadership Development Center, in Crotonville, New York, led by Noel M. Tichy: the idea that leadership needed to be embedded in GE's genes through training. Welch believed that leadership needed to extend beyond the CEO and the senior executive team and reach down through all levels of the organization. It is ironic that in the cult-of-personality adoration that followed Welch's career at GE, this largely democratic and decentralized leadership model that Welch advocated was not given much attention.

"One of the signs of excellence in a manager is the ability to anticipate problems, not just to react them." —Liam Donaldson

The U.S. Army's chief of staff, Gen. Eric Shinseski, pointed out that "mistrust and arrogance are antithetical to inspired and inspiring leadership." He clarified the difference between formal authority, which is about being appointed to a position, and how leadership needs to be learned and practiced.

Learning   A key to learning is thoughtful reflection. Every manager is a teacher, mentoring, working with her own staff; taking the learning and sharing it with others. *See* University.

Learning Organization   Model characterized by a flat-structured organization and customer-focused teams having the ability to exploit employees' willingness to develop a shared vision.

There are four characteristics: constant readiness for change, continuous planning, improvised implementation, and action learning. 3M runs its organization with a campuslike learning atmosphere and emphasizes that 15% of employee time should be devoted to new and open-ended projects.

Learning Style   The way in which someone approaches the acquisition of knowledge and skills. Four learning styles have been identified: The activist likes to get involved in new experiences and enjoys change; the theorist likes to question assumptions and learns best with no time limits; the pragmatist prefers practicality above all else; and the reflector likes to take his time to think things through.

Life Cycle of Technology   A phenomenon that exists in the high-tech industry: the trajectory of purchase trends of newly introduced products. According to Donald Norman, there are two types of consumers in this type of industry: the innovators and technology enthusiasts, and the pragmatists. The first dominate the market early. They are willing to pay the higher price for the products that satisfy their craving. Later, once companies innovate their processes and make their products more afford-able, the latter enter the market.

Norman describes this sequence as "the change from technology-driven products to customer-driven, human-centered ones." He also states that "as long as the technol-ogy's performance, reliability, and cost fall below customer needs, the marketplace is dominated by early adopters: those who need the technology and who will pay a high price to get it. But the vast majority of customers are late adopters. They hold off until the technology has proved itself, and then they insist upon convenience, good user experience, and value."[2]

Although the innovators drive the market, they are a very small percentage com-pared to the pragmatists, who make up the largest portion of the market, once they finally decide to spend. The timing of this decision is of course dependent on the costs; thus, competitors in the second stage of the life cycle are in a good position if their products are priced competitively. *See* Second Mover Strategy.

Linkage   Linking new business opportunities to corporate strategy. New business opportunities need to be linked to the core business, lest they become resource starved and forgo the opportunity to demonstrate their full potential. Intel and Microsoft have disclosed plans for pushing deeper into home entertainment, a hot market for computers—a strategy that is based on the linkage of hardware and soft-ware industries.

Location Advantage   Location advantage is an international business theory that posits that firms locate abroad according to a complex assessment of this advantage. Often location advantage can involve access to inputs, such as a highly educated labor pool, or to sources of raw materials, R&D, or production. Another location advantage may be close proximity to competitors to learn from their technology, practices, and people. An example of location advantage is the information gleaned about competi-tors and new technology when listening to conversations in any given grocery store in Palo Alto (in Silicon Valley). An example of the opposite of location advantage might be Starbucks Coffee's plans to open its first retail location in France early in 2004—Starbucks is hoping to find its place, rather than be scorned, in a country known for corner bistros and cafés.

Logical Incrementalism   Phrase coined by James Brian Quinn to denote an adaptive mode of strategy making that is not based on a fully articulated plan, but instead pro-ceeds as a more nonlinear mixture of planning with spontaneous changes midcourse.

Think of the Third Army Division's arrival at the gates of Baghdad: American field commanders were able to throw out the playbook for a siege of the city and instead push the limits of the city's defense, finding little resistance and entering the city without a pause.

Logicians   Logicians define their concepts and relate them to each other in some logically consistent conceptual system.

Lone Ranger Boss   A lone ranger boss is out on a limb; *see* Isolated CEO. No longer a successful leadership style.

Low-Credibility Committee   A committee formed with no power to implement or take meaningful action.

Low-Hanging Fruit   Something easily obtainable that provides short-term opportunities for quick profit. Usually acted upon quickly because highly accessible to other competitors. For example, the top of a Google search page is now the most valued position in cyberspace—especially if a Web site is trying to lure potential customers. Advertisers pay for ads that run next to Google's search results and can scoop up the low-hanging fruit this investment provides them.

Endnotes

1. Northouse, P. G. (2004). *Leadership: Theory and practice.* Thousand Oaks, CA: Sage.
2. Norman, D. (1998). *The invisible computer: Why good products can fail, the personal computer is so complex, and information appliances are the solution.* Cambridge: MIT Press.

M

Maintainer Strategy The maintainer strategy is to keep the status quo through consistency, standardization, sticking with winning products and processes, and preserving company tradition and reputation. It can be argued that Wal-Mart has a maintainer strategy: They have a winning approach and they are sticking with it, expanding it globally, and never straying far from the views and culture of the now-deceased founder Sam Walton, like the sundown rule (address a customer's issue before the sun goes down).

Management Getting results through people. It is often said that management produces order and consistency whereas leadership produces change and movement. Management is about planning, budgeting, organizing, and staffing. Leadership is more about establishing direction, aligning people, and motivating and inspiring.[1] Henry Mintzberg rightly asked, at the Academy of Management in Denver in 2002, "Whatever happened to management in strategic management?" His point was that strategic management can become so enamored of the complex econometric industry analysis and the linear programming-based implementation schedules that the tricky feat of getting results through people can be ignored.

Management Expressions Managers often like to use clichés in their writing and speech. Metaphorical statements like "That train has already left the station" seem to be more effective. Below are some clichés that bog down management communication.

"the fact of the matter is . . .," "the fact that . . ."

"window of opportunity," "meeting the challenge," "level playing field"

"send a message" (to anyone about anything), as in "The president is sending a strong message to his opponents."

"the take-home message is . . ."

"empowerment" (of anyone or anything)

"a warm, caring environment"

"global" (anything), "cutting edge"

"fully integrated," "fully diversified"

"the bottom line is . . ."

"the good news is blah blah blah and the bad news is blah blah blah"

"bio" as a prefix in new words, e.g., biorational, bioresponsible, bioglobal

"the best of both possible worlds" (or the worst)

"pose a threat"

"taking it to the next level," "pushing the envelope"

Management Science The application of scientific methods and principles to management decision making and problem solving. Encompasses the use of quantitative, mathematical, and statistical techniques. Lies at the opposite end of the spectrum from the various human relations schools of thought.

Managerialism Power in corporation falls to senior managers, who may advance their own interests rather than those of the owner. Often referred to as the agency problem (*see* Agency Theory). Peter Drucker notes that in a corporation, the owner—the institutional investor—is an absentee landlord. These managers can show a preference for acquisition rather than disposal, for executive jets, or for locating the head office a close drive from their suburban home.

Managerial Tasks Managerial tasks include setting agendas, setting time tables, allocating resources, providing structure, making job placements, establishing rules and procedures, developing incentives, and generating creative solutions and taking corrective action, among others.[2] Some good books on the topic are Ken Blanchard and Spencer Johnson's *The One Minute Manager;* Peter Drucker's *The Practice of Management;* and Chester Barnard's *The Functions of the Executive* (more philosophical than typical management books; Barnard delves into the nature of obtaining cooperation). *See also* Management.

Managers If you look in a typical strategic management textbook for managers, you will be redirected to strategic leaders. However, there will always be managers toiling in the vineyard to implement the grand strategic plans. A good way to get insight into the mind-set and dilemmas of the manager is to consider a novel by Sloan Wilson from the 1950s. Like William H. Whyte's *The Organization Man* and David Riesman's *The Lonely Crowd,* this book's title became a catch phrase: *The Man in the Grey Flannel Suit.*

Wilson's best-selling novel tells the story of Tom Rath, who is pursuing a living as a writer in the corporate world of the postwar years. In the course of writing speeches for the corporate president, Rath realizes that the president's success has come at the expense of personal happiness. Ruminating on his own life, Rath is torn between his responsibility to an illegitimate son and his current obligations toward his wife, his children, and his employer. Among the many life-altering decisions Rath makes is his determination to seek out a job that will allow him to spend more time with his family, even if it means a severe cut in salary.

The novel's theme is not dated, and is more relevant than ever: the conflict between an individual's humanistic ideals and the rough-and-tumble capitalist reality. Having been a paratrooper during World War II, Rath quickly sees that corporate bureaucracy has become a postwar extension of military hierarchy and regimentation and that his war record will not make up for a lack of business experience. Executives are the officer corps, the grey flannel suit is the uniform of the day, and the CEO is more than the general, he is a supreme thinker perched at the top of the corporate pyramid. This novel is relevant today because it shows how far America's business conduct had fallen from any ideal of honor and integrity. Success in the pursuit of wealth is seen as a test of character. *See* Existential Strategy.

Marine Corps   "Every marine a rifleman." The Marine Corps is the only branch of the military that has a reading list. The list includes Nietzsche and Camus' *L'Etranger*. The marines are considered "the tip of the spear," have their own history, lore, and tactics. The Marine Corps' birthday is November 10, 1775—the corps is older than the United States. The birthplace was Tun Tavern, Philadelphia. The bloodiest battle of World War II: Tarawa. Marines consider the deadliest weapon on the earth to be the marine and his rifle. You want to win your war? Tell it to the marines! Jar Heads. Dubbed "devil's dogs" for the way they fought the Germans in Belleau Wood, in World War I. The Germans had said that to be the most ferocious was to "fight like an Englishman" until they met the devil's dogs.

It is said that at night marines pray for war; they want to get a promotion, get rid of some of the deadwood. This could be too callous to be true, really just very patriotic, with supreme confidence in their leaders, from their team leader to the president.

The Marine Corps has its own planes, troops, and ships—practically an army, navy, and air force all in one. Marines have taken fewer casualties in its peacekeeping role in Iraq than the army. Lt. Gen. James Conway explains the Marine Corps approach: "We manage the level of violence. If we take fire, we immediately achieve fire superiority and we govern the de-escalation. We don't let the bad guys do that." It was somewhat difficult for the marines to accept that it was army troops who discovered Saddam Hussein in his hole; just some friendly rivalry among the branches of the military.

Market   The grouping of people and organizations unified by common needs and goals. Can also be seen as a gathering of sellers and purchasers to exchange commodities.

Market Analysis   Market analysis can be described as answering the following questions: "Who?" (determining the customers to serve), "What?" (determining the customer needs to satisfy), and "How?" (determining core competencies necessary to satisfy customer needs).[3]

Market Development   Market development consists of marketing present products to customers in related market areas by adding channels of distribution or by changing the content of advertising or promotion. For example, firms that open branch offices in new cities, states, or countries are practicing this approach. Likewise, companies are practicing market development if they switch from advertising in trade journals to advertising in newspapers or if they add jobbers to supplement their mail-order sales efforts.

DuPont used market development when it found new applications for Kevlar, an organic material that police, security, and military personnel use primarily for bullet-proofing. Kevlar is now being used to refit and maintain wooden-hulled boats, since it is lighter and stronger than glass fibers and has 11 times the strength of steel.

Marketing Orientation   A marketing orientation involves a commitment to the marketing concept that the customers' needs and wants are the determinants of the organization's overall direction and its marketing programs.[4]

Martha Stewart Strategy   Every element of your life becomes something marketable. Stewart started with modeling and went on to décor, chefing, her career as an entertaining queen, her magazine of homemaking tips, and so on—subsuming every part of her life into her strategy. Reality TV operates on the same principle.

In 1999, her company goes public and is worth $1 billion by the end of the opening day. In 2003, Martha was indicted for securities fraud and obstruction of justice linked to her 2001 sale of her shares in her friend Sam Waksal's biotech company, ImClone. She later resigned as CEO of Martha Stewart Living Omnimedia. Her yearbook quote in 1959 read, "I do what I please, and I do it with ease." Since her indictment, Martha-philes and -phobes have bought souvenirs from dozens of Web sites. A sample T-shirt slogan, "If her stock sale was legit, you must acquit."

Maslow, Abraham H. (1908–1970)   Most known for his hierarchy of needs, Maslow groups needs into classes and arranges them into a hierarchy, ascending from the lowest need to the highest. Once one set of needs is met, one moves up—in theory—to the next level. The highest, self-actualization, is much sought after, but rarely attained. His book *Motivation and Personality* is his defining work about self-actualization and the hierarchy of needs. Possibly the most expensive paperback you will ever buy, but a classic. See Figure M. 1. Abraham Maslow taught at Alliant International University in the early 1970s.

Matrix Organization   Keanu Reeves does not work there. A matrix organization involves overlapping chains of command that violate Henri Fayol's dictum for unity of command: Basically, you have more than one boss. The matrix structure is meant to increase direct contact among division managers and to act as an integrating mechanism for encouraging and supporting cooperation and sharing of both competencies and resources. In practice, this structure has largely failed to deliver results due to its unwieldy structure.

Maturation of Markets   When products or industry reach that point in the life cycle where demand levels off, they soon decline.

Figure M.1   Maslow's Hierarchy of Needs

MBA   "Not prepared to manage" badge.

Mechanistic Thinking   Concern for efficiency, measurement, evaluation, order, and chain of command.

Mentors   Corporate managers who supervise, coach, and guide selected lower-level employees by introducing them to the right people and acting as their organizational sponsors. Most mentoring is informal, but many organizations use a formal system of assigning mentors.

Merger of Equals   A merger in which the two participating companies are of comparable size, assets, and reputation. San Diego's Idec Pharmaceuticals merged with Massachusetts-based Biogen, supposedly as a merger of equals with Idec paying a purchasing price of $6.4 billion for Biogen, a much larger company. Each is profitable and largely dependent on a single popular drug. The combined company, called Biogen Idec Inc., will be the third-largest biotechnology firm.

Mergers   Mergers are a rapid way to widen the control of resources and strengthen market share without creating new production capabilities internally.

Mergers usually arise because neither company has the scale to acquire the other on its own. A merger has the potential benefit of being friendlier but requires special handling. However, mergers and acquisitions share similar strategic issues.

Although popular press accounts focus on mergers and acquisitions among large firms, they occur with small firms as well. In fact, any combination of sizes is possible.

Small and medium enterprises in Europe have merged to take advantage of the European Single Market and the Euro and to better exploit economies of scale and improve the efficiency of the enterprises. Larger mergers obviously imply greater organizational complexity and are more difficult to coordinate and manage.

The Hewlett-Packard-Compaq merger took place in 2002. When Hewlett-Packard announced its plans to merge with Compaq, feelings were mixed. With a deal as major as this one, which was estimated to be worth around $25 billion, there was much controversy as it was opposed by some factions or backed by others.

Many opponents of the merger, like Walter Hewlett, an HP board member and son of cofounder Bill Hewlett, did not believe that the best way for the company to go was to merge with Compaq. They believed that HP's position was strong on its own. Their printer division gave them an advantage over the other companies. Unlike a PC purchaser, a customer who purchases a printer becomes a customer for a very long time. He has to purchase toner or ink cartridges—components that are very profitable for the company for many years to come. Compaq had a server line that HP believed would allow it to capture and lead that field. The opponents, however, did not see that as a good enough reason to absorb Compaq. In fact, the two main opponents of the deal launched a campaign to stop it. Walter Hewlett was the most visible opponent of the merger, issuing a series of press releases and securities filings over several months urging shareholders to reject the deal. Hewlett argued that the combination would weigh down HP's profitable printer division and overly expose the company to the low-margin PC business. However, so far the HP-Compaq merger seems to be largely successful.

One of the reasons for the failure of the merger of Rover by BMW was the wrong model policy: Rover did not complement the product range of BMW in the mid-size and small car segment. Eventually, after significant losses, BMW was able to sell Rover and continue with its success in the luxury segment.

Mergers and Acquisitions   A merger is a strategy whereby two firms agree to integrate their assets and operations on a more or less equal basis. An acquisition is a strategy whereby one firm buys out the assets of the other firm. Many situations that are touted as mergers end up in effect being acquisitions as one firm dominates the process. A takeover is a special type of acquisition in which the acquired firm did not solicit the action by the acquiring firm, also called a hostile takeover.

Mergers and acquisitions are complicated enough to manage within a single country, but they become even more complex when conducted multinationally. For example, international mergers and acquisitions are confronted with many extra problems such as different languages, cultures, customs, currencies, legislations, political systems, and work ethics.

S. Shiva Ramu defined mergers and acquisitions according to four categories:

1. Savior operation: Firms with financial difficulties look for a potential rescuer.

2. The will to cooperate: Joining forces is clearly beneficial to all parties concerned, with no losers.

3. The protesting acquisition: A merger is approved entirely by many parties; however, the "loser" clearly doesn't see the merger as entirely beneficial.

4. Hostile acquisition: The firm that is purchased completely opposes the deal.[5]

Mergers and acquisitions can also be defined in terms of the stages of production involved or affected:

Vertical integration: Producers or suppliers of a utility seek to extend their operations with a company involved further up or down the supply chain, or extend their operations through organic growth.

Horizontal integration: Across the European energy markets, producers, suppliers, or distributors are merging with, or acquiring, companies providing the same utility or service.

Lateral integration: A company acquires a utility in the same area within the supply chain, or chooses to enter the supply chain at the same level but in a different sector.

Diagonal integration: A company acquires a utility in a different part of the supply chain and in a different sector, such as an electricity producer acquiring a gas supplier.

Mergers and Acquisition Strategy   This is a strategy that allows a company to expand or diversify its capacity to compete. However, it has both a positive and negative aspect. It can work well if the company is well prepared for the change after the merger and devastating if the company has not prepared well. For example, the merged AOL Time Warner cable company faced many problems in terms of quality of services and substitutive services of dial-up and broadband. The executives found that the merger was much bigger and went much faster than they could keep up with, including commoditizing some of these new services. The merger also coincided with the era of the dot-com bust, so Time Warner had to get back to what its core is. The collision of the cultures of two previously separate entities was also a substantial problem. Recently the firm dropped AOL as a moniker, signaling the nondelivery of promised synergy.

Metaphor   Verbal picture.

1. A figure of speech in which a word or phrase that is not literally applicable is used in place of another to suggest an analogy. A metaphor is a comparison not using *like* or *as*.

2. Something used to represent another; a symbol.

From Latin *metaphora*, from Greek *metapherein* (to transfer), from *meta* (among, with, after) + *pherein* (to carry). Thinking and writing in metaphors is a good way to formulate strategy and clarify the mission and vision of the firm. Among examples of useful metaphors are the CEO is a marionette, conductor, architect; the general manager is a foot soldier. The organization can be an amoeba or a well-oiled machine.

Three metaphors of the organization, according to Henry Mintzberg:

1. Organization as a vertical chain on horizontal plane (this is compatible with Porter and his value chain)

2. Organization as a hub, a center, an airport

3. Organization as a web, a network (an example is a high-tech venture in which everyone is a manager/owner)

Metrosexuals   Marketing term that denotes straight urban men willing to embrace their feminine side. Soccer superstar of the club *Real Madrid* David Beckham, with his flair for fashion and style, is a metrosexual icon.

M-Form Organization Structure   Multidivisional structure for control of different businesses (divisions) under headquarters (HQ).

M-form organization structure was first explored in *Strategy and Structure*[6] (Alfred Chandler). Large U.S. and European corporations adopted M-form organizational structures with discrete strategic business units (SBU) in the 1960s and 1970s.

Micromanaging Minutiae   When top management, through a misguided need to control, takes on oversight of tasks that are the purview of those lower in the organization. For example, a medium-sized organization recently had its chief operating officer (COO) spending her time personally signing expense reports to control expenses in a belt-tightening time. We can see this as inappropriate micromanaging.

Mintzberg, Henry (1939–)   Considered by many to be the foremost thinker in business strategy. His doctoral study on CEOs was published as *The Nature of Managerial Work*. Also well-known for developing the Ten Schools of Thought[7] and his keen intellectual skepticism. These ten schools of strategy are brilliant categorizations, a distillation of 30 years of writing in strategic management. However, no categories can be comprehensive, exhaustive, and mutually exclusive. Nevertheless, understanding the ten schools can give some insight into different strategy approaches.

1. Design School

- Sees strategy in the light of SWOT (strengths, weaknesses, opportunities, and threats)
- Clear and unique strategies are formulated
- Deliberate process

2. Planning School

- Strategy formulation is cerebral and formal
- After formal analysis of the industry,
- Strategy is reduced to generic positions,
- Leading to value chains, game theory, and strategy groups

3. Positioning School

- Porter, industrial organization, where the economic analysis of an industry's structure is central to strategy
- Outside-in: analyze industry structure first and then consider firm strategy

4. Entrepreneurial School

- CEO-centric, cult of personality
- Rooted in the mysteries of intuition, vague visions, and broad perspective

5. Cognitive / Mental School

- Constructs strategies as creative interpretations rather than mapping reality

6. Learning School

- Strategies are emergent, and there are many strategists in the organization

7. Power School

- Strategy making is rooted in power,
- A political process involving
- Bargaining, persuasion, and confrontation
- Focuses on common interest and integration

8. Culture School

- Focuses on common interest and integration

9. Environmental School

- Illuminates demands of the environment

10. Configuration School

- Organization is a configuration,
- A coherent cluster of characteristics and behaviors
- Develops a strategy that involves the different layers
- Looks outside the process

The American philosopher and psychologist and author of the first textbook on psychology, William James, said that most of us have one great idea, if we are fortunate. We can use this claim to understand the unifying idea that runs through Mintzberg's work in strategy. Mintzberg's first study, *The Nature of Managerial Work*,[8] looked at what managers do. He simply observed what a number of managers actually did. The myth is that they sit in solitude and contemplate the great strategic issues of the day, that they make time to reach the best decisions, that their meetings are high-powered, concentrating on the metanarrative rather than the nitty-gritty. His finding blew away the managerial mystique. What he found was that managers did not contemplate, but were slaves to the moment, moving from one diversion to the next. Mintzberg found that the median time spent by a manager on any given issue was 9 minutes. Managers do great quantities of work at an unrelenting pace. Their activities are marked by variety, brevity, and fragmentation; their preference is for issues that are current, specific, and nonroutine. They prefer spoken rather than written communication.

Mintzberg found additional characteristics of the manager at work. For example, they act within a web of internal and external contacts (*see* Social Network Analysis) and are subject to heavy constraints, though they can exert some control over the work.

From his study, Mintzberg identified managers' key roles, which he divided into three categories. These are worth reproducing as they are the basis of Mintzberg's reputation among practitioners.

1. *Interpersonal*

   Figurehead: representing the organization to outsiders

   Leader: motivating subordinates, unifying effort

   Liaiser: maintaining lateral contacts

2. *Informational*

   Monitor: overseeing information flows

   Disseminator: providing information to subordinates

   Spokesperson: transmitting information to outsiders

3. *Decisional*

   Entrepreneur: initiating and designing change

   Disturbance handler: handling nonroutine events

   Resource allocator: deciding who gets what and who will do what

   Negotiator: negotiating deals with different constituents within the organization and with outside entities

Mintzberg's final conclusions are that all managerial work encompasses these roles, though the prominence of each role varies in different managerial jobs.

Theory of Management Policy was Mintzberg's first proposed book, a book he has in fact never written. He recently disclosed that each of the books that he has published thus far were started as chapters in that never-ending book. He is still writing it, fortunately for the field of strategic management! Emphasized management as art, science, and craft. Mintzberg wrote an award-winning HBR article describing management as being like a potter working to produce pottery; the key is intimate contact and knowledge of the material that is being molded into a finished product. Throughout his career, Mintzberg has emphasized the emergent rather than planned approach to strategy, and the kernel of this idea was there in his first study, which concluded that executive behavior was fleeting and verbal (so it appears there is little planning going on).

Mission   The overarching purpose or raison d'etre of the firm. Can be arrived at by stating what the firm does and then continually deepening the whats with whys. For example, Phil Night founded Nike in 1971, starting with a series of lightweight racing and training shoes for runners. Nike's mission statement is to bring inspiration and innovation to every athlete in the world.

The mission, even in business, can have an almost religious connotation, which just goes to show that business will harness any concept and exemplifies a general trend of crossover from the religious to the secular.

An example is the Coca-Cola promise: "The Coca-Cola Company exists to benefit and refresh everyone who is touched by our business. The basic proposition of our business is simple, solid and timeless. When we bring refreshment, value, joy and fun to our stakeholders, then we successfully nurture and protect our brands, particularly Coca-Cola. That is the key to fulfilling our ultimate obligation to provide consistently attractive returns to the owners of our business."[9] *See also* Moral Cause. Some recent thinking on the mission downplays the importance of having an actual written statement and instead focuses on the development of an organizational consensus around issues such as the organization's vision, business domain, and competencies.

Mission-Critical Boundaries   Boundaries that can destroy the business if crossed. These boundaries can include regulatory or financial controls. People who cross these boundaries need to be fired to send a signal to reinforce the importance of these boundaries. This can be a key to encouraging thinking out of the box and yet avoiding Enron-style meltdowns.

Mohammed Saeed al-Sahafisms   Iraq's minister of information whose memorable denials that the Americans were anywhere near Baghdad and claims that these same troops were committing suicide at the gates of Baghdad seemed delusional. However, these statements did demonstrate organizational loyalty and commitment, especially when your life is on the line.

"In an age of spin, al-Sahaf offers feeling and authenticity. His message is consistent—unshakeable, in fact, no matter the evidence—but he commands daily attention by his on-the-spot, invective-rich variations on the theme. His lunatic counterfactual art is more appealing than the banal awfulness of the Reliable Sources.

He is a Method actor in a production that will close in a couple of days. He stands superior to truth."—Jean-Pierre McGarrigle[10]

Some sample quotes:

"There are no American infidels in Baghdad. Never!"

"I can say, and I am responsible for what I am saying, that they have started to commit suicide under the walls of Baghdad. We will encourage them to commit more suicides quickly."

They are nowhere near the airport. . . . they are lost in the desert. . . . they can not read a compass. . . . they are retarded."

" . . . They are nowhere [pause] . . . they are nowhere, really."

"Bush doesn't even know if Spain is a republic or a kingdom, how can they follow this man?"

Question: Is Saddam Hussein still alive? "I will only answer reasonable questions."

"They are becoming hysterical. This is the result of frustration."

An existential strategy approach (*see* Existential Strategy) emphasizes authenticity, and these quotes demonstrate how denying the reality of one's experience produces inauthentic viewpoints and statements that are comical in their absurdity. One wonders if some of those involved in recent corporate scandals such as Enron and WorldCom applied a similar through-the-looking-glass logic to their own actions, which were ultimately harmful to both employees and stockholders.

Momentum   Momentum is strength or force gained by motion or through the development of events. Momentum is the energy that is necessary for the implementation of change. Momentum can be created, maintained, or built by leaders to get change to work its way through an organization.[11] Momentum is aided by strategic persistence and commitment to implementing change. Think of momentum as the force that maintains the flight of a 747 jet. After the initial take-off, which takes a burst of enormous energy output and pilot concentration and nerve, there is a continuous momentum that keeps the flight going, that can seem effortless but actually requires steady commitment of resources and commitment to a specific flight path.

"Monkeys at the British Museum"   If an infinite number of monkeys start typing at random, they will eventually produce Shakespeare's *Hamlet*. An infinite number of computers running an infinite amount of time and generating random characters would have the same probability of producing the plays. This is an intuitive argument that may not hold up under rigorous mathematical scrutiny, but it does provide insight into strategy. It demonstrates how seemingly random, unconnected events can form a meaningful sequence and produce a desired result (*see* Complexity Theory).

Moore's Law   In 1965, Intel's Gordon Moore created a "law" that became shorthand for the rapid, unprecedented growth of technology. He predicted that the number of transistors on a chip would grow exponentially with each passing year. At the time, even Gordon Moore never imagined it might still be true today. Intel has developed new technologies that allow it to squeeze one billion transistors on a chip (a far cry from the 2,300 on its first processor).

Moral Cause   Sun Tzu's word for mission. Moral cause needs to be communicated by the leader so as to inspire followers to sacrifice their lives for the leader and her moral cause.

Motivation   The creation of stimuli, incentives, and work environments that enable people to perform at the best of their ability in pursuit of organizational success. Motivating people is a challenge at all levels, to say the least. Most companies are reasonably good at managing the organizational aspects of change and motivation, but are notoriously weak when it comes to managing the people aspects of an organization.

However, motivation and inspiration can energize employees, not by "pushing them in the right direction," but by satisfying basic human needs. *See* Maslow.

Motives   Leaders and managers need to tap into the right motives to get organizational commitment or buy in to change.

Multistep Process   One that involves overcoming a number of sequential obstacles. Basically true of most problem solving.

Multiunit Organization   A feature of the 21st-century economy is the many multiunit systems that operate in several markets, an organizational form that arguably rivals the "M-form" or multidivisional form of the 20th century. The multimarket perspective requires a focus on commitment and mutual forbearance (*see* Mutual Forbearance), and the multiunit perspective emphasizes learning and knowledge transfer theory. DaimlerChrysler exhibits multiunit organization in the auto industry and in its investment in aerospace company EADS. *See* Structure.

Murphy's Law   What can go wrong will go wrong. It is the failure to understand Murphy's law that led to both the Challenger and Columbia accidents. Management just did not allow themselves to think of insulation on the fuel tanks. If they had applied Murphy's law exhaustively, they could have planned for this scenario. A piece of insulation flew off the fuel tanks, hit the wing of the Challenger, and broke the thermal layer open. The managers dismissed it when they saw it. They did not realize the velocity and how it would penetrate the carbon on the plane.

Applying Murphy's law strategically involves exhaustive examination of all possibilities, especially the negative possibilities. They have to do more than they have done.

Mutual Forbearance   When firms agree not to fight over a particular segment of the market so as to avoid mutually assured destruction.

Mutually Assured Destruction (MAD)   Mutually assured destruction refers to the cases when to continue on a course of action would annihilate both parties. The classic example was when Russia and America had enough missiles aimed at each other to destroy one another. *See* Counterintuitive Strategy.

Endnotes

1. Northouse, P. G. (2004). *Leadership: Theory and practice.* 3rd ed. Thousand Oaks, CA: Sage, p. 9.

2. Ibid., p. 9.

3. Hitt, M. A., Ireland, R. D., & Hoskisson, R. E. (1999). *Strategic management: Competitiveness and globalization,* 3rd ed. Cincinnati, OH: South Western College Publishing. 130–135.

4. Govoni, N. A. (2004). *Dictionary of marketing communications.* Thousand Oaks, CA: Sage.

5. Ramu, S. (1999). *Cross-border mergers and acquisitions.* New Delhi, India: A. H. Wheeler Press.

6. Chandler, A. (1962). *Strategy and structure.* Cambridge: MIT Press.

7. Mintzberg, H., Ahlstrand, B., & Lampel, J. (1998). *Strategy safari.* New York: Free Press.

8. Mintzberg, H. (1973). *The nature of managerial work.* Englewood Cliffs, NJ: Prentice Hall.

9. http://www.coca-cola.com/ourcompany/ourpromise.html

10. http://www.welovetheiraqiinformationminister.com

11. Jansen, K. J. (2000). The emerging dynamics of change: Resistance, readiness, and momentum. *Human Resource Planning,* 23:2.

N

NAICS (North American Industry Classification System)   NAICS (pronounced nakes) is the system for classifying business establishments that in 1997 replaced the old Standard Industrial Classification (SIC) system. NAICS is the industry classification system used by the statistical agencies of the United States. It is the first-ever North American industry classification system, having been developed jointly by the United States, Canada, and Mexico to provide comparable statistics across the three countries of North America. The system was developed by the Economic Classification Policy Committee (ECPC) in cooperation with Statistics Canada and Mexico's Instituto Nacional de Estadística, Geografía e Informática (INEGI). For the first time, government and business analysts will be able to directly compare industrial production statistics collected and published in the three North American Free Trade Agreement (NAFTA) countries. NAICS also provides for increased comparability with the International Standard Industrial Classification System (ISIC, Revision 3), developed and maintained by the United Nations. Much strategy research and financial reporting relies on NAICS for standardization purposes.

Narrative Approach to Strategy   The narrative approach works with a story line and literary techniques such as plot, character, and setting to identify patterns in the firm's behavior.

Need for Achievement (n-Ach)   The need for achievement may be defined as the need to master or overcome difficulties. Coined by David McClelland in *The Achieving Society*,[1] reporting on his cross-cultural studies of entrepreneurship in such countries as Japan and Mexico. McClelland concluded that American society best epitomized this n-Ach, which is so essential for entrepreneurial success. American culture glorifies entrepreneurs, whom we see as heroes and household names beaming from the covers of magazines. McClelland noted that typically Protestants had a higher n-Ach than Catholics.

Need for Affiliation (n-Aff)   The person who spends days and nights thinking about how to get other people to love her has a strong need for affiliation. Managers typically have low n-Aff.

Need for Power (n-Pow)   The need for power derives from the need to influence people. A strategic manager's job calls for someone who can influence people rather than someone who likes doing things. According to the late David C. McClelland of Harvard University, a good manager likes power. McClelland argues that socialized power benefits not only the individual but also the organization as a whole. This need for power can be translated into, for example, generating shareholder wealth. Jack Welch was able to channel his n-Pow and n-Ach into increasing the market value of GE from just $12 billion in 1981 to about $280 billion in 2003. Others such as Microsoft's William H. Gates III, Intel's Andrew S. Grove, Walt Disney's Michael D. Eisner, Berkshire Hathaway's Warren E. Buffett, the late Coca-Cola chieftain Roberto C. Goizueta, and the late Wal-Mart founder Sam Walton all created shareholder wealth through a similar McClellandesque socializing of the power and achievement needs.

Needs   Peter Drucker suggested that the primary goal of a business is the *invention* of customer needs. Conventional wisdom, as influenced by marketing orientation, argues instead for the *satisfaction* of customer needs. Although Drucker's formulation sounds more Machiavellian, there is some truth there. *See* Maslow, Abraham H., for his hierarchy of needs.

Negotiation   Negotiation denotes a bargaining process between seller and buyer. The Spanish word for business, *negocios,* puts negotiations at the heart of any business transaction.

Networked Enterprise   The vertically integrated company has given way to the networked enterprise, a structure that is characterized by greater agility and adaptability. Organizations need to maintain secure relations with third-party organizations such as suppliers, technology outsourcers, and government regulators. These include ownership networks, collaboration networks, organizational networks, and marketing networks, to name a few.

Networking   Networking is the process of establishing and maintaining contacts with key managers in one's own organization and in other organizations and using those contacts to weave strong relationships that serve as informal development systems. We can distinguish between interpersonal and interorganizational networks, although there is some overlap, especially at the top management level.

As regards *interorganizational networks,* research suggests that embedded networks, if connected to two or three firms with a deep relationship, can result in groupthink and forgone market opportunities. Normally, however, highly prestigious firms would prefer to partner with a high-status firm. Partnering with one of lower status would lower the firm's own status in the industry.

Firms at the center of a network are better able to evaluate whether a potential partner is worthy of a relationship. Peripheral firms are likely to have many partners. In a dynamic, highgrowth environment, firms are likely to have many partners in arm's-length relationships. As an industry slows, the networks become a mix of arm's-length and embedded relationships.

Industry position and environmental dynamics determine whether the structure of local networks becomes an asset or liability. Generally, highly central firms have few exchange partners. Peripheral firms have either a single sponsor partner or should diversify relationships amongst many partners. When markets grow, firms need flexibility in their networks, and thus must have partners with many allies of their own. When industry growth stops, firms' partners need to drop some of their own allies and strengthen their relationship with the remaining ones. Failure to adhere to these strategies can result in loss of market share.

Positional embeddedness denotes location of the node in the overall industry and within environmental dynamics. In arm's-length networks, each individual is of limited value. Network embeddeness enables or constrains strategic action.

As regards individual networks, research suggests that those organizational members that have the highest number of network ties both inside and outside the organization have the highest creative input to the organization. However, there is an optimal level of network contacts beyond which keeping up with one's network of contacts becomes so onerous that one can no longer engage in the primary creative activity (think of an author who becomes so successful that he is too busy keeping up with his correspondence to find sufficient time to write his next book).

Another key finding in network studies is that there is an optimal density of network contacts; typically, the more contacts individuals have with members of their organization (for example, their social, advice, and innovation networks), the more innovative the organization will be. Some initial findings in a very fruitful and new area for strategy research.

Networks in a Box   Networks in a box are cellular mini power stations that are capable of linking several thousand users in metropolitan areas; good for use in the chaos following war or disaster.

Newbies   New entrants, whether on the firm or industry level; typically have to prove themselves.

New Nepotism or Dynastic Capitalism   New nepotism puts a positive spin on an age-old phenomenon. More and more children are going into the family business (think George W. Bush, movie stars like Kate Hudson, CEOs like Edgar Bronfman Jr., Sofia Coppola); these new successors are opportunistically trading on their famous names and family connections, not being merely passive recipients of family endowments. Adam Bellow,[2] son of the famous writer Saul Bellow, argues that nepotism is at the root of all human cooperation and thus is the basis of all societies. In non-Western societies, nepotism can run rampant, with many examples of corruption, collusion, and nepotism. In the West, nepotism is seen as an obstacle to economic development.

However, dynastic capitalism is prevalent worldwide. Italy provides many examples, both positive and negative, of this phenomenon. Benetton siblings Giuliana, Carlo, and Gilberto built an empire from their family sweater knitting that spans 120 countries with an annual revenue of $9 billion and runs everything from roadside restaurants to cattle ranches. On the other hand, a scandal enveloping the family-owned Italian dairy company Parmalat, once the eighth-largest business in Italy, is an example of dynastic capitalism run rampant. Tightly controlled by founder Calisto Tanzi, who also staffed his empire with relatives, the multinational Parmalat was investigated in 2004 for allegedly defrauding banks and shareholders of $18 billion over 15 years. Tanzi is in jail in Milan and his daughter and son have been dismissed.

NGOs   Nongovernmental organizations, engaged typically in social entrepreneurship. *See* Social Entrepreneurship.

Niche Strategies   Niche strategies focus on a single segment of the market, whether it is defined geographically or by some criterion such as "high end" (e.g., the Ritz Carlton). The important property of the niche strategy is that its power derives from its being exclusionary, excluding pesky or menacing competitors. It is argued that all start-up strategies are by definition niche until the firm acquires enough resources to become a broad-based competitor. An example is Southwest, which started as regional carrier before becoming national airline.

One problem with the niche strategy is that if a small firm discovers an attractive niche, big players in the industry may see the excitement in that niche and use their market power to blow the small firm out of it. For example, Ryka had a niche in women's athletic shoes until Nike and Reebok took notice; we no longer hear much about Ryka. It is often a jungle out there, and a niche strategy is hard to defend in a jungle.

Nonmonetary Incentives   Nonmonetary incentives are motivators that are not financial or even tangible. Herzberg in his famous HBR article, "One More Time, How Do We Motivate?"[3] (an article that though award winning, widely quoted, and frequently reprinted, is nevertheless not widely believed or accepted because his conclusions do not fit with most people's intuitive conviction that money *is* the primary motivator), argues that the true motivators include achievement, recognition, the work itself, growth, responsibility, and peer relationships. Nonmotivating factors include aspects of job environment, working conditions, salary, policy, administration, and supervision.

Nonroutine Assignments and Decisions   Strategic assignments and decisions are by their very nature nonroutine, nonregenerative, and nonrecurring.

Nonsubstitutable Capabilities   Nonsubstitutable capabilities are those that do not have strategic equivalents. For example, many firms have tried to imitate Dell's business model, but without Dell's success, so we can say that this is a nonsubstitutable capability.

Normative Power   Normative power is based on legitimacy and essentially coincides with formal authority in the hierarchy. However, legitimate or actual power may not be normative and relates to who really calls the shots and get things done (for example, your superior's secretary has low normative power but high legitimate or actual power).

Endnotes

1. McClelland, D. (1961). *The achieving society*. Princeton, NJ: Van Nostrand.
2. Bellow, A. (2003). *In praise of nepotism: A natural history*. New York: Doubleday.
3. Herzberg, F. One more time: How do you motivate employees? *Harvard Business Review,* 81:1, p. 87.

Objectives Ends toward which effort is directed and resources are focused. Objectives usually attempt to achieve a firm's strategic vision. Objective setting is given a practical application in "management by objectives" (MBO), coined by Peter Drucker to denote a process whereby the manager and subordinate agree on objectives, thus increasing buyin.

Objectives are strategic intentions stated in categorical terms. For example, "Intention: We will try to knock out the pillbox" is a weakly stated objective. "Intention: Knock out the pillbox" is the categorical statement of an objective. Objectives and goals can be used in strategy interchangeably; usually they are fairly concrete and can often be expressed in quantitative terms, such as an objective to outperform the Standard and Poor's Index or to gain a certain percentage of market share. The risk of stating objectives in quantitative terms is that not reaching the objectives can be demoralizing. Alcan Aluminum discovered that when it could not hit its publicly stated objective of beating the S&P 500.

Objectives in the key areas are the "instrument panel" necessary to pilot the business enterprise, according to Drucker.

Offensive Strategy The U.S. advance on Baghdad is something that military historians and academics will pore over in great detail for decades to come. As a case study of dexterity, audacity, and brilliance in putting the plan into effect, this military example has important implications for a new type of flexibility required in offensive strategies. The U.S. plan was devised to exploit enemy weaknesses and to capitalize on U.S. strengths in weapons technology, communications, surveillance, and skillful maneuver by armor, infantry, and special operations forces; the strategy emphasized flexibility above all else.

Battlefield commanders were encouraged to improvise in a way that some compared to a quarterback calling audibles (*see* Calling Audibles) at the line of scrimmage. For example, when U.S. forces reached the gates of the capital, they threw away their original visions of how to besiege Fortress Baghdad. They expected the Republican Guard to put up a fierce defense and draw them into a street fight. However, when they found the barricades weaker than they expected, army soldiers and marines poured in, hastening the end of the fighting by days if not weeks. Allied commander Gen. Tommy Franks conferred directly with troops in the field while watching them march toward Baghdad.

"They were extremely surprised by just the sheer velocity of the plan," a Central Command official said. "We never gave the enemy a chance to decide and act. They were constantly having to react." In business, an offensive strategy is risky and costly.

Off-Shoring In decades past, millions of American manufacturing jobs moved overseas, but in recent years, the movement has also shifted to the service sector, with everything from low-end call center jobs to high-paying computer chip design jobs migrating to China, India, the Philippines, Russia, and other countries.

Executives at IBM and many other companies argue that creating more jobs in lower-cost locations overseas allows their industries to remain competitive, holds costs down for American consumers, and helps to develop poorer nations while supporting overall employment in the United States by improving productivity and the nation's global reach. Oracle CEO Larry Ellison compares off-shoring to the advent of electricity: "Well, off-shoring is devastating but not nearly as devastating as electricity. When electricity showed up, a lot of people lost jobs. But as we become more efficient in general, products become less expensive. Some people's careers have to change, but that happened massively with the agricultural revolution and the Industrial Revolution." Intel CEO Craig Barrett looks at off-shoring as having a "yin and yang to the issue." He focuses on the opportunity off-shoring creates for Intel: Three billion people are potential customers because the growth of tech-savvy regions in India and China means spin-offs of economic activity, new competitors and customers, and an emerging middle class.

However, Barrett adds, "As a U.S. citizen looking at the future for my grandchildren, I'm more pessimistic." Hewlett-Packard CEO Carly Fiorina calls it "right-shoring," a term that will not make it as an entry in this dictionary.

One Minute Manager Parable published in 1980, the *One Minute Manager,* by Spencer Johnson and Kenneth H. Blanchard,[1] is the story of a hypothetical manager and his hypothetical employees, being interviewed by a hypothetical interviewer who is out to learn how to become a better manager. The interviewer discovers that the One Minute Manager has developed a three-legged process for managing the behaviors of others:

1. One Minute Goal Setting

2. One Minute Praisings

3. One Minute Reprimands

This book has been criticized for making complex business situations seem black and white. This approach is a forerunner of the *Who Moved My Cheese?*[2]—an allegory that was also wildly successful. The literary, allegorical, and parabolic approach to strategic management has some power and value.

OODA Loop   OODA loop is the process that John Boyd observed fighter pilots executing during dogfights: another strategy by acronym. The pilots **O**bserve what the enemy is doing, **O**rient themselves to this action, **D**ecide what to do next, and **A**ct. Our action unpredictably changes the other's sense of the situation, requiring an immediate adjustment. If we repeatedly take unpredictable actions faster than the other side can reorient themselves and react, we are getting inside their decision cycle (also a Boyd coinage) and they lose any coherent grasp of the situation and succumb to mental paralysis. As Boyd puts it, "their minds fold back on themselves."

Boyd emphasized the importance of orientation in his formulation. When there is an intuitive understanding of the rapidly changing environment, the sequence can move rapidly from initial observation to action. This certainly applies to a firm in a competitive market, which can profit from speed of communication and reaction.

A key element of Boyd's thinking was the emphasis on trust and cohesion within the group (*see* Social Network Analysis). When there is trust and group cohesiveness and the rallying around a common goal, then the lower levels in the hierarchy understand the overarching objectives and can therefore implement their own independent OODA loops without waiting for the orders from on high, because they know already how to harmonize the mission. The German army's perfection of blitzkrieg in the Second World War was a good example of this. Boyd's thinking, although originating in the air force, currently has a strong influence on Marine Corps strategy as well as in the business world. Boyd encapsulated his ideas in a 14-hour slide show, "A Discourse on Winning and Losing."[3]

Open Standards   Previous thinking argued that standards are critical if new industries are to evolve. However, this view is being challenged by the open standards argument for industry evolution.

Industry and technology standards are emerging through market dynamics instead of by government edict. Many industries have a de facto open standard: No government agency dictates standards and no vendor dominates them, and the technology is available by license to anyone. A proprietary standard, like the Apple operating system for many years, can be a source of competitive advantage. However, this competitive advantage is becoming increasingly short-lived through the process of reverse engineering and other sophisticated patent-circumventing competitive techniques for imitating proprietary technologies and destroying the value of the invested capital. Think of how Microsoft's Windows technology destroyed the value of Apple's operating system.

The sources of competitive advantage are shifting from patents and technology to cost, quality, speed, and access to suppliers and distribution channels. This is why many industries and firms that had previously invested significantly in R&D are now outsourcing that function to the young entrepreneurial firms that they subsequently acquire or enter into strategic alliance with. Open standards allow greater strategic flexibility.

Open Systems   Systems theory involves the conceptualization of open systems—systems that integrate external and internal feedback loops.

Operational Effectiveness   Achieving business performance by aligning and improving core operational processes and supplier chains with business direction and customer needs, and managing market pressures to deliver better value to customers than your competitors. Think Southwest Airlines.

Operational Innovation   Operational innovation uses inventions to transform inputs into products and services in a new and better way, raising productivity or lowering costs. New economic reality calls for new ways to organize work to meet changing human needs.

Optimize the Portfolio   In a highly competitive market, it is crucial to develop alternative capabilities that could be profitable by meeting customers' needs. One way to do this is to offer a high level of variety of products. Another is to find new potential markets or tap into new customer behavior. For example, McDonald's has franchises worldwide, but the franchises in any given country make special adaptations to customer preferences in that country. In Thailand, McDonald's offers hamburgers that are a mix between American and Thai-style recipes. These new products are innovations well adapted to the different markets. A perhaps better example is the recent foray of McDonald's into more upscale dining with its new venture, Chef Mac's, recently opened in New Orleans. Modeled after a similar eatery in Orlando, Florida, the new restaurant will have chandeliers, leather couches, stylish tiles, and upgraded restrooms—all this to optimize the McDonald's portfolio within the deteriorating fast-food industry.

Organization   In the classic sense, an organization is an entity with rules and controls necessary to keep a business running smoothly, but that can act to constrain or suffocate innovation.

Organizational Change   Organizational change denotes that process of incorporating new strategies and distinct cultures into an organizational repertoire. Beeson[5] describes three ways of looking at organizational change. The first view is **deterministic change,** a mechanical or linear view, which is based on an early systems perspective of organizations as machines that are the product of rational thought. In this model, change is driven by top managers and is planned in an orderly, logical fashion. The second view, **equilibrium-based change,** is represented by the organic or cybernetic models of the organization. Change is seen as an adaptive response by the organization to maintain itself within a shifting environment. The third model, **transformational change,** views the organization as dynamic and capable of revolutionary and evolutionary moves as it shifts between stability and instability. This third stage draws on theories of chaos, complexity, and self-organization from the natural sciences.[6]

Organizational Culture   *See* Culture, Organizational.

Organizational Learning   Prahalad and Hamel describe organizational learning as "The acquisition of new knowledge by actors who are able and willing to apply that knowledge in making decisions or influencing others in organizations."[4]

Organizational learning moves valuable knowledge and experience from those individuals who possess it and across the organization as a whole. Citicorp supplies an example of the process of organizational learning: It uses a variety of practices in its management of expatriate employees so as to capitalize on their knowledge and experience and the networks they developed while working overseas and to leverage that knowledge to the organization as a whole.

Organizational Politics   Chester Barnard, in his elaborate and painstaking philosophical treatise on the nature of cooperation, *The Functions of the Executive,* was the first to point out that in addition to the formal hierarchy in the organization, there is an informal hierarchy. The formal organigram captures the former and is based on a linear logic; the latter is based on a nonlinear logic of informational control, power plays, and suppressed values (for example, the paranoia implicit in rules of engagement like "shoot to kill, not maim"). Think of Karl Rove, political adviser to George W. Bush, BlackBerrying people wildly during a meeting with presidential staff, confidentially messaging various participants in the meeting. This is organizational politics at work.

Organizational Sociology   The roots of strategy that gave us the ideas resource dependence, organization, ecology, institutionalism, social networks, and culture.

Organization Building   Like nation building, on a smaller scale. An essential task postmerger, when a new entity has to emerge.

Organization Man   A term derived from the title of William Whyte's best-selling book of sociological analysis (1956). Whyte's concept of the organization man is of somebody who fully accepts, to the point of being absorbed by, the organization's values and objectives. This absorption was perhaps appropriate when there was a bond of loyalty between the organization and the employee. However, this loyalty has disappeared. In more recent decades, work has evolved into a more self-fulfilling, self-actualizing mode. The emphasis is no longer on loyalty to one company, but rather on loyalty to achievement, or to being part of a "hot" technology or project, or simply to one's own career.

Outsourcing   The procuring of services or products from an outside supplier or manufacturer in order to cut costs. Many companies like Nike outsource their manufacturing. It has been suggested that pharmaceutical companies could recognize that their expertise lies more in sales and marketing and outsource their R&D.

India's Wipro Ltd. is a world-class provider of high-quality software to such clients as Compaq, Home Depot, Nokia, and now Sony. In 2002, Wipro landed a breakthrough deal that allowed it to expand its repertoire and client list. Sony Corp gave Wipro a $5 million contract to write information-technology applications for its TV and computer assembly plants in the United States. Sony expects to save 30% through cutting costs by hiring low-cost Indian engineers. There is a mutual benefit; Sony benefits from lower costs, while Wipro adds a giant to its repertoire, which definitely adds prestige to its reputation.

Ownership Caps   Ownership caps place a legal limit on equity stake in a firm. Ownership caps are a kind of governmental blockage of monopolistic practices. Since the government can and does have a substantial impact on the market structures in many business segments, the instruments they use to regulate markets are of great interest to anyone wanting to succeed in strategic management. The European Union has been using ownership caps as an antimonopolistic device, changing the competitive landscape and blocking some United States–based acquisitions such as the unconsummated GE-Honeywell acquisition.

Endnotes

1. Johnson, S., & Blanchard, K. (1983). *One minute manager.* New York: Penguin Putnam.

2. Johnson, S. (1998). *Who moved my cheese?: An amazing way to deal with change in your work and in your life.* New York: Putnam Press.

3. Coram, R. B. (2003). *The fighter pilot who changed the art of war.* Boston: Little, Brown.

4. Prahalad, C. K., & Hamel, G. (1996). *Competing for the future.* Boston: Harvard Business School Press.

5. Beeson, I., & Davis, C. (2000). Emergence and accomplishment in organizational change. *Journal of Organizational Change Management,* 13:2.

6. Ibid.

P

PAEI Production Administration Entrepreneurial and Integration. PAEI is an acronym for a method of evaluating the contribution and area of strength of each person on a team. In a self-evaluation, at least one of the letters needs to be in lower-case to denote an area of weakness. To rate oneself with equal strength in every area denotes an attempt to project perfectionism. This is a tool from consulting practice that is used toward the goal of producing a well-balanced team.

Paradigm Thomas Kuhn, in *The Structure of Scientific Revolution,* argues that it is a mistake to suppose that we can describe the facts in neutral-observation language. What you see in the organization is a function of your paradigm or worldview, which encompasses the set of assumptions that you use to describe a situation. A paradigm, according to Kuhn, is a set of assumptions shared as a social agreement among scientists. Whether you describe people as terrorists, illegal combatants, militants, or freedom fighters depends on what paradigm you share with others. Andy Grove neatly summed up his business paradigm in the title of his autobiography *Only the Paranoid Survive.* This is a paradigm also shared by Nike in its beat-all-to-win philosophy.

Parallel Organization A parallel organization is a team function set up alongside the organization to implement change.[1] The parallel organization is composed of:

1. A sponsor group of senior leaders who initiate the process and provide morale support and funding

2. A steering committee that represents a cross-section of all levels

3. One or more design groups that work on specific changes

Together, these teams function alongside the regular organization. This parallel organization is responsible for planning and managing the change process.

Paralysis by Analysis The inability of managers to make a decision as a result of a preoccupation with meetings, administrative duties, and analytical data. Can occur most often in horizontal organizations where there are conflicts between different hierarchical levels.

Path-Goal Model   Victor Vroom of Yale argued that performance is a multiplicative function of motivation (M) and ability (A): Performance $= f(M, A)$

Motivation to perform a task is assumed to vary with (1) the utilities of outcomes associated with the performance of that particular task and (2) the instrumentality (belief that performance and outcome are linked) of performance to achieve or avoid certain outcomes. The path-goal model argues that getting the right task right helps to determine human satisfaction.

Performance   Difficult to measure in a complex and dynamic environment. Nevertheless, performance is at the heart of the study and practice of strategic management.

Persona   The actual and implied themes in the annual report or other company documents project the firm's persona, or image, to its interested stakeholders.

Peter Principle   People rise to their level of incompetence.

Plan B   Plan B is the first alternative to Plan A. Always having a plan B is a good way to run a career, a business, or one's day-to-day life.

Planful Opportunism   The planful things you do in life are: know your skill set, know your values, and know who you are, according to Noel M. Tichy, leadership guru at GE. He emphasizes that although you don't know when an opportunity is going to pop up, if you have done your homework on the planful part, you can quickly make effective decisions.

Planned Approach   This approach is characterized by its repetitiveness and its cyclicality, using a process of diagnosis, action, and evaluation. Criticisms of the planned approach are that it assumes that all members of the organization can get on the same page and that it is mostly suited for environments that are relatively stable and predictable.

Planned Performance   Planned performance means setting and meeting the stakeholders' expectations such as profits, positive cash flow, growth, and debt reduction. Traditional financial performance analysis would be figuring out the firm's liquidity, efficiency, and profitability from the financial information in the firm's 10-K.

Planning   Process of setting objectives and goals and formulating policies and procedures to meet organizational objectives. Planning can be either long term (strategic) or short term (operational) or both. Igor Ansoff might be included in this particular school of thought, where all possible (foreseen) contingencies are planned for.

Platform   A product used as a basis for building more complex products or delivering additional services. *Eine Wurst, drei Grosse:* "one sausage, three different lengths"; this expression means three different products made from one original mold. The Honda Accord is available in three different widths, with a total variation of 20%, to adapt to different international markets.

Pluralism   Pluralism is a worldview in which the world is not monolithic. A number of institutions exist that interact, cooperate, and sometimes come into conflict. Events then become less predictable. Different institutions come out on top at different times. Postmodern writers borrow Bakhtin's notion of carnival to convey the sense of the pluralism of many voices having a say in a somewhat chaotic manner. Think of how relative minorities can achieve a clear voice in the discourse, such as the Chiapas Indians did through their revolt in Mexico. The Internet is continuing to fuel a more pluralistic world. Marketers respond to this by investigating and servicing ever-increasingly narrow and distinct target markets.

In a pluralistic society, cliques and pressure groups must be allowed to have their say. This can be applied in an organizational setting to a certain extent. One goal can be to avoid the tyranny of the majority. It is very demanding of leaders to encourage the expression of minority opinions, so that factions are not pushed around by an overbearing majority. Democracy is based on the principle of pluralism. One definition of democracy is majority rule with respect for and protection of the rights of minorities; otherwise, the result can become tyranny of the majority. This is the conundrum in setting up democracy in Iraq: Although the majority are Shiite, the rights of the Sunni and Kurdish minorities must be respected. The same issue of pluralism is becoming more pressing in the business world.

Take the example of innovation: Innovation has a creative-destructive effect both within and outside the organization. Outside the organization, it destroys the value of capital invested—as wireless technology destroys the value of the previous investment in cables. Within the organization, innovation destroys the value of previously acquired expertise in the former technology. So the minority of innovators within a firm must be protected against the majority of experts. Another pluralistic dilemma for organizations are the myriad social responsibility issues where the firm needs to respond to the priorities of many activists.

POLEing   Planning, organizing, leading, and evaluating. An acronym describing a shopping list, clothesline, laundry list in management.

Porter's Diamond Model   A diagram developed by Michael Porter showing four conditions: demand; factor endowments; related and supporting industries; and firm strategy, structure, and rivalry. All four conditions must usually be favorable for an industry to develop and sustain a competitive advantage.[2]

Portfolio Planning (BCG Growth/Share Matrix)   Portfolio Planning (BCG Growth/Share Matrix) offers an analysis of industry growth rate by relative market share to show overall competitive strength and cash-generation potential of a firm. Products are analyzed and categorized as question marks, cash cows, dogs, and stars. Popular in the 1980s.

Portfolio Strategy   It is a corporate-level strategy that minimizes risk by diversifying investment among various businesses or product lines. Like an investor who invests in a variety of stocks, portfolio strategy guides the strategic decisions of corporations that compete in a variety of businesses. For example, it could be used to guide the strategy of a company like 3M, which makes 50,000 products for 16 different industries. Similarly, it could be used by Johnson & Johnson, which has 170 divisions making health care products for the pharmaceuticals, diagnostics, consumers, and health care professionals markets. Just as investors consider the mix of stocks in their stock portfolio when deciding which stocks to buy or sell, portfolio strategy provides guidelines to help managers acquire companies that fit well with the rest of their corporate portfolio and sell those that don't.

Position Power   Power based on position within the organization. Becoming less valid and relevant.

Postcorporate World   A world of nonhierarchical, entrepreneurial firms with no middle managers.

Power   The ability, either innate or learned, to compel or direct others to do what you want them to do, voluntarily or otherwise. Having the ability to influence others can be derived from rank or status, or even from personality.

Some argue, like Charles Reich in *The Greening of America,* that it is not the misuse of power that is evil, but the very existence of power that is evil. A more reasonable approach argues that some use of power beyond the traditional organigram reporting relationships is necessary to get organizations to change and grow, move forward, and accomplish things.

Pragmatism   Pragmatism is described by Andy Reinhart and Nassim Majidi as a way European companies have survived in their markets.[3] Namely, when developing strategies and courses of action, the companies focus on the practical consequences of ideas or propositions. Pragmatism is an American philosophy most prominently propounded by William James.

Prahalad, C. K. (1941–)   Prahalad's work focuses largely on the ability of large organizations to maintain competitive vitality when faced with international competition and changing business environments. Prahalad cowrote *Competing for the Future* with Gary Hamel.

Price Competition   It has been suggested that in any business, competing on price is a last resort—what you do when there is nothing more you can offer the customer over the competition. Dell's whole business strategy could be construed to be based on this idea of competing on price. Was it Dell that brought out a flat-panel Windows all-in-one computer in 2003? You get what you pay for, and if you pay for a Dell, you get a computer that is at best almost as good as the competition.

Prisoner's Dilemma   From game theory, the calculations that each individual who is being questioned separately from her partners in crime makes as to whether the others are going to confess. If others confess, her confession loses its value as a bargaining chip. Oligopolistic competition often involves a prisoner's dilemma component.

Problem Solving Systematic approach to overcoming obstacles or problems in the area of management. Steps in the problem-solving arena can include recognizing a problem, defining a problem, generating solutions, picking the best solution available, implementing the solution picked, and finally, evaluating the effectiveness of the solution. Organizations need to share the problem with teams and departments, not just the solution. Otherwise, the organization may short-circuit all the wisdoms of the world.

Process Consulting This is a buzzword. Process consulting facilitates the change process in a firm. Many consulting firms usually provide only training to address the client firm's needs. Others provide a diagnosis of the firm and a report of findings and recommendations, leaving implementation to the firm. Process consulting not only diagnoses the problems but also ensures that implementation is carried out. Process consultants analyze the environment (internal and external), then start the strategic transformation process by training employees to implement the recommendations.

Process consultants' main aim is to provide sustainable solutions. They provide knowledge to the company in such a way as to ensure that employees can carry on from where the consultant leaves off; that is, they provide sustainability. The client firm needs to absorb, or internalize, the knowledge, not just pay consultants for training. Process consulting imparts this knowledge and creates change agents capable of sustaining the transformation processes.

Product Development Product development involves substantial modification of existing products that can be marketed to current customers through established channels. This strategy is often adopted either to prolong the life cycle of current products or to take advantage of a favorite reputation or brand name. The idea here is to attract satisfied customers to new products as a result of their positive experience with the firm's initial offering.

The telecommunications industry provides an example of product extension by product modification. To increase an estimated 8%–10% share of its $6 billion corporate user market, MCI extended its direct-dial service to 146 countries, the same as those serviced by AT&T, but at lower average rates. Another example is Nabisco, which, to maintain its position as leader, pursues a strategy of developing and introducing new products and expanding its existing product line; Spoon Size Shredded Wheat and Ritz Bits crackers are but two examples of new products that are variations on existing products.

Product-Development Council

1. A group of globe-trotting senior executives that monitors consumer trends and establishes priorities for product lineup.

2. Could be seen as a kind of central nervous system in a multinational corporation: It senses changes in the environment and relays them to subordinates such as department heads, product-development teams, or outsourcing partners and suppliers.

IKEA, founded by Inguar Kamprad, is an example of successful outsourcing. The entire IKEA strategy and global ambition is a good model. IKEA exhibits original and consistent corporate strategy and organizational structure coupled with smart and sharp tactics.

At IKEA they do it backward:

Step 1: Pick a price.

Step 2: Choose a manufacturer.

Step 3: Design a product.

Step 4: Ship it.

The most critical key component in this successful formula or algorithm is for the product-development council to identify coming trends as well as solve customers' problems with product design. Take one "problem" recently identified by the council: Around the world, the kitchen has slowly replaced the living room as the social and entertaining center of the home. Consequently, today's kitchens need to project comfort and cleanliness to guests while also reflecting the gourmet aspirations of the host.

We might just replace the word "council," which sounds a bit too authoritative and structured, with the word "team" or "group." This term is actually very to the point: Put "product" above anything else and all the "strategy" should work around the "product": The resulting term is "product-strategy team."

Product or Process Innovation   James Utterback[4] argues that there are two kinds of innovation: product innovation and process innovation. Companies first innovate their products, but then, to be successful, they must also innovate and refine their processes. Process innovation is essential to mass marketing as a means of bringing price down and quality up, but it also requires standards, procedures, and administration. Many companies get caught up in this process phase and forget about further product innovation.

Once process innovation sets in, it puts the whole company into an efficiency mode, with little time, energy, or inclination to look beyond the current narrow ways into whole new approaches. Thus, there is a clash between the culture of experts versus innovators.

Hewlett-Packard has been doing process innovation recently by focusing on efficiency and cutting costs. However, because PCs are a mature or declining industry, there is a real threat from new entrants who do not have the same fixed-cost forces working against them. This is the reason small, nimble new companies can take over through product innovation that can creatively destroy the value of previous investment. These small companies move faster and are willing to take risks. They have a lot less to lose, and a whole lot more to gain.

Professional Intellect   The capacity to manage human intellect and to convert it into useful products and services is the critical executive skill in a knowledge economy.

Profit According to Peter Drucker, profit is not the cause but the result of the performance of a business in marketing, innovation, and productivity. Profit is the reward for risk, because business activity is economic and it always attempts to bring about change that profit measures.

Profitability The ability of any company to operate in the "long run" depends on attaining an acceptable level of profits. Strategically managed firms characteristically have a profit objective (at least they should!), usually expressed in earnings per share or return on equity.

Propositions Propositions explain the relation between two variables.

Prosumerism As consumers gain access to more information and start exercising their new options, the balance of the power shifts dramatically from manufacturers and distributors to consumers. Businesses have to become "pro" consumers to respond to this newfound power. The spread of television in emerging markets and the Internet worldwide gives consumers access to vast amounts of information.

Public Relations Public relations is a management function, because it manages the relations between the company and its publics. It is a bridge between the organization and its environment. The PR function helps firms to establish and maintain communication, involves the management of issues, helps management to stay informed on every communication aspect, and effectively serves the various publics by using research and being ethical and clear. The acronym of the components of public relations is RACE: Research, Action, Communication, and Evaluation.[5] It also gives a flavor of the time pressures involved. Public relations people counsel management by giving advice and taking actions. Grunig points out that "Nowadays, by the turn of the new century, PR is becoming a part of management and the PR specialists also becoming strategic counselors who are more involved in management decisions, strategic planning and other management functions."[6]

The Catholic Church's handling of priests' sexual abuse of minors in the United States is an example of poor public relations policy, which culminated in Frank Keating's incurring the wrath of many bishops for his blunt remarks about their complicity. When Keating, former governor of Oklahoma, resigned as the head of a 13-member board of prominent Catholic laypeople, he gave an interview to the *Los Angeles Times* in which he likened the bishops to la Cosa Nostra in their willingness to cover up wrongdoing.

Pulsetaker A cultivator of relationships that allow her to monitor the ongoing health and direction of the organization. Some characteristics of the pulsetaker:

- It is not always easy to see who these people are.
- They have sparse links, but these links are diverse and used frequently.
- They are first to sense changes in the wind and to intervene in subtle but powerful ways.
- They are prairie dogs, poking their heads out of their burrows to see what is going on.

"Putting the Monkey on the Other Guy's Shoulders"   Colorful phrase for successfully delegating.

Endnotes

1.   Axelrod, R. H. (2001). Why change management needs changing. *Reflections: The SOL Journal,* 2:3.

2.   Porter, M. (1990). *The competitive advantage of nations.* New York: Free Press.

3.   Reinhart, A., & Majidi, N. (2003, May 12). Europe's borderless market: The net. *BusinessWeek.*

4.   Utterback, J. (1994). *Mastering the dynamics of innovation: How companies can seize opportunities in the face of technological change.* Boston: Harvard Business School Press.

5.   Seitel, F. (2004). *The practice of public relations.* Upper Saddle River, NJ: Pearson Prentice Hall.

6.   Grunig, J., & Hunt, T. (1984). *Managing public relations.* New York: Holt, Rinehart & Winston.

Quality   Characteristics and features of a product or service that affect its ability to meet stated or implied needs. Typically, quality can be managed through TQM and performance standards and indicators.

Even a company that makes its name on quality and distinction, like Prada, Tiffany, and Baccarat, is not immune to tumbling from the heights. Take the case of Mercedes-Benz. Customers have started to complain that Mercedes isn't making them like they used to. As a brand, they have fallen from first place in most major quality and durability studies like the J. D. Power & Associates study. DaimlerChrysler is scrambling to address these issues as their cars have lost their top-selling position to the Lexus division of the Toyota Motor Corp.

Quality Standard   Framework for achieving a recognized level of quality within an organization. Achievement of a quality standard demonstrates that an organization or company has met the requirements laid out by a certifying body.

R

Radical Innovation   Radical innovation, also called sustainable innovation (as opposed to incremental innovation), involves the big changes that cause industry growth. Wal-Mart was a radical innovation that a company like Sears was unable to successfully respond to. Gary Hamel states that the challenge of companies is to make innovation an everyday part of their operations. Radical innovation is found in all industries and comes in all shapes, sizes, and forms—from the Starbucks in-your-pocket debit card to the Southwest Airlines out-of-the-box economic model.

RAND Corp.   Research and Development. Famously brilliant independent, private, nonprofit think tank that consistently solves strategic problems in an innovative way.

Rational Actor Model   Often viewed as the ideal, the rational actor is a comprehensive and systematic leader responsible for strategic thinking who marshals his or her followers to simultaneously take action to implement his or her decisions. There is a strong alignment between strategy and action and works best with benign and predictable environments.

Reasoning Through a Problem   Breaking a problem into its component parts is a key step in reasoning through a problem. This analytical aspect of strategic planning is based on the principles of Cartesian logic. Winston Churchill exemplified this approach when, after the battle of El Alamein, in Egypt, he noted: "This is not the end. It is not even the beginning of the end. But, it is, perhaps, the end of the beginning." Anything consists of the beginning, middle, and the end. Once you have that clear, you can apply that principle to the various subsections of the problem. Now, instead of having three sections you have nine. For more tools for reasoning through a problem, *see* Case Method and Strategic Management.

Reciprocal Cooperation   Referring customers to your "competitor" if the client's needs would be better served there. In this type of referral, cooperation needs to be repaid in kind. This can boost business and minimize unnecessary competition. For example, companies competing in the same business areas may not be focusing on the same market; for example, one may have more focus on consumer segment and the other on manufacturing clients.[1]

Reengineering Reengineering is the radical redesign of business processes for dramatic improvement, as originally outlined by Michael Hammer and Jim Champy. In their continuous striving for better performance, greater cost efficiency, and better customer service, some large companies are discovering the benefits of reengineering. The application of the reengineering effort typically involves bringing 15 to 20 young information system experts from a high-priced consulting firm like the Boston Consulting Group. These experts redesign the workflow and set new procedures and rules covering all aspects of business and organizational functions. In the end, they typically come up with new designs heavily based on a new computer-networked system with considerable reduction in the workforce needed.

There are many controversial questions as to the real benefits of reengineering and the extent of its desirability and efficiency in the workplace. CEOs are attracted to reengineering because of the prospect of greater efficiency and a less cumbersome, less bureaucratic chain of command. On the other hand, there are risks from "corporate anorexia"—removing "fat" may excessively reduce the social capital needed for value innovation.

Reflective Mindset Managing the self. *See* University.

Related Businesses/Diversification Businesses are said to be related when there are competitively valuable relationships among the activities comprising their respective value chains. The appeal of related diversification, then, is exploiting these value chain matchups to realize a $1 + 1 = 3$ performance outcome and build shareholder value. Related diversification has been shown to be, on the average, more profitable than single-business or unrelated-business diversification.

Relational Capital Relational capital has to do with the care, love, trust, and commitment that underpin the alliances and networks an organization engages in. Relational capital also derives from the leadership and the charisma of the CEO. It involves establishing close relationships with the client, competitors, suppliers, and employees.

Starbucks illustrates the rise of relational capital. Starbucks uses a multidimensional alliance strategy to turn a commodity, coffee, into a powerfully differentiated brand. This strategy was driven by a visionary CEO, Howard Schultz, who knows how to leverage relational capital. Starbucks' success proves that relationships are as important as physical capital, a model of a new competitive landscape.

Starbucks opens more than 1,200 stores a year. How do they continue to grow the business? In 20 years, Starbucks has spent $20 million on advertising (by contrast, P&G spends $30 million annually on its Pampers), and Starbucks has experienced 2,000% growth over the past 10 years. The answer is in relationships. "Starbucks starts and ends with core values. . . . The core values emanate from and around relationships with people," says a Starbucks VP. Relationships are central to sustained superior performance, moving beyond a transactional mind-set to trust-based, mutually beneficial long-term associations. The key constituencies are customers, suppliers, alliance partners, and employees (especially baristas or coffee brewers).

Starbucks is a model of relationship-centric organization. Relationships are the core asset in communication and collaboration. A good example is the story of the baristas and frapuccino blended beverage. The idea for the frapuccino blended beverage came from Starbucks baristas in Southern California, who had many requests for this drink. Initially thinking this type of beverage did not fit with the Starbucks concept, Schultz relented and introduced it, and it became wildly successful. Schultz now describes his initial veto of it as "the best mistake I never made."

Suppliers are also considered partners. Starbucks pinpoints where on the value chain it wants to focus and shed noncore operations. Licensing and cross-branding are a core strategy of Starbucks. It also effectively uses business alliances, international retail store licensing, grocery channel licensing, warehouse club accounts, direct-to-consumer joint ventures such as HMS Host (the largest airline concessionaire), Barnes and Noble (one of their most successful cross-licensing ventures), Albertson's and Safeway, United Airlines, and Sodexho and Compass (food service companies). For example, Schultz sees the baristas as the communicators of its brand. He creates and sustains an environment that encourages empowerment.

Relational Contracting   Relational contracting involves the kind of mutually beneficial alliances and contracts—for example, between a manufacturing firm and its supplier—that is characteristic of the Japanese kerietsu system.

Reliability   Reliability is a measure of the consistency of responses to a survey or questionnaire item. If different researchers administer the test or different subjects respond and there is consistency in results, the test is reliable. The caveat is that though the research method is reliable, it may not be valid; it may not actually measure the phenomenon that you want to understand.

Research and Development and Commercialization   Commercialization involves transforming an idea into a tangible product. According to the National Science Foundation, $292 billion were spent in the United States in national research and development (R&D) in 2002. Industry invested 72% of those expenditures and the federal government accounted for $80 billion. This funding was provided to federal laboratories (30%) and universities (25%) with the remainder going to small and large businesses. The general perception is it takes 15–40 years to transform an idea into a tangible product. Additionally, only a small percentage of intellectual property (patents) is actually commercialized.

Resilience   Resilience is the ability to dynamically reinvent business models and strategies as circumstances change. Strategic resilience, Gary Hamel argues, is not about responding to a onetime crisis or about rebounding from a setback. Resilience is about continuously anticipating and adjusting to trends that can permanently alter the earning power of a core business. It's about having the "capacity to change before the case for change becomes desperately obvious."[2]

Resource-Based View (RBV)   A perspective on strategic management associated with names like Barney, and Prahalad and Hamel. The resource view is an inside-out perspective that starts with the unique capabilities of the firm and then chooses to extend those capabilities into various markets. This resource view is compatible with the notion of core competences.

Prahalad and Hamel introduced the notion of core competence that is central to the RBV: "A capability or skill that provided the thread running through a firm's businesses, weaving them together into a coherent whole."[3] The idea is that the firm is run as a portfolio of competencies, not just as a portfolio of businesses.

RBV emphasizes the benefits of building and maintaining strategies that exploit existing stocks of human, physical, financial, reputational, social, and organizational capital. It also looks at strategies that explore new sources or resources not currently existing in the organization. RBV emphasizes that these resources need to be valuable, unique, and difficult to imitate. The resource-based view is contrasted with adaptive strategy, which emphasizes fitness with the environment.

Coca-Cola versus Pepsi is a competitive situation we all recognize. Analysts often cite Coke as the clear leader. They cite Coke's superiority in tangible assets as well as intangible assets. They also mention that Coke leads Pepsi in several capabilities to make use of these assets effectively—managing distribution globally, influencing retailer shelf allocations, marketing savvy, and speed of decision making to take quick advantage of changing global conditions. The combination of capabilities and assets creates competences that give Coke several competitive advantages over Pepsi that are not easily duplicated. Like the RBV of the firm, Coke's underlying premise is that it differs in fundamental ways from Pepsi because it possesses a unique "bundle" of resources.

Risk   Risk involves the possibility of suffering damage or loss in the face of uncertainty about the outcomes of actions or circumstances. Attitudes toward risk exert considerable influence on strategic choice. Where attitudes favor risk, the range of strategic choices expands and high-risk strategies are acceptable and desirable. Where management is risk-averse, the range of strategic choice is limited and risky alternatives are eliminated before strategic choices are made.

Risk-tolerant Nokia has been doing better than its risk-averse cell phone rivals like Motorola. Risk-tolerant managers lean more toward opportunistic strategies with higher payoffs. Risk-averse managers lean more toward conservative, safe strategies that have a probability of reasonable returns.

Risk Management   Risk management is a process for incorporating sufficient flexibility in all aspects of plans, strategies, and tactics. This involves adapting strategies and tactics to incorporate unforeseen future events, both favorable and unfavorable. It can also be defined as steps the organization takes to minimize threats to efficiency or profitability. Often, companies take out insurance against financial loss as well as implementing security and safety measures.

Risk Mitigation Programs   75% of the Fortune 1000 CEOs have risk mitigation programs that cover such day-to-day activities as mail processing, travel, protection of employees, and protection of infrastructure. However, these programs may be defining risk and security too narrowly.

Risk Trade-Offs   Pursuing one strategic priority usually means giving other strategic priorities less attention. A defense policy analyst at RAND Corp. explained these trade-offs when analyzing the 148,000 American troops on the ground in Iraq following the war: "While the U.S. could take Iraq with three divisions, it couldn't hold Iraq with three divisions." The planners had anticipated disorder and looting—but decided that other risks such as oil field fires, refugee flows, or famine were more dangerous. The RAND analyst notes that when you plan, you assess various risks and then you accept that you can't do everything—"that's life. . . ." In Iraq, there were certain risks that the coalition decided to invest more resources in, and there were other risks that they understood they could not address to the same extent. These trade-offs are not tidy and lead to unpredictable outcomes.

Rivalry   Firm rivalry has to do with the moves and countermoves that firms engage in to jockey for position within an industry. Two signs of intense rivalry in an industry would be the price wars or advertising wars that we see rampant in the fast-food industry and the cola and beer industries.

Rock Drill   Assembling an interdepartmental task force with the goal of planning a huge task in a very short time with many unknowns.

Role Blur   It is, at times, hard to tell, just by looking, exactly what work or family roles people are playing. For example, The sleepy-looking dad who stands at the corner bus stop with your kids may be telecommuting for a Japanese software firm. Role blur is very common in California, as evidenced by many CEOs running around in jeans and sneakers.

Role of the CEO   The CEO's personal values, aspirations, and ideals are a key component of corporate strategy. The CEO role includes assessing market opportunities, corporate competences and resources, her own personal values and aspirations, and finally, her obligations to various segments of society. *See* Mintzberg for a list of the 10 roles of the CEO.

Root Cause Analysis   A technique used in problem solving to identify the underlying reason why something has gone wrong. By asking why, one can examine the root cause between cause and effect.

This approach has been criticized on the grounds that it presupposes a single source of the difficulty, while in reality, the situation may be, and often is, more complex.

Rumsfeld's Rules   Many young White House interns show up at work on their first day and receive a copy of memos and lists stapled together titled "Rumsfeld's Rules." Reputed to be the best 20 pages ever compiled on how to serve the president ethically and effectively. These must-read rules can be good guides for aligning managerial behavior with firm strategy. Examples include:

If in doubt, don't. If still in doubt, do what's right. Things have to pass the smell test.

Move decisions out to the Cabinet and agencies. Strengthen them by moving responsibility, authority and accountability in their direction.

Your performance depends on people. Select the best, train them and back them. The "best and brightest" approach to hiring. Recruitment is undervalued in most companies. If the staff lacks policy guidance against which to test decisions, their decisions will be random. Top management needs to agree on a limited number of strategic management initiatives. These goals will in turn drive the demand for certain technology applications and other implementation tools that are needed for the firm to become more productive.

Be above suspicion. Set the right example. *See* If in doubt, don't. If still in doubt, do what's right.

Endnotes

1. http://www.bcentral.com/articles/wuorio/185.asp?LID=33278
2. Hamel, G., & Välikangas, L. (2003). The quest for resilience. *Harvard Business Review,* 81:9, p. 52.
3. Hamel, G., & Prahalad, C. K. (1999). *Competing for the future.* Boston: Harvard Business School Press.

S

Sarbanes-Oxley Act of 2002 The legislation intended to regulate corporate governance in the United States, drafted in the wake of the accounting, leadership, and governance scandals at such large companies as Enron, Tyco, and WorldCom. One provision is that CEOs and CFOs personally certify the accuracy of their financial statements to restore investor confidence.

Scaling Fitting the means to the end. Using Big Bertha to blow the head off an ant is a problem—a high-powered method applied to an insignificant end.

Scanning Environment In a turbulent environment, managers must allocate attention in such a way as to develop useful new strategies for coping with a changing environment.

Scenario Scenario writing has been described as "making up stories about the future." It has been said that a scenario has "a hypothetical, likely or unlikely, development or situation; a development which is described as caused to some extent by the actions and reactions of various actors: a desirable or non-desirable development or situation."[1]

Martino states that scenarios serve three basic purposes: (1) to display the interactions among several trends and events in order to provide a holistic picture of the future; (2) to help check the internal consistency of the set of forecasts on which they are based; and (3) to depict a future situation in a way readily understandable by the nonspecialist in the subject area.[2]

The scenarios written for the war in Iraq said that there would be no real resistance; planners did not anticipate guerrilla Iraqis in SUVs. The 507th Maintenance Company got caught in hostile fire and 11 soldiers died and 7 were taken prisoner. The company could have been in the middle of a big combat unit—a tank at the front and one at the back—but they were not expecting to be under attack.

The ambush of the 507th Maintenance Company on March 23, 2003, was a turning point in the war against Iraq. It exposed the fragility of the U.S. support lines. It was the deadliest day of the war for the coalition forces up to that point. The videos of the American prisoners and dead were demoralizing international news.

One of the soldiers killed in that ambush had told his father as he shipped out to Iraq, "Don't worry about me, I will be 100 miles from the front." Because of a lack of scenario planning, the 507th did not have hand grenades or antitank guns. It was not part of the scenario that they would get lost, take a wrong turn, and lose the protection of their combat unit. They found themselves in a situation where nearly everything that could go wrong did go wrong (*see* Murphy's Law). "The route they were given was Route Blue to Route Jackson to Route Blue again," noted a Special Forces friend of some of those killed in the 507th. "They went Route Blue all the way and that is what cost them."

Schnaars notes that scenarios do not pretend to predict the future but rather present a set of possible futures.[3] The value of a forecast depends on the validity of underlying assumptions. There are typically several sets of assumptions that can be offered upon which various scenarios can then be constructed. While scenarios sometimes lack specificity and accuracy, they do focus attention on causal processes and crucial strategic inflection points.

Scenario Planning   A technique that requires the use of a scenario in the process of strategic planning. Scenario planning aids in the development of corporate strategy. This technique is normally used in the face of uncertainty. Shell Oil is a big proponent of using scenario planning.

Scenario planning is one key tool in the management of technology innovation, a process that allows strategy development teams to imagine several possible futures.[4] They then outline and describe the different futures that might or could occur as if they had already happened, and develop plans for attaining each future. Management can then use this information to determine which scenarios set the most feasible strategic direction.

Schumpeterian   Joseph Schumpeter, an early-20th-century Austrian economist of the institutional school, coined the term "creative destruction" to denote those situations in which innovations destroy the value of investments in the previous technology or infrastructure; thus, the terms Schumpeterian rents or Schumpeterian innovation. Schumpeter was one of the first economists to posit the entrepreneur as central to the success of the capitalist system. This is why we now often see Schumpeter referred to in hip strategy magazines such as *Fast Company* or *Strategy + Business*.

Scientific/Analytical Explanation   Scientific/analytical explanation includes the following: (1) a general proposition, (2) a statement about certain given conditions, and (3) an empirical proposition in the form of a deduction from 1 + 2.

Scientific Approach   Hypothesis testing is only one of the steps in scientific investigation, but it seems to be the one that North American strategic management academics overly emphasize. Perhaps what is also needed is careful observation, patterning the process by setting up a diagnostic grid. Perhaps we need to look for a new telescope. Galileo formulated his scientific view after making use of a recent invention, the telescope. Science does not make eternal statements; we constantly need to develop new instruments and new hypotheses.

Scientific Study L. J. Henderson in his lectures on the methods of science outlined that the final task in scientific study is "the clear, explicit, and logical formulation of all relevant observations, analyses, and conclusions."[5]

Second Mover Strategy This is a strategy where the risks and costs of innovation are borne by the first mover, who is the innovator, pioneer, or leader in new technology. Microsoft has a classic and wildly successful second mover strategy whereby they were not the first to see the value of the graphical user interface (Apple was) or the first to see the excitement in the Internet (Netscape was ahead of them) but profited magnificently from the vision of others.

Self-Assessment and Adjustment It has been said that there are four levels of learning:

1. Unconsciously incompetent

2. Consciously incompetent

3. Consciously competent

4. Unconsciously competent

Self-Contained Community Module Each unit has its own generator for power, an ATM, wireless communications, a library with computers hooked up to vast databases to provide information on jobs and other services. This was the idea of a recent graduate from the Wharton Business School and is being tested out in Iraq.

Self-Efficacy Self-efficacy is defined as one's belief that he or she can effectively and successfully pursue certain actions and that self-efficacy grows with hard-won achievements.[6] Self-efficacy is important because many studies have linked high self-efficacy to entrepreneurial success.[7] Self-efficacy refers to a judgment of one's capability to accomplish a certain level of performance or desired outcomes. According to Bandura, individuals gradually accumulate self-efficacy over time through greater accomplishments.[8] Specifically, someone who has a high level of self-efficacy is more likely to set a higher or more challenging goal, which in turn raises the level of motivation and performance. A high level of self-efficacy can help individuals maintain their efforts until their initial goals are met.

Research shows that efficacious individuals not only pursue more challenging activities but also tend to persevere longer.[9] By definition, an entrepreneur with a high level of self-efficacy, who truly believes in his or her capability to execute all of the requirements to perform a task successfully, is more likely to see the positive potential outcomes that might accrue from a new venture. As a result, the entrepreneur may sustain more effort through the entrepreneurial process to achieve these positive outcomes.

Serial Acquirer A firm that has no time to build a technological base, so instead buys one. For example, Symantec, a global software technology company based in

Cupertino, California, enhanced its antiviral software into a full-scale enterprise security company by acquiring little companies for $1 million each. It acquired L3 Network Security, Brightmail Inc., and Axent Technologies Inc. in a span of two years. This can be a strategy to acquire both talent and technology rapidly.

Shareholder Value Analysis (SVA) Calculation of the value of a company by looking at the returns it gives to its shareholders. Importance is placed on managers and CEOs maximizing the wealth of the company's shareholders. SVA = Net Income/Share Value.

Short-Term Wins Payoffs appear in a short time period, for example, within a quarter. There is a danger in generating short-term wins at the expense of long-term strategy.

Situational leadership Originally, situational leadership suggested that a given leader could adapt different leadership styles, say, participative or autocratic, depending on the situation or on follower readiness. A more recent interpretation of situational leadership holds that there are various leader roles in any group. Thus, a leadership based on individual skills or qualities could be replaced by the group approach to the problem of leadership.

Skunk Works An organized, fast-moving group that works on the edge of (sometimes just outside) the organizational structure. Main purpose is to accelerate the innovation process without the usual bureaucracy. First introduced at Lockheed Martin and later lionized in 1984 by Tom Peters in *A Passion for Excellence.*

Smith, Adam (1723–1790) Adam Smith was an eighteenth-century professor of moral philosophy at Glasgow University. Smith studied economics by interviewing businessmen and visiting workshops. He opens his 1776 *Wealth of Nations* with a detailed description of a pin factory illustrating the merits of specialization and division of labor, which should be mandatory reading for all students of business. Smith's theory of enlightened self-interest highlights the fact that while firms exist to make a profit, the pursuit of these profits could transform one's selfish interest into useful service for the common good. He also advocated the "invisible hand" of the marketplace, where price and demand are set by the marketplace.

For example, in deciding their course of action during the potato famine in Ireland, British government officials and administrators rigidly adhered to Smith's theory, known as laissez-faire (in French, meaning "let it be"), which advocated a hands-off policy in the belief that all problems would eventually be solved on their own through "natural means." Throughout the entire famine period, the British government did not provide massive food aid to Ireland for fear that English landowners and private businesses would be unfairly harmed by resulting food price fluctuations. In adhering to laissez-faire, the British government also did not interfere with the English-controlled export business in Irish-grown grains. Throughout the famine years, large quantities of native-grown wheat, barley, oats, and oatmeal sailed out of ports such as Limerick and Waterford for England, even though local Irish were dying of starvation.

Smith wrote, "People of the same trade seldom meet together, even for merriment or diversion, but the conversation ends in a conspiracy against the public, or some contrivance to raise prices." This is an astute observation that needs to be applied to the Enrons or WorldComs of the future.

Snafu   As a noun, applies to a bad situation, especially one resulting from incompetence. As an adjective, means marked by confusion; chaotic. Or when used as a verb: to throw into disorder or confusion. U.S. military acronym for Situation Normal, All Fouled Up.

"But the Burger King snafu is potentially damaging, Cohen said."[10]

"In a conference call, chief executive Steve Snyder said the snafu was literally a cut-and-paste error in an Excel spreadsheet that we did not detect. . . ."[11]

Social Capital   Refers to the actual and potential resources individuals obtain from knowing others, being part of a social network with them, or just from being known to them and having a good reputation.

Social capital for an individual is a type of credential, a social identity badge of distinction, that can be converted into significant tangible benefits for the firm as a whole. The benefits for the firm of having employees with high social capital include enhanced access to knowledge and increased cooperation and trust. The more people one knows, the more information one receives, and presumably the greater the accuracy of the information. Social capital translates into financial outcomes and thus social capital is positively related to the compensation received by both managers and CEOs.

Social Entrepreneurship   Social entrepreneurship comprises endeavors undertaken with the view to achieve a socially beneficial goal rather than for the profit motive.

Social Network Analysis (SNA)   The study of the degree of connectedness or communication among actors within and across boundaries. Researchers study the proliferation of joint ventures and interorganizational networks and other linkages among firms, and also among nonfirms. Organizational innovation and organizational learning are closely related to networking. The degree of connectedness of communication among actors within and across boundaries is a current theme of research. A recently developed SNA growth model shows how the diffusion of productive knowledge takes time and is more rapid within firms than between firms.

Many studies relying on social networking use analysis techniques to locate actors within networks; their locations are measured by a construct termed centrality. The most common software used in SNA is called UCINET. Three centrality measures (degrees, betweenness, and closeness) are used to show, for example, that networks with low centralization scores do not have single points of failure, but are resilient in the face of many intentional or random failures.[12]

One of the basic arguments in SNA was first put forth in the 1950s by an American sociologist who wrote about the strength of weak ties. His example was looking for work. When you're looking for a job, it is not your strong ties (for example, close friends) who are going to help you find the job (because they are likely in the same position as you) but more likely your weak ties (friends of friends, relatives of friends).

Karen Stephenson, a social network theorist, studies what she calls the calculus of human exchange and developed a quantum theory of trust. She considers organizations the modern-day equivalent to the trade networks of the past. Stephenson completed her doctorate on technology company Bolt, Beranek and Newman (BBN) in Harvard's anthropology department, developing a formula for ranking the significance of individuals as knowledge conduits. BBN designed the packet-switching technology of the Internet and chose the symbol @ to demark e-mail addresses.

Stephenson argues that an organization's ability to implement any new strategy depends primarily on the way knowledge courses through its networks. And to determine that she asks the following strategic questions using SNA: Is the CEO a hub? Does a gatekeeper dominate a particular strategic product or region? Are the relationships among top executives devoid of trust? Are informal networks being rewarded?

SNA has been used to cultivate and increase collective cognitive capability of companies in the following instances: J. P. Morgan, to facilitate the merger with Chase Manhattan; IBM, to reengineer itself; HP, to foster innovation; U.S. Defense Advanced Research Projects Agency (DARPA, which created the original design of the Internet), for Information Awareness, the counterterrorism branch of the agency. With SNA, the key is putting the right people in the right places and fostering new opportunities for them to talk with each other.[13] SNA focuses on the executive organization as a communication system.

Societal Considerations   Andrews was one of the first in the strategic management field to insist that the CEO, as the architect of purpose, needs to incorporate societal consideration: the broader implications of firm choices on different stakeholder groups, such as environmentalists or feminists. *See* Role of the CEO.

Soft Manager   A soft manager invites candid feedback from her employees, and can even admit when she is wrong! Aligned with the emotional intelligence school of thought.

Special and Mysterious   Best strategies are simple, heroic, and bold.

Special Forces   Special Forces are those units in the military that specialize in covert or highly risky missions, such as the navy's SEALs and the army's Rangers. For example, in the Second Gulf War, Special Forces were involved in sniper-versus-sniper duels with Saddam's Fedayeen loyalists in Baghdad, saving army Pfc. Jessica Lynch, behind-the-lines reconnaissance, and searching for weapons of mass destruction. The Iraq war follows the Special Forces–dominated Operation Freedom in Afghanistan. The strategic issue is whether these special warfare units are now effectively becoming key players in full-scale wars.

In the First Gulf War, Special Forces were peripheral, but in Afghanistan and the Iraq War, they have become central to the war effort. In large numbers, 250 SEALs and 500 naval special-warfare personnel in Iraq and Kuwait gave the forces the ability to sustain larger-scale operations and to conduct multiple operations simultaneously. However, the situations they face are best described as fuzzy, the missions are not black-and-white. When the Special Forces are used to this extent, do they lose their elite status and specialized impact?

Specialization   Coordination of specialized parts or units to accomplish the purpose or goals of the formal organization. Types of specialization include geographic, temporal, associational, and functional. *See* Smith, Adam.

Sponsor   An active supporter of a project or innovation. The sponsor is ideally at higher levels of the organization (such as on a top management team) who mobilizes resources and moral support for the implementers (like the champion, who is a leader of the implementers, and her team of doers).

Stakeholders   Individuals, groups, or organizations having a financial, contractual, ethical, or political interest in the decisions or actions of a specific organization. As we transform into a more global and pluralistic society, the number and complexity of these relationships among stakeholders are growing. There is a transfer of power from the institutional managerial hierarchy to the multiple stakeholders.

Stakeholders' Legitimacy and Power   The stakeholders' power can be viewed as being related to the extent of their access to critical resources.[14] Legitimacy and power are related in the case of the stakeholder. Legitimacy can be derived from exchange, legal right, moral right, or simply an interest in the outcomes of the organization's actions, and its fate. Stakeholders gain (or are granted) legitimacy when they are perceived by others to have the right and capacity to participate.

Static Efficiency   Efficiency that is derived from existing resources. Because returns from exploiting existing resources are generally more certain and reliable than those from exploring new resources, the old can often drive out the new. So, resource-rich firms often focus on what they have and fail to explore new resources that may be needed for strategic change and evolution. A good example of a firm that declined to rest on its laurels of static efficiency is Intel in the early 1980s, when Andy Grove decided to abandon their lucrative (though with declining margins due to Japanese competitors) memory chip business to go into the unknown world of integrated chips. We all know how well that has gone.

Static Efficiency and Dynamic Efficiency   Returns from exploiting existing resources (static efficiency) are generally more certain than those from exploring new resources (dynamic efficiency). The former often drives out the latter.

Storytelling and Strategy, or PHAT   Robert Dickman, a founder of FirstVoice Communication who has consulted for firms such as the Ford Motor Company,

Mattel, and SAIC, uses his training as a Buddhist, his pre-Socratic philosophical training, and his experience as an acting and directing coach to bring storytelling to corporate strategy. His acronym (*see* Strategy by Acronym) is PHAT to capture the storytelling aspect of strategy. **Passion:** The emotions of a story allow us to anchor the strategic issue in our memory. Think of transformative leaders who can sell their mission based on passion, like Lee Iaccoca saving Chrysler through sheer force of personality. His passionate message was what is good for Chrysler is good for America. **Hero:** Does the story provide a clearly defined point of view? Think of the storytelling that went on at Wal-Mart, for example, in their very successful "buy American" campaign, during which the heroic Wal-Mart championed or at least bolstered America and in part the struggling manufacturing sector (of course, this campaign was in part based on fiction, as the items were often actually manufactured wholly or partly outside of the United States). **Antagonists:** Are there obstacles that confront the hero? For example, Microsoft's spin on their court case with the Department of Justice: the entrepreneurial, innovative firm versus big government. **Transformation:** Does the story have the power to change the life of the audience? Think of how WiFi is trying to sell their wireless connections in public places as a transformative, liberating technology, turning Starbucks more completely and conveniently into your office.

Strategic　Strategic denotes significant resource commitment and may involve the survival of the firm or entity. *See* Tactical Action.

Strategic Action　A significant commitment of specific and distinctive organizational resources. Typically, a strategic action is difficult to implement and reverse.

Strategic Alignment　Strategic alignment involves matching the internal resources and capabilities of the organization to the constraints and opportunities of the environment. Andrews, for example, calls it "fit" whereas Ansoff calls it strategic alignment. A basic tenet in strategic management is that a key determinant of the firm's long-term success, and even survival, is its ability to sustain strategic alignment with the environment.[15]

Strategic Alliances　Agreement between two or more organizations to cooperate in specific business arrangements. One goal for a strategic alliance would be to gain competitive advantage. Increases in the numbers of alliances are due in part to globalization and the uncertainties and complexities associated with it.

A strategic alliance is distinguished from a joint venture because the companies involved do not take an equity position in one another. In many instances, strategic alliances are partnerships that exist for a defined period of time during which partners contribute their skills and expertise to a cooperative project.

In some instances, strategic alliances are synonymous with licensing agreements. Bell South and U.S. West, with various marketing and service competitive advantages valuable to the European market, have extended a number of licenses to create personal computer networks in the United Kingdom.

Strategic Allocation of Attention Managers serve a significant function in the organization by interpreting events and framing choices. The executive worldview or allocation of attention sets the strategic tone for the organization. Leaders have the formal authority to prescribe interpretations, so how their own interpretations shift can be highly significant in shaping the strategy and character of the firm. This is part of the strategic architecture that sets the direction of the firm.

Strategic Architecture of the Firm The fossil that forms from the preference, whims, inspirations, and insights of the top management team. The architectural approach to business is grounded in the work of some recent authors.[16] Strategic architecture is the unique means of bringing together organizational resources to deliver value to customers and shareholders.[17] For example, the shopping mall is a strategic architecture that allows retailers collective access to lower rent and high volume of people traffic. Starbucks is a strategic architecture to allow for a third place (home and work being one and two, or two and one depending on your priorities) that allows for socialization and ersatz European experience.

Strategic Capability Strategic capability denotes the size and type of resources available for pursuing a particular strategic goal. For example, upon his retirement, the U.S. Army's chief of staff, Genera Eric Shinseski, made the point that Secretary of Defense Donald Rumsfeld's choices constrained the strategic capability of the army. With more than 370,000 soldiers, or 70% of the army, now deployed in 120 countries, the strategic capability of the United States to pursue a doctrine of preemption is constrained. In Shinseski's farewell speech, he warned of the dangers of pursuing a 12-division strategy with a 10-division army. This gets to the heart of strategic capability.

Strategic Debate A wide-ranging exploration of the issues that face a company, looking at standard business issues like technology and industry trends, but strategic debate also includes the "humanities" or soft-side topics such as ethics; the reason for existence of the firm; the meaning of debt versus equity (à la Enron); pushing the envelope in business, accounting, financing, ethics; and so on. Strategic debate is an important tool for top management teams to blue-sky and look at the big issues: "Looking at the field, what are the big issues?" "Can we take a little bite out of those big issues?"

Occasionally in meetings, the discussion is elevated to the level of debate. Executive debates not only have a certain entertainment value, they sometimes help to clarify a situation.

Strategic Decision-Making Models The Harvard Business Case method trains business students in a three-step process: Assess a situation, accept and outline options, and take appropriate action (*see* Case Method).

President Bush, the first president of the United States with an MBA, exemplified this approach to decision making in a political situation in 2003. Enmeshed in an internal struggle in his administration over whether and how to send U.S. peacekeeping troops to Liberia, Bush also made an appeal for time in making a decision that would have repercussions on military strategy as well as on domestic politics. He said that once his strategy is decided, "I will let people know whether or not I'm airborne." But until then, "I'm just gathering enough information to be rational in what we do." Bush consistently uses this Harvard Business Case approach whether the issue is stem cell research or a response to the 9/11 attacks.

Kathleen Eisenhardt, an advocate of the chaos/complexity theory of managing, outlines a four-elements model of effective decision making.[18]

The first one is **building collective intuition** that enhances the ability of a top management team so they can see threats and opportunities more quickly and accurately. In high-velocity markets, there is often little time for formal meetings or for the careful consideration of extensive information. Executives, the thinking goes, consider limited, decision-specific data, concentrate on one or two alternatives, and make decisions on the fly.

This approach is congruent with the studies of executive behavior as outlined by Mintzberg, where the day is filled with fleeting encounters of 2 to 3 minutes. From extensive real-time information, these executives build a collective intuition that allows them to move quickly and accurately as opportunities arise.

The second approach is **stimulating quick conflict** to improve the quality of strategic thinking without sacrificing significant time. Eisenhardt argues that conflict stimulates innovative thinking, creates a fuller understanding of options, and improves decision effectiveness. Without conflict, decision makers commonly miss opportunities to question assumptions and overlook key elements of the decision.

The third approach is maintaining a **disciplined pace** that drives the decision process to a timely conclusion. The team launches the decision-making process promptly and keeps up the energy surrounding the process. Moreover, it cuts off debate at the appropriate moment.

The last approach is **defusing political behavior** that creates unproductive conflict and wastes time. The focus is on a collaborative, not competitive, approach setting limits on politics and, more generally, interpersonal conflict.

Strategic Dissonance   A discrepancy between upper management's intended strategy and the strategy actually implemented by lower levels of management.

R. A. Burgelman describes a situation at Intel regarding dissonance, quoting then CEO Andy Grove:[19]

Don't ask managers, What is your strategy? Look at what they do! Because people will pretend. . . . The fact is that we [Intel] had become a non-factor in DRAMs with 2–3% market share. The DRAM business just passed us by! Yet, many people were still holding to the "self-evident truth" that Intel was a memory company. One of the toughest challenges is to make people see that these self-evident truths are no longer true. . . . I recall going to see Gordon Moore [Intel's founder] and asking him what a new management would do if we were replaced. The answer was clear: Get out of DRAMs [and focus on microprocessors]. So I suggested to Gordon that we go through the revolving door, come back in, and just do it ourselves.

Strategic Focus   "If not here, where?[20] Schelling asks. Strategic focus is the collective obsession of the organization, focusing on what the organization is in agreement with is the most salient or prominent goal. There has to be an element of the herd instinct, where even a random group of people will converge on a prevailing judgment of the direction of the group.

Strategic Groups   Strategic groups, a concept coined by Michael Porter, are companies that emphasize the same strategy. In general, within these groups, competition is higher than with the rest of the industry. Porter argues that it is important to analyze the strategy of competitors and identify possible strategic groups in order to forecast competition and future strategies.

Coke and Pepsi form a strategic group; they have a similar strategy of heavy emphasis on advertising and a broad product line. Cadbury Schweppes would be more of a niche player, not in the Coke and Pepsi strategic group. Intel and AMD belong to the same strategic group as they are both selling microchips. Competition between them has been fierce.

Strategic Inflection Point   A strategic inflection point (the term was coined by the former CEO of Intel, Andy Grove) indicates a major paradigm shift, or dramatic change in strategy, that a firm may need to make after reaching a fork in the road. At Intel, Grove abandoned the memory chip business in the 1980s when he realized that Japanese low-cost competitors were not beatable. This presented a strategic inflection point, and Grove bet the company on the semiconductor industry, and won big by basing Intel's strategy on differentiation rather than low cost. A strategic inflection point is any of those rare moments when something creates a "$10 \times$ change"—a change 10 times greater than your average everyday change. On a personal level, a strategic inflection point might be getting laid off, or adolescence. In technology, the arrival of the Web was just such a moment.

The IBM story presents a strategic inflection point: Watson Senior is distraught about the loss of exclusive control of punch card technology through a Justice Department ruling, so Watson Junior says, in effect, "That's great, let's give it to them and move into computers."

Strategic Intent   Strategic intent represents a tangible corporate goal or destiny that is a stretch for the organization. It also involves a worldview about the competitive position a company hopes to build over the long term.

Strategic Management   Strategic management as a practice includes the general management of firms for long-term performance and covers the functions and tasks of general management and the strategies they develop. Strategic management is the plan a company implements to gain competitive advantage in its industry. Strategic management can also be seen as the ability of top managers to achieve the firm's goals through a system built by those top managers and by other people within the organization; it is actually a system (rather than a plan) that allows managers and employees to respond to situations without necessarily referring to a plan.

Strategic management is also cycle that starts with the process of exploring, analyzing, and interpreting the firm's capabilities and strengths and the threats in its operating environment, then goes on to setting objectives, allocating resources, interpreting the outcomes, and exploring again. Building on Mintzberg's original turn of phrase, it has been said that strategic management is a stream of decisions and actions that lead to the development of an effective strategy to help achieve corporate objectives. Strategic management, it can be argued, necessarily involves innovation, new ideas, new opinions, and new optics on the world that need to be created, discussed, debated, and perhaps introduced into the firm beginning at the top management level. The cases of Enron, WorldCom, Marconi, and other recent corporate debacles suggest that this innovative strategic debate is not sufficiently widespread. Many boards are too quick to support rather than question the CEO (*see* Corporate Governance).

As a field of inquiry, strategic management can be considered fragmented: so many topics and silos of functional areas. Some consider strategic management a subfield of economics and industrial economics (the powerful Porter approach) and consequently often neglect the behavioral area. Others argue that it needs to stick close to the general manager: their point of view, behavior, and activities (the Harvard Business School approach, propounded by authors such as John Kotter). Mintzberg maintains that strategy cannot be separated from management, although it has been consistently in the past.

Strategic management is a process that assures the future success of profit and not-for-profit organizations through planned renewal of their technologies, products, markets, and sociopolitical relationship with their environments. Some helpful definitions include:

- Strategic management is a process, needed to plan for the future.
- A favorite definition of strategic management is not necessarily a technique or a conceptual model that can reduce uncertainty to zero, but rather tools and frameworks that can help managers to assess the level of uncertainty they face and to tailor appropriate strategic response.
- Strategic management creates freedom of action for executives by defining internal and external goals and allowing the middle manager to work within these confines.
- Strategic management is not a box of tricks or a bundle of techniques. It is analytical thinking and commitment of resources to action.
- Remembering the past, being aware of the present, and having capacity (mind-set) for envisioning the future are essential premises for building a strategy.[21]
- Napoleon said, "Strategy is the art of making use of time and space. I am less wary of the latter than the former; space we can recover, time never."

According to Chaffee,[22] strategy is viewed in three distinct but sometimes-conflicting ways: linear strategy, adaptive strategy, and interpretive strategy. The linear model has been used by most researchers and focuses on planning and forecasting. The second model is described as adaptive and most closely associated with "strategic management." This model "tends to focus the manager's attention on means" and is largely concerned with "fit." The third, interpretive model is a minority view that sees strategy as a metaphor and, therefore, not as something that can be measured but rather viewed in qualitative terms.

We can conclude that strategic management practitioners and academics are the integrationists; both need to look at what management is and what it is not.

Strategic Myopia   Strategic myopia refers to managers' inability to "see"—a failure to interpret or predict the firm's business environment, rejecting those things that are unknowable out of hand as "unrealistic or impractical." A fatal strategic error. Remedy: Implement LASIK procedures or get out what Prahalad and Hamel call the strategic crystal ball and start focusing on that unknowable future.

Strategic Pathway   A disciplined sequence of strategic priorities established by managers who then place great importance on them. Many times, however, managers can tend to underestimate market size and overestimate their organization's share of it.

Strategic Planning   The process by which an organization formulates and implements important decisions across different levels and functions of the organization. Organizations conduct strategic planning to formulate long-range goals and then to select activities to achieve each of those goals, meant to ensure that the organization is successful.

Today's gurus of strategy urge companies to democratize the process—once the sole province of a company's most senior officers—by handing strategic planning over to teams of line and staff managers from different disciplines.

Electronic Data Systems Corp., which manages large-scale data centers, has opened its strategic-planning process to a broader range of players. Four years ago, EDS launched a major strategy initiative that involved 2,500 of its 55,000 employees. The company picked a core group of 150 staffers from around the world for the year-long assignment. The group ranged from a 26-year-old systems engineer who had been with EDS for 2 years to a sixty-something corporate vice president with a quarter of a century of EDS experience. Similar approaches have been used by a wide range of companies, including Marriott Hotels and Helene Curtis Industries.

Strategic Repositioning   Companies reposition themselves in order to be more efficient in the future. The repositioning process may bring some extra costs for the short-term period. An important requirement is that strategic repositioning must support the company's strategic plan. Schlotzsky's Inc., the franchiser of quick-service deli restaurants, applied strategic repositioning in the year 2000. The company was willing to sacrifice its earnings in the next year (2001) in order to improve its balance sheet, reduce debt, and increase profit margins for the year 2003.

Strategic Thinking   Not being on automatic pilot. Strategic thinking means being a doctor rather than a pharmacist. A doctor makes complex assessments and judgments, whereas a pharmacist, though highly trained, merely follows the prescription.

Top management is largely responsible for strategic decision making; however, strategic thinking needs to occur at all levels of the organization. Agree on the goal and then let others do their own self-reflection.

Dr. Jagdish Seth advocates asking, "Are we doing the right thing?" This focuses attention on the big picture of the organization.

Strategic thinking involves making decisions and taking actions based on having a definite purpose in mind, with an understanding of the environment and with an emphasis on creative solutions that marry firm purpose and the environment in new and effective ways.

Strategy   Lance Armstrong in 2003, upon winning Le Tour de France for the fifth consecutive year and tying the previous record of wins, stated, "I think this year I had to rely more on strategy than physical gifts or fitness. . . . I will be back, and I don't plan on being this vulnerable. I won't make the same mistakes again. But, you know, maybe it was good for me to have a rough year." Lance also gave credit to his USPS team for ensuring the win. The lessons of how important strategy is, how to meticulously go over your performance and learn from your mistakes, the importance of making mistakes and having a rough time, and the necessity of a strong team to back you up are all appropriate grounds for or contributors to business strategies.

Some useful insights and definitions of strategy include:

"The determination of the basic long-term goals and objectives of an enterprise, and the adoption of courses of action and the allocation of resources necessary for carrying out these goals." (Chandler, 1962)[23]

"A pattern of resource allocation that enables firms to maintain or improve their performance." (Barney, 1997)[24]

"Top management's plans to attain outcomes consistent with the organization's missions and goals." (Wright et al., 1992)[25]

Strategy is understanding the big picture, consumer megatrends, and the little things that matter, also understanding the competition's weakness and exploiting it and making good partners.

Strategy Implementation   Once the goal is determined, strategy implementation involves allocating resources, and setting up a structure that must include information systems, roles and relationships, and incentives and controls of performance.

Leadership is decisive in strategy implementation. Andrews[26] was the first to clearly differentiate strategy formulation (mission, goals, etc.) from implementation, as defined above.

A good analogy for getting a handle on a modern view of implementation is, How does one move one employees from being a good pharmacist to being a good doctor? The answer would include thinking assertively and working creatively around unexpected problems. A pharmacist cannot add value to a prescription. She can impress with her service but not with a decision. A doctor assesses complex situations, makes important diagnoses, and outlines a plan of action. This view of strategy implementation has the implementer also involved in the formulating, thus breaking the false formulation/implementation dichotomy that Andrews first introduced.

Strategy in Motion   Making strategic decisions and moving forward while realizing your decision may need to change. This is one of the strategic leadership practices used by Intel IT in order to move forward in a technology market filled with more detours and surprises than patterns.[27]

Strategy of Culture   Strategy of culture involves basing your marketplace strategy on the legacy of the culture of the institution. The *New York Times* has brand integrity and strategy of culture based on an encyclopedic approach to the news that hearkens back to its coverage of World War II. The *Times* was the only American newspaper to cover every front of the war, filing stories every day on, say, the Congo or Alaska, even if they were only a few lines.

In 2003, when the *Times* discovered that one of its reporters, Jason Blair, was fabricating stories, this strategy of culture slowed down their response to the problem. It seems that this failure to respond quickly was not a journalism-school but a business-school problem. When one of the editors was challenged on the veracity of Blair's work, the editor pulled a quarter out of his pocket and said here, go and get yourself a job. This offhand comment shows how the institution was too rigid, suppressing the information from the bottom, and thus it seemingly could not change. Once the truth broke through, the board finally fired the two editors and the reporter to maintain brand integrity and reassert its strategy of culture: an encyclopedic culture of news with integrity.

Strategy Roots   Some of the roots of strategy include military, cold war, sports, metaphysics, cybernetics, psychology, and economics.

Strategy Rules

1. There are no general rules.

2. There may be exceptions to Rule 1.

3. "Getting there quickest with the mostest." U.S. Army

4. "Don't let the best be the enemy of the good."

Stress   Responsibility for people always causes more stress than responsibility for things—equipment, budgets, etc. A study done for NASA found that administrators were much more subject to stress than engineers or scientists.

Stretch Goals   Jack Welch coined the term to denote those objectives that are seemingly unobtainable with present resources.

Structure   The design of an organization through which the enterprise is administered, according to Alfred D. Chandler (1962).[28]

Henry Mintzberg in his book *The Structure of Organizations*[29] describes the five configurations as Simple Structure, Machine Bureaucracy, Professional Bureaucracy, Divisionalized Form, and Adhocracy.

The **Simple Structure** is typically seen in entrepreneurial firms and in firms that experience crisis or extreme hostility, since it is very flexible and adaptive—in effect, organic and centralized. This centralization is a double-edged sword because power is centered in one person who thus becomes the critical factor. This person's health is vital to the health of the structure.

The **Machine Bureaucracy** is very efficient, which is its force. But innovation is rare, and if it happens, it is despite the structure, not because of it. Operating efficiency is achieved in a simple, stable environment; if the environment becomes complex and dynamic, the machine bureaucracy is often unable to respond effectively to the changes and loses competitiveness. Also, the coordination mechanism and design parameters of the machine bureaucracy frequently result in low worker morale.

The **Professional Bureaucracy** focuses on standardization of skills, not on work process as with the machine bureaucracy. The professional bureaucracy does share the machine bureaucracy's lack of innovativeness, but for different reasons. The professionals' focus is on perfecting their skills, not on developing new skills or developing innovations. This focus, together with the inflexible structure, is ill suited for new outputs.

The **Divisionalized Form** is Chandler's M-form or multidivisional form, with relatively independent structures within the divisionalized structure. This structure is typically seen in market-based firms. Often there is a duplication of functions, departments, and so on, to minimize the reliance of one division on others. Also, the top management team in the divisionalized structure is concerned with the portfolio of strategic business units, whereas the division manager is focused on market-based strategies. Prahalad and Hamel have extensively criticized this form, which they call SBU (strategic business unit) management, because they feel that it does not fit well with the strategic exigencies of globally competitive environment. Specifically, they argue that managing a firm as a portfolio of assets neglects the synergies or core competences that cut across SBUs.

The **Adhocracy** is the most potentially innovative and potentially inefficient structure of the five. Strategy is not formally formulated but developed through the process of individual decisions over time. The mutual adjustment and strategy process leads to inefficiencies, but there is also a gain in effectiveness (doing the right things, instead of doing things right).

Mintzberg recognizes the limitation of these ideal structures in the real world. Consequently, he further synthesizes his findings into a pentagon with an ideal structure located at each corner; according to Mintzberg, each structure is some combination of pulls among the five in search of a harmonious structure in the organization. In this way, Mintzberg is able to include all variations among the ideal structures.

Sun Tzu   Wrote *The Art of War* in approximately 490 BCE. "The way of war is a way of deception. When able, feign inability; when deploying troops, appear not to be; if [the enemy] is weak, stir him to pride. If he is relaxed, hurry him; if his men are harmonious, split them." This emphasis on manipulation of the enemy through deception and dissimulation, as John Minford observes, is at the heart of Sun Tzu's strategic thinking. The key is to protect and maintain ambiguity, giving the enemy or competitor pause to wonder, question. The classic example of this is the Allied invasion of Normandy. The Allies succeeded to some extent in confusing the Germans as to the location of the actual landing. Although not totally misled, Hitler had enough uncertainty that the delayed response that was crucial to the success of the operation occurred.

SuperCEO   Like a supermodel: Jack Welch, Lou Gerstner, Bill Gates, Michael Dell—household names, now celebrities; the cult of personality.

Supply Chain Management   Supply chain management is the integrating of a network of suppliers, factories, warehouses, distribution centers, and retailers through which raw materials are acquired, transformed, and delivered to the customer. The details vary from industry to industry, but in general, the importance of trust and providing a product by working together is what makes this management theory a success.[30] The idea of supply chain management: Multicompany groups, functioning as one extended enterprise, make optimum use of shared resources (people, processes, technology, and performance measurements) to achieve operating synergy.[31]

Sony has developed it own supply chain management strategy that has given it a respectable place among some other companies in the same industry. Supply chain management has played an important part in Sony's success by allowing it to comply with costumer demands in a competitive environment. An example is Sony's assembly plants called *maquiladoras* that are located in Mexico's main cities along the U.S. border.

After analyzing the U.S. business environment, Sony managers concluded that California had everything the company needed such as a successful economy, available labor, and a location that facilitated the shipment of components from Japan. Given all the advantages that California offered, Sony established its San Diego Manufacturing Center. Sony later realized its San Diego plant needed production support closer to home and set up a facility in Tijuana, Mexico, in 1985. Sony took advantage of human and natural resources that were available in Mexico such as cheap labor, lack of government regulations, and ample space availability to construct warehouses. This decision to locate an assembly plant in Mexico was a key element in their supply chain management strategy. Sony has followed NAFTA policies, which states that any assembly plant established in Canada, the United States, or Mexico has to buy at least one of its components from one of these countries.

Another example is the North African Division of Coca-Cola, which found that investing in the technical support of its bottlers allowed benefits to be realized by its rivals. A local African bottling company began production of a soft drink brand, "Softa." It had access to already highly developed packaging suppliers groomed by Coca-Cola. This included the cap suppliers and the suppliers of plastic and glass bottles and cases. This shows the dangers of operational effectiveness through supply chain management. Supporting suppliers over whom one has no control can confer benefits on one's rivals.

Surfing Model of Strategy   A model of strategy developed by James Brian Quinn in a talk at the Academy of Management. He suggested: Go out beyond the waves and hang there and look for waves, where one can see patterns of what is happening, and then paddle over to where the action is. However, it is the wave that has to push, the wave of new technology. It is arrogance for the company to think it is the wave. It is a moving frontier, a lot of beautiful waves out there. The other issue is, When do you get out?

Sustainability   There is no one single definition for sustainability, but in the business context, it means for an organization to consider not only economical needs but also environmental and social/community needs. In times of public criticism of bad business practices such as dubious accounting practices or "sweatshops" in developing countries, it has become a strategy (or at least part of it) for companies to follow guidelines for sustainability to establish public trust in them. For example, Adidas-Salomon focuses on sustainable business practices as their executives believe that good corporate citizenship will not only improve their environment but also company performance in the long run.

Sustainable Competitive Advantage   A sustainable competitive advantage exists when a firm is able to protect a value-creating strategy from imitation by other firms—perhaps because it is too costly to imitate or too intricate. For example, the competitive advantage that Southwest Airlines had for so long seemed to be embedded in the unique corporate culture of the firm that allowed for the lowest costs in the industry. However, the arrival of JetBlue demonstrates that these sustainable competitive advantages are not indefinitely sustainable.

SWOT Analysis   An assessment of Strengths, Weaknesses, Opportunities, and Threats. This is used in the early stages of strategic planning. SWOT analysis can aid in the problem-solving stages as well as making employees recognize the need for change.

SWOT analysis is a widely used technique through which managers can create a quick overview of a company's strategic situation. It is based on the assumption that an effective strategy derives from a sound fit between a firm's internal resources (strengths and weaknesses) and its external situation (opportunities and threats). A good fit can maximize a firm's strengths and opportunities and minimize its weaknesses and threats.

Strength is a resource advantage relative to competitors and the needs of the markets a firm serves. It is a distinctive competence when it gives the firm a competitive advantage in the marketplace. Strengths arise from the resources and competences available to the firm.

Weakness is a limitation or deficiency in one or more resources or competences of a firm relative to those of competitors that impedes the firm's effective performance.

Opportunity is a major favorable situation in a firm's environment. Identification of a previously overlooked market segment, changes in competitive or regulatory circumstances, or technological changes might represent opportunities for the firm.

Threat is a major unfavorable situation in a firm's environment. The entrance of new competitors, slow market growth, and new regulations can represent threats to a firm's success.

Synergy Synergy exists when the value created by business units working together exceeds the sum of the value those same units create when working independently: the harmonization of the direction and operation of separate organizations into a whole entity. Synergetic activity typically needs to be carefully planned, analyzed, and implemented.

Synergy is the technique used to defeat ordinary arithmetic where $2 + 2 = 4$ and replace it with a strategic arithmetic where $2 + 2 = 0, 1, 2, 3, 4, 5, 6 \ldots n$. This is a more useful way to look at it than thinking that $2 + 2 = 4$. For example, a Comcast-Disney union would marry the USA's No. 1 cable and broadband company to an entertainment giant that owns the ABC network, ESPN, and Disney's film business. The two could team to sell services and content to broadband and digital customers. This synergy could be good for consumers, because phone companies might fight back with better technology, choices, deals, and service.

However, there is also a common phenomenon of negative synergy or illusory synergy, as many merger managers know, such as those at DaimlerChrysler. The lack of a cultural and strategic fit is one of the main causes of failures in mergers.

System A system is a set of objects that interact regularly or interdependently to form a unified whole.

System Lock-In System lock-in occurs when a firm creates high switching costs in order to keep customers. Coca-Cola has greatly benefited from system lock-in. Its main strength has been its brand products, led by its flagship brand, Coca-Cola. It has also entered into distributorship channels with restrictions such that the branded fountains and coolers it provides to various outlets can be used only for its products. Of course, the bottlers can buy the concentrate only from the Coca-Cola Company.

Systems Principles Some systems principles as they relate to organizations:

1. The whole is more than the sum of its parts. A related concept is synergy: the effectiveness of combined action.

2. Organizations are goal seeking.

3. The cybernetic idea of feedback loops affects system operation and equilibrium.

4. Systems seek a stable equilibrium point (according to neoclassical economics or linear systems), or equilibrium is a state of degrading and decay of the system (according to complexity theory).

5. Systems are arranged hierarchically (linear systems).

6. The principle of equifinality: A system can achieve the same end state from a variety of beginning states ("There is more than one way to skin a cat").

Systems Theory   In systems theory, it is assumed that the organization and its environment can be understood as a set of interrelated parts. The organization functions like a living creature, goal seeking and trading with its environment—importing things, transforming them through an at-times mysterious process, and finally exporting them to the environment with value added for a profit. Taken to its logical extreme, the universe is seen as a set of systems interfacing. Also taken to its logical extreme, systems theory as applied to strategic management can lead to compulsive obsession—the filling in of boxes and hierarchal diagrams of missions leading to visions leading to strategies to objectives to goals to projects, budgets, and action plans with a feedback loop to mission. Argg!! This presents the danger of turning strategy into a bureaucratic exercise that the famous Austrian economist Joseph Schumpeter advised would choke the entrepreneurial spirit of creative destruction out of capitalism.

Systems theory was an academic movement with great promise for strategy in the early 1960s, with proponents from Carnegie Mellon like George Steiner and his protégé Igor Ansoff. However, it failed to deliver as a way to understand and study strategy. The hands-on, clinical, anecdote-based Harvard Business School Case Study method won out, with Andrews and later Porter taking a more practical approach. Systems theory has been rehabilitated somewhat with the nonlinear logic of complexity theory. Somewhat. The main nonmathematical proponent of complexity theory is Kathleen Eisenhardt of Stanford,[32] and maybe also Tom Peters.[33]

Systems Thinking   This is a term made popular by Peter Senge in his book *The Fifth Discipline: The Art and Practice of the Learning Organization.*[34] Systems thinking borrows from physics, one such borrowing being Newton's law that for every action there is an equal and opposite reaction. Another example is that nature abhors a vacuum.

Senge enumerates five learning principles, with the fifth being systems thinking. Systems thinking, according to Senge, involves the idea that organizations are holistic patterns of interconnected parts. Senge explores "system archetypes" that recur among different organizations. Some of his insights regarding systems are as follows:

1. Today's problems come from yesterday's solutions.

2. The harder you push, the harder the system pushes back.

3. Behavior grows better before it grows worse.

4. The cure can be worse than the disease.

5. Faster is slower.

6. Cause and effect are not closely related in time and space.

7. Small changes can produce big results—but the areas of highest leverage are often the least obvious.

8. You can have your cake and eat it too—but not at once.

9. Dividing an elephant in half does not produce two small elephants.

10. There is no blame.

Senge has mastered the strategic art of thinking in metaphors.

Endnotes

1. Schwarz, B., Svedin, U., & Wittrock, B. (1982). *Methods in futures studies: Problems and applications.* Boulder, CO: Westview.

2. Martino, A. (1983, Oct.). Fraudulent democracy. *Economic Affairs,* 4:1, p. 148.

3. Schnaars, S. (1989). *Megamistakes: Forecasting and the myth of rapid technological change.* New York: Free Press.

4. Intel Corporation. (2003). *Strategic leadership: Strategic management during uncertain times.* IT@Intel. http://www.intel.com/ebusiness/it/research/pp023306

5. Henderson, L. J. (1970). *On the social system.* (Bernard Barber, ed.). Chicago & London: University of Chicago Press.

6. Bandura, A. (1997). *Self-efficacy: The exercise of control.* New York: W. H. Freeman.

7. Koen, P., Markman, G., Baron, R., & Reilly, R. *Cognition and personalities as predictors of resource attainment among corporate entrepreneurship.* The Stevens Institute of Technology. http.www.babson.edu

8. Bandura, A. (1986). *Social foundations of thought and action: A social cognitive theory.* Englewood Cliffs, NJ: Prentice Hall.

9. Bandura, A. (1997). *Self-efficacy: The exercise of control.* New York: W. H. Freeman.

10. Scott, L. Coke on thin ice with Burger King. *The Monterey Herald* (California); June 19, 2003.

11. Drew, C. Excel snafu costs firm $24m. *The Register* (UK), June 19, 2003.

12. Krebs, V. (2002). *Knowledge networks—Mapping and measuring knowledge creation and re-use.* orgnet.com

13. Ibid.

14. Solomon, E. (2001). The dynamics of corporate change: Management's evaluation of stakeholder characteristics. *Human Systems Management,* 20:3.

15. Barr, P. S. (1998). Adapting to unfamiliar environmental events: A look at the evolution of interpretation and its role in strategic change. *Organization Science: A Journal of the Institute of Management Sciences,* Nov/Dec, 9:6.

16. Zachman, J., & Sowa, J. Information Systems Architecture. David Nadler and Michael Tushman, Organization Architecture. ttp://www.istis.unomaha.edu/isqa/vanvliet/arch/isa/isa.htm. Nadler, D., Tushman, M., & Nadler, M. B. (1997). *The power of organizational architecture.* New York: Oxford University Press.

17. Lynch, R. L., Diezmann, J. G., & Dowling, J. F. (2003). *The capable company: Building the capabilities that make strategy work.* Malden, MA: Blackwell.

18. Eisenhardt, K., & Brown, S. (1998). *Competing on the edge of chaos.* Boston: Harvard Business School Press.

19. Burgelman, R. A. (1994). In fading memories: A process theory of strategic business exiting dynamic environments. *Administrative Science Quarterly* 39, p. 24. Burgelman, R.

(1994, March). Fading memories: A process theory of strategic business exiting dynamic environments. *Administrative Science Quarterly,* 39, Issue 1, pp. 24, 33.

20. Schelling, **?.** (1960). *The strategy of conflict.* pp. 111–114. Cambridge, MA: Harvard University Press.

21. By Peter Drucker (Marie Rankin Clarke, Professor of Social Science and Management at Claremont Graduate University in Claremont, California, which named its Graduate Management Center after him in 1987.)

22. Chaffee, E. E. (1985). Three models of strategy. *Academy of Management Review* 10, 89–98.

23. Chandler, A. (1962). *Strategy and structure.* Cambridge: MIT Press.

24. Barney, J. B. (1997). *Gaining and sustaining competitive advantage.* Reading, MA: Addison-Wesley.

25. Wright, P., Kroll, M., & Parnell, J. (1992). *Strategic management: Concepts.* London: US Imports & PHIPEs.

26. Andrews, K. (1971). *The concept of corporate strategy.* Homewood, IL: Dow Jones-Irwin.

27. http://www.intel.com/eBusiness/it/research/pp023306_sum.htm

28. Chandler, A. (1962). *Strategy and structure.* Cambridge: MIT Press.

29. Mintzberg, H. (1979). *The structure of organizations: A synthesis of the research.* Englewood Cliffs, NJ: Prentice Hall.

30. Fox, M. S., Barbuceanu, M., & Teigen, R., (2000). Agent-oriented supply-chain management. *International Journal of Flexible Manufacturing Systems,* 12:2/3, pp. 165–188 [found by KG oline].

31. Kuglin, F. (1998). *Customer-centered supply chain management: A link-by-link guide,* pp. 3–4. New York: AMACOM.Amacom

32. Eisenhardt, K., & Brown, S. (1998). *Competing on the edge of chaos.* Boston: Harvard Business School Press.

33. Peters, T. (1988). *Thriving on chaos: Handbook for a management revolution.* New York: HarperCollins.

34. Senge, P. (1990). *The fifth discipline: The art and practice of the learning organization.* New York: Doubleday/Currency.

T

Tacit Bargaining Describes negotiation among parties without having any explicit contract. In the automobile industry, for example, in the days of the Big Three, Ford and Chrysler would wait until GM made a change in prices or in the warranty and then would follow accordingly. The term was made famous by T. C. Schelling in *Strategy of Conflict*,[1] where he discussed such everyday activities as dealing with the possibility that you and your wife will get separated in a shopping center: How do you know where to rendezvous with her—at the information desk, at the café, at her favorite store?

Tacit Knowledge Knowledge within the firm falls into two main categories: explicit knowledge and tacit knowledge. Explicit knowledge is relatively easy to code and very external in nature. Tacit knowledge, on the other hand, is harder to code and extract, and is very internal in nature. Most organizations have concentrated their knowledge management efforts on developing effective links between the management of explicit knowledge and external communications systems. (*See* Knowledge Management.)

Tacit knowledge, not explicit knowledge, is generally the source of a firm's core competence and competitive advantage and is thus the more important of the two; it is the glue that binds explicit knowledge together, and it is essential for the effective use of information in decision making. Not only does it need to be discovered, extracted, and captured, it has to be creatively disseminated so that it can be efficiently shared and used to extend the knowledge management base. Perhaps it is also the more important component of knowledge management, insofar as the collaboration that it encourages leads to quantum shifts in knowledge rather than incremental linear enhancements.

Tacit knowledge may not be able to be codified or documented in the same way that explicit knowledge systems can, because it is knowledge that is the result of human experience and the senses. For example, when a cook bakes a cake, the recipe is the explicit, documented knowledge needed to begin, but to arrive at the final product, the cook must know when and how to combine all the elements to create a truly good cake. This is done using the human senses and experience. This is the essence of tacit knowledge.

The effect of tacit knowledge on innovativeness and the economic outcomes of the creation of knowledge cannot be managed, only enabled. Thus, attempts to control and administer creativity and innovation generally fail to achieve the desired outcomes and will result in the inefficient use of already limited resources, time, and energy. Though understood and applied by those possessing it, tacit knowledge is not easily communicated or fully described to others, and is difficult to replicate or imitate. The skills of a master craftsworker are not learned from a textbook or class, but through years of experience and apprenticeship.

Tacit knowledge is strategically important because it consists of the why and the experience portions needed to make good business decisions in often turbulent environments. Tacit knowledge management systems are hard to implement and even harder to maintain, but many firms and software makers are attempting to develop systems that enhance the tacit knowledge of the firm and hence its ability to innovate. These systems include e-mail search engines, resident experts, and systems intended to enable experts to document their expertise. In a knowledge economy, tacit knowledge is a key to innovation and is very hard for competitors to imitate.

Tactical Action   Tactical action is taken to fine-tune a strategy; it involves fewer and more general organizational resources than strategic actions and is relatively easy to implement and reverse. A classic tactical action is lowering price as a competitive lever.

Tactics, Competitive

Military tactics are like unto water; for water in its natural course runs away from high places and hasten downwards. So in War, the way is to avoid what is strong and strike at what is weak. Water shapes its course according to the nature of the ground over which it flows; the soldier works out his victory in relation to the foe whom he is facing.

Therefore, just as water retains no constant shape, so in warfare there are no constant conditions. The five elements—water, fire, wood, metal, earth—are not always equally predominant; the four seasons make way for each other in turn. There are short days and long, the moon has its periods of waning and waxing. He who can modify his tactics in relation to his opponent, and thereby succeed in winning, may be called a heaven-born captain.[2]

The only way for a business to survive over time is to adapt to change; if the business doesn't change, it won't survive. Water does not have any shape, it is always changing. If you put it in a round container, it will be round. If you put it in a square container, it will be squared. If you put it over a fire, it boils; if you put it in a cold area, it freezes. Water can adapt to everything no matter where you put it—it will take the form of its surroundings. In business, it is necessary to adapt to different market environments and always be open to change.

Napoleon, for example, used the tactics of concentration, relying on speed, and shock action to win his objectives. He also organized his divisions into subunits so that they could act independently.

Talents Those innate qualities of the individual that can be leveraged to create value for the customer. A key to strategy is mapping the talents of the individuals onto the firm's value creation model. A distinction can be made between talents and skills. Talents are more open-ended and can be leveraged onto new products and areas of innovation. Managing talents can mean not managing by numbers but by value creation and problem solving.

Tall Organizations Tall organizations have many layers of management. The cost of these hierarchies is high overhead and often lack of a customer-driven approach. The opposite is the flat organization.

Target Critical Vulnerabilities Analyze and probe competitors with the aim of identifying and rapidly exploiting those weaknesses that will do the greatest damage to their competitive position.[3] For example, in Iraq, constant bombing in the southern no-fly zone during the run-up to the war significantly degraded Iraqi air defense and communication networks, thus targeting critical vulnerabilities.

Task Force In a task force, the task is always the primary consideration. The German military in 1940 was the first to recognize that combat formations should be designed, trained, and applied to a particular task and then disbanded. Its success in building task forces of combat engineers, armored infantry, paratroopers, and bombers brought the static fortresses of France and Belgium to a state of ruin. Britain and the United States took to the idea with great enthusiasm, and soon task forces that cut across conventional military structures, processes, and values were ubiquitous. This later led to the concept of project management. Modern versions of task forces include the cross-functional (global, new product development) team.

Teaching Organization As opposed to the learning organization, the teaching organization focuses on disseminating useful information that contributes to the bottom line throughout the organization. For example, when executives go to training sessions and seminars, in a teaching organization, they are required to teach the relevant knowledge gained within their own organization. It is a well-known truism that if you want to learn something, you need to teach it. In the knowledge industries, people need to be getting smarter every day, which teaching can achieve.

Team Building Team building involves the grouping of a mix of people and the development of the skills required to achieve agreed-upon objectives.

One example is Crotonville, GE's "in-house university" where groups of aspiring executives meet to discuss and debate real-world issues affecting GE.

Teamwork For a group to work well as a team, according to Tushman,[4] three elements need to be present: teamwork, common goals, and the open sharing of information. Effective teamwork requires leadership, a critical group function that involves managing both the internal and external network of the team (*see* Social Network Analysis) and involves continual assessment of when to take action.

Technical Knowledge The business of patenting knowledge. Knowledge is a form of capital and has to be protected.

Technological Forecasting The methodology and practice of technological forecasting uses future studies as planning tools as they interrelate social, environmental, and technological factors. The area of technological forecasting merges into several adjoining areas:

1. Management of technology and innovation

2. Economic forecasting, time series, and the like

3. Social aspects of technological change

4. Futurology

Technological forecasting includes "all efforts to project technological capabilities and to predict the invention and spread of technological innovations."[5]

Architects, urban planners, industrial engineers, systems engineers, political scientists, military experts, futurologists, and corporate planners are all involved in technological forecasting. Some tools for technological forecasting include Delphi, trend extrapolation, historical analogy, and scenarios. For example, at Monash University in Melbourne, Australia, there is a project designed to describe the future of virtual environments created by global electronic networks. The outcomes of the research will be a description of possible virtual environment futures, an analysis of the emerging issues for groups and individuals, and a critique of existing business and market models in the light of these possible futures. This technological forecasting study is using the Delphi technique.

Such rapidly developed and revolutionary technological changes and innovations as lasers, satellites, desalination, and hybrid cars have prompted many firms to invest significantly in technological forecasting. Knowledge of probable technological developments helps strategic planners prepare their firms to benefit from this kind of change. Both brainstorming and the Delphi technique are two effective approaches in technological forecasting.

Technology To be first with a new technology is often fatal; it is usually better to come second after seeing the mistakes the innovator made and then take it from there.

Two technology companies that got it right are Microsoft and IBM, because neither fell in love with its technology. Technology is more than an engineer's game, as Carly Fiorina has pointed out. A good example of the danger of being first is the British development of the first four-engine jet airliner, the de Havilland Comet, in the mid-1950s. Two planes crashed almost right away. The cause turned out to be metal fatigue, an unknown condition at that time. Neither de Havilland nor the British airline industry recovered from this disaster, while Boeing learned from de Havilland's mistake and came out with the 707. Lockheed and McDonnell quickly followed suit and the American airline manufacturers were dominant for a time.

Technology Strategy Significant investments aimed at improving customer service and exploring ways to provide more personalized product offerings and services—while lowering costs and increasing operating efficiency.

Standard & Poor's characterized industry leader CVS is poised to benefit from the growth in health care spending and from effective cost-control measures, superior use of technology, and a focused expansion strategy. CVS was one of the first in the industry to install a chainwide automatic prescription-refill system. CVS has introduced its Excellence in Pharmacy Innovation & Care (EPIC) system, a multiyear project that reengineered the way its pharmacists communicate and fill prescriptions. EPIC strives to improve quality assurance and customer service while reducing labor costs. CVS also is implementing the Assisted Inventory Management (AIM) system, which more effectively links CVS stores and distribution centers with suppliers to speed the delivery of merchandise to its stores. This helps reduce out-of-stock positions and lower investment in inventory. All these technology strategy programs seem to work better with pithy acronyms. From a strategic management perspective, we suspect the term "technology strategy" as often it is more operational than strategic. It is worth noting that James Brian Quinn developed his idea of logical incrementalism (*see* Logical Incrementalism) from his technology strategy courses; these courses became the model for some of the pioneer courses in strategic management.

Technostructure John Kenneth Galbraith has argued that the corporate officials who run organizations form the technostructure and are the decisive players in contemporary society. This is in part the message of the antiglobalizers (who like to refer to themselves as being anti the negative effects of globalization). The technostructure, then, is made up of corporate oligarchs who focus on the advancement of their own status. In an increasingly pluralistic word, they need to satisfy the shareholders, the customers, activists, regulatory agencies, governments, and creditors. Galbraith makes the point that the dismal science of economics is intimately interwoven with the art of politics.

Ten Schools of Strategy Formulation According to Henry Mintzberg, from *Strategy Safari: A Guided Tour Through the Wilds of Strategic Management,* the entire field of strategic management can be categorized in ten schools as follows:

Design School Sees strategy in the light of SWOT; clear and unique strategies are formulated in a deliberate process.

Planning School Strategy formulation is cerebral and formal.

Positioning School After formal analysis of the industry, strategy is reduced to generic positions, leading to value chains, game theory, and strategy groups.

Entrepreneurial School CEO-centric, rooted in the mysteries of intuition, vague visions, and broad perspective.

Cognitive/Mental School Constructs strategies as creative interpretations rather than mapping reality.

Learning School   Strategies are emergent, and there are many strategists in the organization.

Power School   Strategy making is rooted in power, a political process involving bargaining, persuasion, and confrontation.

Cultural School   Focuses on common interest and integration.

Environmental School   Illuminates demands of the environment.

Configuration School   Organization is a configuration, a coherent cluster of characteristics and behaviors; develops a strategy that involves the different layers, looks outside the process.

Ten T System   Tell them what you are going to tell them, tell them, tell them what you told them. All great speeches are content-free. The speech is about the process of the speech.

Thanatos   Death Force. The forces of decline and destruction that kick in when the organization and its people stop growing. Analogy of *Decline and Fall of the Roman Empire,* by Edward Gibbon—resting on their laurels and getting lazy.

Theory in Strategic Management   It has been said that there is nothing quite so practical as a good theory. First, all research does not have to be theoretically grounded. Second, good managers bounce back and forth between the conceptual level and action level (i.e., Jack Welch)—true also of good researchers.

Theory Versus Practice   Aristotle argued that there are two kinds of professionals: Those who practice but do not teach what they practice and those who teach but do not practice what they teach. Increasingly, management theory is important to the practitioner, as the power of ideas is multiplied in a knowledge-based economy.

A recent article in the *Harvard Business Review* outlined the following points about the value of theory. Good theories are valuable because they help make predictions. They also help us interpret the present, to understand what is happening and why. The article highlights three aspects of theory building:

1. The importance of explaining what causes an outcome

2. The process of categorization that enables theorists to move from tentative understanding to reliable predictions

3. The importance of studying failures to building good theory

The application of a theory is the central theme of the book *The Innovator's Solution.*[6] In the late 1990s, Lucent Technologies Inc. applied an entrepreneurial approach to its three operating divisions by reorganizing them into 11 hot businesses. The idea was that each business would be run largely independently, as if it were an internal entrepreneurial start-up.[7] There is nothing quite as practical as a good theory.

Theory X   Theory X is Douglas McGregor's theory of autocratic leadership or management that is predicated on the following assumptions about employees: They dislike work, avoid responsibility, have little ambition, are motivated by fear and money, and therefore need to be forced, controlled, directed, and threatened.

Theory Y   Theory Y is Douglas McGregor's theory of democratic leadership or management that is predicated on the following assumptions about employees: They like work, naturally work toward goals, seek responsibility, are imaginative, creative, and clever, and are motivated by empowerment. It has been suggested that with reference to Theory X and Theory Y, individuals tend to see the organization through bifocal lenses: When they are looking upward in the hierarchy, they wish to be seen through Theory Y lenses, but when they look down their bifocals at their subordinates, they tend to see with Theory X lenses.

Think Globally, Act Locally   Coca-Cola has been experiencing a realignment phase since the company adopted the slogan Think Globally, Act Locally. The North African Division (NAD) of Coca-Cola was dissolved in December 2000 and various functions moved to the constituent regions. The reasoning behind this was to get customer bonding through proximity. This allowed NAD associates to work closely and jointly with bottlers while interacting with customers to anticipate customers' needs and to jointly develop new products. NAD conducted various training sessions for productivity improvement involving sharing best practices in the system, Excellence in Maintenance programs, Quality Assurance, and Customer Service. Because of the investment the bottlers put into such training, any change in the partnership would result in large switching costs, not to mention the breakup clauses in the agreement, which would naturally be prohibitive.

Time and Task Management   An attempt to control the amount of time spent on completing a task in order to maximize personal efficiency.

Time-Based Theory of Conflict or Maneuver Warfare   A theory developed by John Boyd that is premised on operating at a higher tempo than your enemy or opponent. For example, the First Marine Division struck far into the Iraqi lines three days before the First Gulf War officially started. By sweeping around strong points and attacking from the rear, rather than directly assaulting the enemy, the marines brought about such confusion that the Iraqis brought in reinforcements for what they thought was the spearhead of the U.S. invasion. In the confusion, 15 Iraqi divisions had surrendered to two marine divisions.

Time Horizon   Functional tactics identify activities to be undertaken now or in the immediate future. Business strategies focus on the firm's posture 2 to 5 years out. Delta Airlines has been known to commit itself to a concentration/market development business strategy that seeks competitive advantage via differentiation in its level of service and focus on the business traveler. Its pricing tactics are often priced slightly higher than industry averages, but it often lowers fares on select routes to thwart low-cost competition.

In other words, Delta's overall business *strategy* is focused 5 years into the future, but its pricing *tactics* can change daily.

Top Management Succession Strategy   You have all theses positions—chairman, CEO, vice president, and the like—that at times need to be shuffled, such as after a merger. A succession strategy is necessary to ensure complete control and continuity.

Top Management Teams   Managers and executives at the higher levels of an organization. The CEO will sometimes feel the need to accomplish a special task or solve a problem outside the norm of regular business by creating and organizing top management teams.

Total Customer Solutions Strategy   The North African Division of Coca-Cola does this through support services such as the provision of branded coolers at a nominal fee. It also provides containers for the distributors and transportation of the products to the distribution points.

Training   Mark Twain: "Training is everything, the peach was once a bitter almond. . . ."

Transaction Cost   Costs incurred in completing a transaction. For example, a joint venture has the transaction cost of setting up the equity investment or drawing up the contract that will govern the collaborative effort. Investment bankers profit from the transaction cost of an initial public offering (IPO).

Transformational and Transactional Leadership   Transactional leadership develops from the exchange between leaders and subordinates wherein the leader provides rewards in exchange for the subordinate's performance. This exchange is mostly used for nonstrategic changes that are incremental. Transformational leadership goes beyond transactional leadership by motivating subordinates to identify with the leader's vision and therefore sacrifice their self-interest for the well-being of the whole organization. Thus, transformational leadership is appropriate for strategic or revolutionary changes.

Traumatic Change   Describes situations like the introduction of the Model-T Ford. Though it was called the horseless carriage, it put the horse and cart out of business. And bear in mind that the internal combustion engine was developed only because the oil companies in Pennsylvania had to find a use for the liquid that was left after they extracted the paraffin for use in lamps. Hence the term gasoline engine.

Trend Extrapolation   A forecast using trend extrapolation can be generated by "observing a change through time in the character of something and projecting or extrapolating that change into the future."[8]

Growth curves are used in trend extrapolation. For example, the growth in height and weight of an individual can be charted, and will commonly display a pattern, which indicates a leveling off around early adulthood. So too can the growth pattern of a technology be plotted and charted in a similar fashion. For example, trend extrapolation could be used to chart and forecast the number of cell phone users.

However, trends and patterns are susceptible to sudden unpredictable changes. Schnaars[9] gives an example of a misuse of trend extrapolation by electronics firms in the case of their television manufacturing. Through the 1950s and the 1960s, television sets steadily grew larger. As American firms continued to make large, cabinet-based systems, Japanese firms began to concentrate on making portable sets. While the American firms acted on the belief that the existing trend toward larger sets would continue, the actual trend within the marketplace shifted toward a greater variability in size.

Trust   The belief that people will do what they promised. In strategic alliances and joint ventures, it is not possible to state all expectations and this is where the implicit aspect of trust comes in. Trust means assuming that your partner will act in accordance with your interests even if there is an opportunity to gain an unfair advantage. This unforeseen opportunity to take advantage is the test of trust. Trust implies an ability to predict a person's behavior during the course of this relationship. In trusting, firms and individuals make themselves vulnerable if they trust, hoping people will not take advantage of that vulnerability. These issues are especially crucial in interfirm alliances that center on innovation, with the threat that your venture partner will appropriate your new technology and set itself up as a competitor.

Trust is also a key issue within the firm, especially one that is based on innovation. Network studies (see Social Network Analysis) have shown that firms with higher levels of trust are able to generate greater innovation. This is what Karen Stephenson was referring to when she wrote, "Trust is the utility through which this knowledge flows."

Turbulence   A term that captures the level of change and unpredictability of the environment. Igor Ansoff used this idea extensively in his later writing, developing a 1–5 scale of turbulence levels.

Drucker has this to say about turbulence and strategic management: "There is but one certainty regarding the times ahead, the times in which managers must work and perform. This certainty is that there will be turbulent times. In turbulent times, the first task of management is to make sure of the firm's capacity for survival; to make sure of its structural strengths and soundness; and to make sure of its capacity to survive a blow, to adapt itself to sudden change, and to avail itself to sudden change and new opportunities." He wrote this in 1974 and it is even more true today.

Turnaround   Bringing a distressed company back from the brink of failure, and setting a more healthy course of action. Recognized stages that precede a turnaround include secrecy and denial, blame and scorn, problem avoidance, and helplessness.

For any one of a large number of reasons, a firm can find itself with declining profits. Among these reasons are economic recession, production inefficiencies, or even innovation breakthroughs by competitors. In most cases, strategic managers believe that such a firm can recover if a concerted effort is made over a period of time to fortify its distinctive competences. Such a strategy is known as turnaround. It can include, but is not limited to, cost and asset reductions.

Endnotes

1. Schelling, T. (1980). *The strategy of conflict.* Cambridge, MA: Harvard University Press.

2. Sun Tzu. (1996). *The art of war.* (Ralph Sawyer, Trans.). Boulder, CO: Westview Press.

3. Clemons, J. A., & Santamaria, V. (2003). *The Marine Corps way: Using maneuver warfare to lead a winning organization.* New York: McGraw-Hill.

4. Tushman, M. L., & Anderson, P. (1997). *Managing strategic innovation and change.* New York: Oxford University Press.

5. Ascher, W. (1979). *Forecasting: An appraisal for policymakers and planners* (rev. ed.). Baltimore: Johns Hopkins University Press.

6. Christensen, C. M., & Raynor, M. E. (2003). *The innovator's solution.* Boston: Harvard Business School Press.

7. Christensen, C. M., & Raynor, M. E. (2003). Why hard-nosed executives should care about management theory. *Harvard Business Review,* 81:9, p. 66.

8. Cornish, E. (1977). *The study of the future.* Washington, DC: World Future Society; Cornish, E. S. (2003, July-August). The wild cards in our future. *The Futurist.*

9. Schnaars, S. (1989). *Megamistakes: Forecasting and the myth of rapid technological change.* New York: The Free Press.

U

Unbundle To separate units or products into separate entities. For example, in Europe, many utilities have unbundled their operations and effectively created distinct business units separating, say, generation from supply.

Uncertainty When planning for their company's long-term growth, uncertainties are the what-if scenarios that keep executives up at night. Uncertainty includes technology, because new technologies can put market share at risk and affect the stability of their industries. Another uncertainty that has gained prominence is political stability. Security and property rights are uncertain in much of Latin America, Asia, and Africa, shrinking the opportunities in these emerging markets. The September 11 attacks demonstrated that the disorder flowing from failed governments can affect even mature economies. Schwartz argues that companies can look forward to a rosy future of high-tech efficiency, as long as they dedicate resources to ensure the stability of the governments and economies of the countries where they operate.[1]

Uncertainty Analysis An approach designed to assess the extent of change in a variable caused by uncertainty at the time the input parameters are being estimated.

Undercommunicating Not communicating sufficient information for the troops to have moral cause (*see* Moral Cause). This is common after a merger when management has a bunker mentality.

Ungluing The breaking up of traditional supply chains or other relevant groups by taking control of the elements of the mutual interest that holds the relationship together.

University The university or academy is a place to reflect, step back: creating a thoughtful environment where people can reflect on their experience. Managers, strategic or otherwise, are very busy doing; this dictionary and other university experiences should allow them to reflect on what they are doing, identify concepts at work in their business life, encounter new theories, and return to the fray with double-loop learning (*see* Argyris, Chris).

Unreason Thinking the unlikely and doing the unreasonable that can lead an individual or organization to achieve success.

Unrelated Diversification   Unrelated diversification refers to investment in industries that are not related to the primary business of the firm. Formerly called conglomerate diversification, unrelated diversification does not have a good track record for profitability. An example is the Canadian distiller Seagram's acquisition of Universal (the Hollywood studio), which it later divested. Many said this was motivated by Edgar Bronfman Jr.'s unfulfilled yearnings to be a Hollywood screenwriter rather than being based on sound business decisions.

Endnote

1. Schwartz, P. (2003). *Inevitable surprises: Thinking ahead in a time of turbulence.* New York: Gotham Books.

V

Validity Validity is an aspect of research design and knowledge management that indicates to what extent a research instrument is measuring what you intend to measure. Validity means it is appropriate to the end you have in mind.

Value Value in the present business mind-set is usually defined in terms of the worthy utility or importance of a good or service to a customer, but there is also the view that value to other stakeholders such as the shareholders or owners should be taken into account (*see* Pluralism). Value is best understood in future terms: what you are going to do next, not what you've done.

Value-Adding Intermediary Someone (usually the distributor) who adds value to a product before selling it to the customer. An example is adding a modem or extra software to a computer before it goes onto the market.

Value-Based Management Value-based management drove many of the leveraged buyouts and takeovers in the 1980s. In value-based management, CEOs became increasingly focused on the stock market valuation of their firms. Strategic objectives at times were set aside as the overriding objective of maximizing shareholder value relative to the industry average price/earnings ratio superseded all other goals.

Value Chain This approach describes a way of looking at a business as a chain of activities that transform inputs into outputs that customers value. Value chain analysis attempts to understand how a business creates customer value by examining the contributions of different activities within the business to that value. Porter's value chain divides these into primary activities (inbound logistics, operations, outbound logistics, marketing and sales, and service) and support activities (firm infrastructure, human resources, technology development, and procurement).

One example of a successful use of the value chain is the Gap clothing stores. The Gap, with more than 3,000 stores worldwide, applied the value chain approach to look at specialty clothing to identify key value activities around which they could build a long-term competitive advantage. The company identified four components to take advantage of: (1) product development, where store employees play a key role in selecting clothing for sale in its stores; (2) inbound logistics, where, not unlike Wal-Mart, the Gap has a highly computerized delivery system; (3) operations, where every Gap store is the same, a clean, well-lit store for the harried customer to shop in; and (4) human resource management, where Gap employees receive no commission but do receive above-industry-average base pay.

Value Creation Value creation has to do with problem solving. A key to value creation is to find ineffective activities and drive them out of the organization. Reprioritization.

Value Innovation In the knowledge-based economy, strategy must focus on expanding existing markets or creating new ones, not beating the competition. Value innovation makes the competition irrelevant by offering fundamentally new and superior buyer value in the existing market. We can apply this to the case of Samsung Electronics' cellular phone business in Asia. Samsung entered the business in the late 1980s along with its biggest competitors, Nokia and Motorola. These two brands dominate the cell phone business worldwide. While these two companies spent many years competing and gaining dominance in the market, Samsung was focusing on different applications for its cell phones.

The president of the cell phone division focused on value innovation. He noted that the average person carries his cell phone for more than 13 hours in his hand or belt strap, but uses it for only 25 minutes a day, so the president gave instructions to the R&D department to survey the market and see what other uses they could give to the cell phone. The ideas they came up were the following: e-mail, organizer (palm pilot), games, photo camera, and live conference (with a small camera so you can actually see who you are talking to). Soon Samsung started to add all these features to its cell phone. In a few years, Samsung grew from being ranked about 10th worldwide to 3rd worldwide and is getting closer to Motorola, which is No. 2.

Value Map Maps the level of value the market recognizes in a product or service that helps to differentiate it from other products or services in that particular market.

Value Migration Value migration is a term that denotes the movement of growth and profit opportunities from one industry player to another. Sears Roebuck & Co. found the idea of value migration to be a useful model for understanding its excruciatingly long decline. To strategy guru Adrian Slywotsky, value migrated throughout the 1980s from the outmoded business designs of such retail incumbents as Sears and Montgomery Ward to new, more competitive ones such as specialty stores, superstores, and discounters that were better able to satisfy customers.[1]

Values Set of beliefs or standards that the organization (i.e., organizational values) and its stakeholders (i.e., personal values) believe in and operate from. Organizational values are utilized to guide the day-to-day operations, serving as a linkage between mission (i.e., present operations) and vision (i.e., intended direction).

Values are the organization's code of conduct, which sets it apart in a behavioral sense.

VANE model   A person's values, attitudes, needs, and expectations affect how the person feels, perceives, and behaves. *See* Existential Strategy.

Venture Management   Venture management is generally used in larger organizations to create a smaller, more entrepreneurial atmosphere. The purpose of doing so is twofold. First, it can force the release of built-up innovation and talent from promising young employees. Second, it can have the added benefit of cutting existing bureaucracy and management systems indicative of larger companies.

Vertical Integration   When a firm's strategy is to acquire other firms that supply it with inputs such as raw materials or customer inputs such as warehousers for finished products, then vertical integration is involved. If a shirt manufacturer acquires a textile producer—by, say, purchasing its common stock, buying its assets, or exchanging ownership interests—the strategy is vertical integration.

Amoco emerged as North America's leader in natural gas reserves and products as a result of its acquisition of Dome Petroleum. This backward integration by Amoco was made in support of its downstream businesses in refining and in gas stations, whose profits made the acquisition possible.

Virtual Reality Classrooms   Learning linked by technology rather than shared physical space. Will help to blur the knowledge/skills barrier. Requires high-speed connections.

Vision   For now, we will simply define vision as a mental picture of a compelling future situation. Vision originates from creative imagination. It is also a powerful driving force. Viktor Frankl talks about the importance of vision in the quest for meaning (*see* Existential Strategy).[2]

Drucker notes, "To adapt is too dangerous because it means you are always running behind, you have to find a way of getting ahead—call it vision, call it mission, call it cause . . . it is basically taking responsibility for shaping events. . . ."[3] (*See* Mission and Moral Cause.)

Volvo Mode   The safety-first approach of Sweden's best-known car. Overly conservative in style, as were the Volvos of earlier decades.

Vulnerability   In the movie *Annie Hall,* the heroine is appealing to the viewer in many ways. She is wishy-washy, cute, directionless, and even vulnerable to many outside influences. However, in business, vulnerability is seen as a negative, a sign of weakness, making the firm ripe for a takeover or decline.

Endnotes

1. Slywotsky, A. (1996). *Value migration: How to think several moves ahead of the competition.* Boston: Harvard Business School Press.
2. Frankl, V. (1997). *Man's search for meaning.* New York: Pocket Books.
3. Drucker, P. (2001). *The essential Drucker.* New York: HarperBusiness.

W

"Walking the Talk" People (CEOs and top managers) who do what they say they are going to do are often cited as being trustworthy, someone who can lead an organization and have credibility doing so—someone who "walks the talk."

War War is traditionally thought of in terms of hostility between nations or states; in business, we see competition as a form of war. Sun Tzu notes about war, "This is the art of handling large masses of men. In night fighting, then, make use of such signals as fires and drums, and in fighting by day, of flags and banners, as means of influencing the ears and eyes of your army. A whole army may be robbed of its spirit; a commander in chief may be robbed of his presence of mind."[1]

Motivation is one of the key elements in handling large masses of people, and therefore one of the most important elements in a company because without it you can't do anything. In the maquiladoras in Tijuana, there are many activities to motivate workers on the production lines. For example, every month the production line that produces the most TV sets wins a field trip to a local park or beach. The company takes them out for a full day and makes carne asade, with drinks and music. After the president of this particular maquiladora came up with this idea, production increased by 10%. Thus, the lessons of *The Art of War* can be applied to companies without focusing on the idea of destruction of competitors (*see* Frenemies, Co-Opetition).

War Gaming War gaming is an effective tool for assessing a firm's vulnerability and resilience to identified risk factors. War gaming involves strategic simulations that present mock crises to gauge how well executives and staff are prepared to face serious business discontinuities. Usually, a real-time simulation that typically plays out over a 2-day period where one group makes a move and others respond is particularly revealing of vulnerabilities. Booz Allen Hamilton, a strategic management and technology consulting firm, sponsored a port security war game in October 2002 just after West Coast ports in the United States were shut down by labor unrest. Participants in the war gaming included representatives from government agencies, supply chain–intensive industries, and contract logistic providers.

Ways to Compete

1. Bring new products to market more quickly.

2. Diversify, as in Barnes and Noble's foray into music.

3. Shift product emphasis, as U-Haul did by expanding its product line to include accessories.

4. Consolidate, as in the merger of Exxon and Mobil.

5. Combine online and physical stores, as CompUSA did.

Weakness(es)   "If you know the enemy and know yourself, you need not fear the result of a hundred battles."[2] Weaknesses of competitors can be exploited, for example, in hostile takeovers. Comcast's 2004 attempt to take over Disney exploited the weakness of CEO Michael Eisner's battles with Roy Disney.

White Space Opportunity   Lewis Platt, former chairman of Hewlett-Packard, defines white space opportunity: "My role is to encourage discussion of the white spaces, the overlap and gaps between business strategies." White space opportunity refers to the new areas of growth possibilities that may not be exploited because they don't naturally match the skills and plans of existing business units.

Whiz Kids   American characteristic. Robert McNamara was an example of a whiz kid, with disastrous results in his application of linear programming techniques to the war in Vietnam. Whiz kids are young upstarts—the best and the brightest. Often they arrive at companies in teams or cohorts.

Withdrawal Tactic   Plans to exit a competitive situation or a market. Texas Instruments wrote down $600 million in computer inventory in 1985 as a withdrawal tactic to exit the personal computer industry.

Work Trends for the 21st Century   Tinkering with time, being two places at once, role blur (*see* Role Blur), a super global-travel class, involved working dads, grieving at work.

Worldview   Worldview selectively limits information attended to and interpreted. It also limits the range of alternative solutions to the issues that have been identified. All information is filtered through a worldview (*see* Paradigm).

Endnotes

1. Sun Tzu. (1996). *The art of war.* (Ralph Sawyer, Trans.). Boulder, CO: Westview Press, p. 33.
2. Ibid., p. 2.

X, Y, and Z

X, Generation   Generation X came after the baby boomers; born between 1965 and 1980. Known for their college education, dissatisfaction with typical corporate careers, and a certain cynicism. Gary Hamel argues that if you don't have generation X members on your board, you are not doing strategy well. Those coming after generation X are the millennials (1981–2000), who generally want to be taken seriously. If, for example, you ask the 12-year-old millennial next door to watch your cat, offer to pay her to show you value her time.[1]

Xerox Architecture   Xerox architecture can be synonymous with lost opportunities through high-tech innovation and insufficient commercialization (some would say imagination). The classic Xerox architecture lost opportunity was the mouse and the graphical user interface: Xerox developed both at its PARC labs well before Apple, but did not seize the commercialization potential, and Steve Jobs and Apple reaped the benefits.

Xistentialism   Emphasizes authentic choices that reflect values and posits that dynamic actions and decisions define the company rather than static states. *See* Existential Strategy. In an uncertain world where competitive advantage is insecure, setting strategy becomes an existential exercise.

Yummie   Young upwardly mobile manager into existentialism.

Zeitgeist   Zeitgeist means worldview. Every manager and top management team has a unique worldview or zeitgeist that colors their interpretation of the environment and their decision process. An example would be Nike's ultracompetitive win-at-any-cost zeitgeist.

Zen and the Art of Motorcycle Maintenance   Brian Kenner, CEO of Learning Framework, a California software company, describes the book *Zen and the Art of Motorcycle Maintenance: An Inquiry Into Values* (1974), by Robert Pirsig, as one of his favorite "management" texts. He cites one of the most memorable anecdotes of the book: Phaedrus, a rhetoric teacher, asks his students to produce a composition on Bozeman, Montana. One of his students approaches him to complain bitterly about the activity since she doesn't "know" anything about Bozeman. This is every manager's challenge, getting one's staff to create something new where nothing existed before. This is innovation.

The student desperately wants to be allowed to write about a topic for which she can draw from her existing knowledge. The professor had hoped she would set aside this old information. He uses an effective strategy to focus her on a smaller target, to get her thinking in new ways by asking her to write about the main street of Bozeman.

She still cannot get the creative juices flowing. Finally, he has her focus on the opera house of Bozeman starting with the uppermost left-hand brick. This strategy breaks the innovative logjam and the student quickly writes many pages of insights about the Bozeman opera house. The lesson learned is that strategies are tools of focus to limit the use of our past experiences and to force us to create new value. Many more management insights are contained in this book.

Zero Defects   A philosophy that aims to produce goods that are 100% perfect. Developed in the early 1960s in the United States by Philip Crosby, zero defects has the aim of eliminating the smallest defects at all levels.

Zone of Agreement   The zone that exists when there are simultaneously over-lapping acceptable outcomes for the parties. This zone is particularly important in negotiations. For example, a seller has a particular minimum price that he or she will accept, while buyers have a particular maximum price to which he or she will agree to buy. The zone of agreement is the zone between the seller's minimum selling price and the buyer's maximum buying price.

Zone of Indifference   This is that area where subordinates will follow directions without question. Also related to indifference curve (*see* Indifference Curve), where a number of combinations of consumer items offer equal value to the individual. We hope the dictionary has not left you indifferent!

Endnote

1. Raines, C. (2003). *Connecting generations: The sourcebook for a new workplace.* Menlo Park, CA: Crisp Publications.

Bibliography

Ansoff, Igor. (1965). *Concept of corporate strategy*. New York: McGraw Hill.

Barnard, C. (1971). *The functions of the executive*. Cambridge, MA: Harvard University Press.

Barney, J. B. (1997). *Gaining and sustaining competitive advantage*. Reading, MA: Addison-Wesley.

Brandenburger, A., & Nalebuff, B. (1996). *Co-opetition*. New York: Doubleday Dell.

Brown, S., & Eisenhardt, K. (1998). *Competing on the edge: Strategy as structured chaos*. Boston: Harvard Business School Press.

Chandler, A. (1962). *Strategy and structure: Chapters in the history of the American industrial enterprise*. Cambridge: MIT Press.

Cusumuo, M., & Murkides, C. (2001). *Strategic thinking for the next economy*. San Francisco: Jossey-Bass.

Cyert, R., & March, J. (1963). *A behavioral theory of the firm*. Englewood Cliffs, NJ: Prentice-Hall.

D'Aveni, R. (1994). *Hypercompetition*. New York: Free Press.

Drucker, P. (1993). *The practice of management*. New York: HarperBusiness Press.

Drucker, P. (2003). *The essential Drucker: The best of sixty years of Peter Drucker's essential writings on management*. New York: HarperBusiness Press.

Hamel, G., & Prahalad, C. K. (1996). *Competing for the future*. Boston: Harvard Business School Press.

Kaplan, R., & Norton, D. (2001). *The balanced scorecard*. Boston: Harvard Business School Press.

Kotter, J. P. (1996). *Leading change*. Boston: Harvard Business School Press.

Mintzberg, H. (1994). *Rise and fall of strategic planning*. New York: Free Press.

Mintzberg, H., Alstrand, B., & Lampal, J. (1998). *Strategy safari*. New York: Simon & Schuster.

Porter, M. (1990). *The competitive advantage of nations*. New York: Free Press.

Porter, M. (1998). *Competitive advantage: Creating and sustaining superior performance*. New York: Free Press.

Senge, P. (1990). *The fifth discipline: The art and practice of the learning organization*. New York: Doubleday/Currency.

Sun Tzu. (1996). *The art of war*. (Ralph Sawyer, Trans.). Boulder, CO: Westview Press.

About the Authors

Photo © Natalie Fiocre

Louise Kelly is Professor of Strategy at Alliant International University, in San Diego, California. She is coauthor of *An Existential Systems Approach to Managing Organizations*. Her areas of research and consulting include international entrepreneurship, top management teams, leadership, and social networks, and she has published in the journals *Entrepreneurship, Theory and Practice* and *Journal of World Business*. Africa and Mexico have been the main centers for her research. Her doctorate in strategic management is from Concordia University in Montreal.

Chris Booth is a doctoral student at Alliant International University. His current academic focus is the role of strategic management in government and nonprofits. He holds a Master of Public Administration from the University of Nebraska and a Bachelor of Arts in English from Humboldt State University. Chris's diverse academic background is matched only by his varied personal background, which includes having firewalked and having paraglided off mountains in northern California. Chris is currently an avid lawn bowler.